The Future of Forens Psychology

The Future of Forensic Psychology: Core Topics and Emerging Trends is an authoritative text that presents state-of-the-art research from rising stars in the field. Presented in an accessible way, it draws on cutting-edge research to analyze both core topics and current trends in forensic psychology.

Borne out of the internationally recognized *House of Legal Psychology* doctorate programme, the book features eighteen authors from different international contexts who evaluate current and emerging topics in the field. The book is divided into three parts: "Eyewitness memory and testimony", "Investigative interviewing", and "Deception detection and legal decision-making". Each section contains in-depth research and includes classic topics such as factors affecting eyewitnesses and determining deceit in investigations. The book also covers newer exciting developments within the field, including credibility in asylum contexts, alibis, and the cross-cultural aspect of interviewing.

Offering an insightful summary of the field today, this book is an indispensable read for students and researchers of forensic psychology, legal psychology, and criminology. It will also be of great interest to practitioners in the judicial system.

Sara Landström is a professor of psychology at the University of Gothenburg, Sweden. Her research interest is legal and investigative psychology. She has published over 50 research papers in international peer-review journals, edited a Swedish handbook on legal psychology and frequently serves as an expert witness in criminal cases and as an expert in governmental investigations.

Pär Anders Granhag is a professor of psychology at the University of Gothenburg, Sweden. He has been working in the field of legal psychology for over 30 years and has published over 300 research papers and ten books. He has served as an expert witness in over 50 legal cases and has given seminars to different groups within the legal field for 25 years.

Peter J. van Koppen is a psychologist and emeritus professor of legal psychology at the Faculty of Law of VU University Amsterdam and a professor of legal psychology at Maastricht University, the Netherlands. He has served as an expert witness in many cases, advised police teams frequently and published 35 books, 125 articles, and 100 chapters in edited volumes on various subjects in legal psychology.

The Future of Forensic Psychology

Core Topics and Emerging Trends

Edited by Sara Landström, Pär Anders Granhag and Peter J. van Koppen

Routledge
Taylor & Francis Group

LONDON AND NEW YORK

Cover image: Sara Landström

First published 2023
by Routledge
4 Park Square, Milton Park, Abingdon, Oxon OX14 4RN

and by Routledge
605 Third Avenue, New York, NY 10158

Routledge is an imprint of the Taylor & Francis Group, an informa business

British Library Cataloguing-in-Publication Data
A catalogue record for this book is available from the British Library

ISBN: 978-1-032-31195-1 (hbk)
ISBN: 978-1-032-31194-4 (pbk)
ISBN: 978-1-003-30854-6 (ebk)

DOI: 10.4324/9781003308546

Typeset in Bembo
by Apex CoVantage, LLC

Contents

List of contributors   vii

Introduction   1
SARA LANDSTRÖM, PÄR ANDERS GRANHAG
AND PETER J. VAN KOPPEN

PART I
Eyewitness memory and testimony   7

1 **Misreporting episodic memories: causes and
   consequences for the criminal legal system**   9
   JOANNE RECHDAN AND ANDREW CLARK

2 **Intersections between metamemory and
   eyewitness testimony**   22
   RENAN BENIGNO SARAIVA

3 **The effects of acute stress on eyewitness memory**   33
   CAREY MARR

PART II
Investigative interviewing   45

4 **Cross-cultural investigative interviews**   47
   NKANSAH ANAKWAH

5 **Cognitive barriers to obtaining information during
   investigative interviews**   58
   NICOLE ADAMS-QUACKENBUSH

 6 Lack of cooperation in witness interviews   68
    ALEJANDRA DE LA FUENTE VILAR

 7 Priming in investigative interviewing: A critical review   78
    DAVID A. NEEQUAYE

 8 Pragmatic inferences in investigative interviewing   88
    MEGHANA SRIVATSAV

 9 The discouraging past and promising future of
    research on innocent suspects' alibis   95
    SHIRI PORTNOY

10 Interviewing suspects with the Strategic Use of
    Evidence (SUE) technique   105
    SERRA TEKIN

PART III
Deception detection and legal decision making   115

11 Lie detection in forensic interviews   117
    HANEEN DEEB AND ALEKSANDRAS IZOTOVAS

12 Trust, doubt, and symptom validity   127
    IRENA BOŠKOVIĆ

13 Risk assessment and the influence of bias   139
    JENNIFER KAMOROWSKI

14 Tunnel vision and falsification in legal decision-making   148
    ENIDE MAEGHERMAN

15 Fact-finding in asylum cases   160
    TANJA VAN VELDHUIZEN

    Index   171

Contributors

Nicole Adams-Quackenbush, PhD, is a lecturer at Newcastle University, United Kingdom, where she conducts research exploring information-gathering, decision-making, and cognitive biases.

Nkansah Anakwah, PhD, is a lecturer in forensic psychology at Birmingham City University, United Kingdom, with research interests in eyewitness memory and investigative interviewing in cross-cultural contexts.

Renan Benigno Saraiva, PhD, is a senior lecturer in forensic psychology at the University of Portsmouth, United Kingdom. His research interest is applied cognition in forensic settings and eyewitness memory.

Irena Bošković, PhD, is an assistant professor of forensic psychology at Erasmus University Rotterdam, the Netherlands. She has an expertise in response bias in forensic assessments.

Andrew Clark, PhD, is a lecturer in forensic psychology at the University of Bedfordshire, United Kingdom. His research interest is memory in legal contexts.

Alejandra De La Fuente Vilar, PhD, is a senior research associate at the University of Portsmouth, United Kingdom, interested in psychological, social and cultural factors that affect information elicitation in investigative contexts.

Haneen Deeb, PhD, is a senior research associate in the Department of Psychology at the University of Portsmouth, United Kingdom. Her research interests lie in investigative psychology and specifically in lie detection in forensic settings.

Aleksandras Izotovas, PhD, is a researcher at Mykolas Romeris University, Vilnius, Lithuania, with a research interest in investigative interviewing and deception detection.

Jennifer Kamorowski, PhD, is an assistant professor in criminal justice at Plymouth State University in New Hampshire, USA, and her primary research interests include the use of risk assessment instruments and cognitive bias in legal and expert decision-making.

Enide Maegherman, PhD, is a lecturer at University College Maastricht, the Netherlands, with research interests in investigative interviewing and legal decision-making.

Carey Marr, PhD, is currently a research fellow at the University of New South Wales, Australia, where she is conducting research related to forensic mental health.

David A. Neequaye, PhD, is a Researcher at the University of Gothenburg, Sweden. His research is primarily focused on investigative interviewing.

Shiri Portnoy, PhD, is a lecturer in forensic psychology at the Department of Psychology, School of Social Sciences, Humanities and Law, Teeside University, United Kingdom and a chartered psychologist of the British Psychological Society whose research has focused on innocent suspects' verbal behaviour during police interviews.

Joanne Rechdan, PhD, is a lecturer in psychology at Bournemouth University, United Kingdom. Her research interests include social and cultural influences on episodic memory, metamemory, investigative psychology, and minority access to justice.

Meghana Srivatsav, PhD, is the founder and lead consultant at Forseti Consulting, India. Her research interests lie in investigative and counter-terrorism interviewing.

Serra Tekin, PhD, is a lecturer in psychology at London South Bank University, United Kingdom, and her research focuses on information elicitation in investigative interviews.

Tanja van Veldhuizen, PhD, is an assistant professor in legal psychology at the Department of Criminal Law and Criminology at VU University Amsterdam, the Netherlands. Her research focuses on credibility assessments and investigative interviewing practices in different legal contexts.

Introduction

Sara Landström, Pär Anders Granhag
and Peter J. van Koppen

From the days of old, the study of law seemed to be an exclusive terrain for lawyers (Stein, 1999). In some ways, that is odd. The rules of law in the form of statutes, jurisprudence, and precedents do not exist to please legal scholars— they exist to regulate society by influencing people's behaviour (Crombag, 1994). Regulating society is more the province of disciplines other than the study of law, like economy, sociology, and psychology. The applied research field of legal psychology, or forensic psychology as it is often called, has two main tasks. The first task is to study law as a behavioural technology and consider questions like why and in what form can we expect legal rules to work to reach desired goals (van Koppen et al., 1988). The second task is to study those individuals that operate the law. Let it be the technical detective processing a crime scene, the police officer deciding to make an arrest, or the judge or jury who is deciding a case. And let us not forget the witness telling a story of what has been observed, the suspect who is making a confession and the complainant disclosing abuse—they are all humans, and thus the operation of law is heavily influenced by individual behaviour. In that sense, forensic psychology has the whole breadth of law as its subject and is relevant to administrative law, civil law, and criminal law alike. Traditionally, however, forensic psychologists tend to focus on criminal law and on the issues that are laid out as three cornerstones in this volume: "Eyewitness memory and testimony" (Part I), "Investigative interviewing" (Part II), and "Deception detection and legal decision making" (Part III).

In this volume, young forensic psychologists present their subjects of expertise. This follows in a tradition that is longer than many lawyers seem to realise. In the early 1900s, a German psychologist by the name of William Stern (1871–1938) ran research on the *Aussagepsychologie* (psychology of testimony). He led laboratory research in a manner that is still en vogue in forensic psychology, such as showing subjects photos and having them tell what they have seen afterwards. Sometimes he would let his subjects be interviewed in a suggestive manner and concluded that "a faultless recollection is not the rule, but the exception. And even an oath does not protect against memory errors" (cited in Sporer, 1987, p. 115). The pioneering work of Stern and his associates led to so-called *Wirklichkeitsversuche* (mock crimes) committed in university

DOI: 10.4324/9781003308546-1

classrooms across Europe. Stern also served as an expert witness in courts, and decades later, many forensic psychologists would follow suit. One of those who conformed to Stern's research was the German psychologist Hugo Münsterberg (1863–1916), who pioneered forensic psychology in the United States. Without telling anybody how Stern had influenced his work (Shaw et al., 2013), he explored the psychology of eyewitness testimony with attention to its accuracy (Bornstein & Penrod, 2008). Hence, Stern and Münsterberg laid the groundwork for the applied research field of forensic psychology. But, just like the subject of psychology in general, forensic psychology went into a dark parenthesis during and after World War II (Teigen, 2006). The rebirth of the subject took place in the 1970s and 1980s, with much thanks to the American psychologist Elizabeth Loftus. In her now-classic work, she demonstrated that human memory is malleable and that questions and information that witnesses receive after an event can reconstruct their memory of the event (Loftus & Palmer, 1974). Since then, the pace of development has been strong. In the 1990s, Saul Kassin and Katherine Kiegel became famous by demonstrating that subjects can be brought to make false confessions simply by being accused of destroying a computer by touching the alt-key, even though they never did (Kassin & Kiechel, 1996). Hans Crombag and his colleagues, Willem Albert Wagenaar and Peter J. van Koppen, showed that it was rather easy to lead people to believe they had seen footage of a particular Boeing 747 crashing in an apartment building, even though no such footage exists (the crash happened though; Crombag et al., 1996). Daniel Simons and Daniel Levin demonstrated that eyewitnesses may be blind to changes as they successfully switched one man for another without their subjects noticing it (Simons & Levin, 1998). During the 2000s, the research field of forensic psychology has expanded dramatically and turned into one of the fastest-growing areas of psychology. Today, it is virtually impossible to stay up to date on all the research that is being produced in the area, which is why this volume comes in handy as it offers state-of-the-art chapters that take stock of the new knowledge that is produced within forensic psychology. Knowledge that extends from core topics—such as the study of factors that may influence eyewitness testimonies and the cues used by legal practitioners to determine whether an eyewitness testimony is reliable or not—to emerging trends—such as the study of cross-cultural investigative interviewing and assessing credibility in asylum contexts.

One noticeable development in forensic psychology is that, in difference to the pioneering individual researchers' initiatives and the efforts mentioned previously, today's initiatives tend to take place within the framework of organized research groups and centres. At the beginning of the 2010s, three such centres decided to join forces; Maastricht University in the Netherlands (Faculty of Law and Faculty of Psychology and Neuroscience), the University of Portsmouth in the United Kingdom (Department of Psychology) and the University of Gothenburg in Sweden (Department of Psychology). Not only did these centres share an interest in legal psychology, but each of them also had a long-standing tradition of producing high-quality research. Representatives—including the editors of this volume—from the three centres worked out a proposal that was submitted in response to a call from the Erasmus Mundus Joint PhD degree. On the third attempt, the proposal was granted financial support, and that was the start of the *House of Legal Psychology*. The program started in September 2013 and finished in September 2020 and provided 26 graduate students from around the world a unique opportunity to start a career in legal psychology with ideal conditions for conducting and learning about research while working with experts in the field. The students that were accepted to the program came from countries in which forensic psychology is well developed, for example, Germany, Israel, the Netherlands, the United Kingdom, and the United States of America. But the program also came to include students from countries where forensic psychology thus far is less developed, such as the Ukraine, Bolivia, India, Ghana, Trinidad and Tobago, Turkey, and Lebanon. The House of Legal Psychology was, from the very start, a truly international program perfectly tailored to bring forth new scholars into the field of forensic psychology.

The students that were accepted to the program were fully funded for three years. Three years is a short time to finalize a PhD thesis, but impressively, most students were able to meet this deadline. The program was set up so that each student stayed at one of the centres for two and a half years, which became the student's home department. The remaining six months were spent at one of the two other centres. This guaranteed that each student experienced more than one research environment during their PhD years. Another key component of the program was that each year a summer school and a winter school were organized by one of the participating centres. On these occasions, all students currently in the House came together for a week to present and get feedback on their ongoing research, take part in lectures and seminars by senior researchers in the field, and get to know one another through social activities. Looking back at the now completed program, several things stand out. The international aspect of the program was not only about bringing together students from different corners of the world. The international aspect also served as a major injection for the three centres running the program as many of the international students came to stay after they had finished their PhD and became faculty members. Another thing that stands out is the quality of the work that the PhD students managed to achieve, mirrored both in their theses and in the chapters in this volume. A third thing that stands out is the themes for the PhD theses. Themes that may best be described as prior gaps in the literature. Many of these important gaps are now filled, thanks to the students that worked in the House of Legal Psychology. In this volume, seventeen of these former students contribute with their expertise within the field.

The House of Legal Psychology showed that forensic psychology attracts students from across the globe. But as the students quickly came to learn, forensic psychology is not as glamorous as it is portrayed in TV shows and podcasts. In fiction, crime investigators often have access to hard evidence, such as DNA samples, hair fibres, or fingerprints. In reality, these types of evidence are often unavailable or not relevant, and eyewitness testimonies play an important role in the criminal legal system today as they did in the old days. The first part of the book, "Eyewitness memory and testimony", therefore, includes three chapters on this core topic. Chapter 1 provides an overview of characteristic eyewitness memory errors. Chapter 2 discusses the links between eyewitness testimony and metamemory research, and Chapter 3 presents an up-to-date account regarding the effects of acute stress on memory performance. Information gathering interviews with victims, witnesses, and suspects of wrongdoing are central to crime investigations. To elicit accurate and detailed accounts, the police need to adhere to best practice investigative interviewing practices. Hence, the second part of this volume, "Investigative interviewing", is the most comprehensive and comprises seven chapters on the new and future challenges in this domain. Chapter 4 discuss the importance of attending to culture to receive information from interviewees, and Chapter 5 focuses on the different ways investigators inadvertently create barriers that prevent interviewees from disclosing valuable information. Chapter 6 discusses the fallacy that all witnesses are cooperative and forthcoming and proposes a cost-benefit analysis framework to understand factors that affect witness cooperation. Chapter 7 follows up on the same note presenting an examination of whether social influence techniques such as priming can facilitate the disclosure of information. This is followed by three chapters on suspect interviewing specifically. These chapters discuss topics such as perceived interviewer knowledge (Chapter 8), innocent suspect's alibi generation and provision (Chapter 9), and gives an overview of the Strategic Use of Evidence (SUE) technique (Chapter 10). The third and final part of this volume, "Deception detection and legal decision making", includes five chapters on varying legal decisions and challenges. It begins with an overview of the research on deception detection (Chapter 11), followed by a summary of the detection of intentionally falsely reported symptoms (Chapter 12). Chapter 13 discusses risk assessment instruments employed to evaluate violent, sexual, or criminal recidivism, and Chapter 14 provides an overview of legal decision-making and the dangers of confirmation bias and tunnel vision. The volume ends with Chapter 15, which summarizes the available empirical psychological evidence on credibility assessments in asylum cases.

References

Bornstein, B. H., & Penrod, S. D. (2008). Hugo who? G.F. Arnold's alternative early approach to psychology and law. *Applied Cognitive Psychology*, *22*(6), 759–768.

Crombag, H. F. M. (1994). Law as a branch of applied psychology. *Psychology, Crime and Law*, *1*(1), 1–9.

Crombag, H. F. M., Wagenaar, W. A., & van Koppen, P. J. (1996). Crashing memories and the problem of 'source monitoring'. *Applied Cognitive Psychology*, *10*(2), 95–104.

Kassin, S. M., & Kiechel, K. L. (1996). The social psychology of false confessions: Compliance, internalization, and confabulation. *Psychological Science*, *7*(3), 125–128.

Loftus, E. F., & Palmer, J. C. (1974). Reconstruction of automobile destruction: Example of interaction between language and memory. *Journal of Verbal Learning and Verbal Behavior*, *13*(5), 585–589.

Shaw, J., Öhman, L., & van Koppen, P. J. (2013). Psychology and law: The past, present, and future of the discipline. *Psychology, Crime and Law, 19*(8), 643–647.

Simons, D. J., & Levin, D. T. (1998). Failure to detect changes to people during a real-world interaction. *Psychonomic Bulletin and Review, 5*(4), 644–649.

Sporer, S. L. (1987). Gedächtnis in vitro und in vivo: Von Hermann Ebbinghaus' sinnlosen Silben bis zur experimentellen Pädagogik und zur Aussagepsychologie. In W. Traxel (Ed.), *Internationales hermann ebbinghaus symposium* (pp. 107–119). Passavia.

Stein, P. (1999). *Roman law in European history*. Cambridge University Press.

Teigen, K. H. (2006). *En psykologihistoria*. Liber.

van Koppen, P. J., Hessing, D. J., & Van den Heuvel, G. A. A. J. (Eds.) (1988). *Lawyers on psychology and psychologists on law*. Swets & Zeitlinger.

Part I

Eyewitness memory and testimony

1 Misreporting episodic memories

Causes and consequences for the criminal legal system

Joanne Rechdan and Andrew Clark

This chapter is dedicated to the memory of the inimitable Dr James Ost (1973–2019).

Eyewitness testimony plays an important role in the criminal justice system. The testimony of confident witnesses is often a determining factor in jury decision-making (Semmler et al., 2012). Yet, research has shown that memory is fallible, and many wrongful convictions have resulted from mistaken eyewitness testimony (Gould & Leo, 2010; West & Meterko, 2015). Memory errors can occur because of external influences or internal processes. Examples of the former include misinformation received through communication with other witnesses, suggestive interviewers, or the media. However, the process of memory retrieval is complex enough to pose its own challenges, and memory errors need not be the result of external influence. Internal processes, often operating in conjunction with external social influences, can shape how we recall life events over successive retellings. In this chapter, we will review some of the means through which an individual's memory for an event may be altered and consider the consequences of such alterations in legal contexts.

Reconstructive memory

In his book, *Remembering* (1932), psychologist Frederic Bartlett (1886–1969) proposed that memory is a reconstruction and therefore not necessarily a faithful reproduction of past events. This reconstruction is guided by *schemas*—general organising structures that aid in the creation of memories and guide their later retrieval (Roediger & DeSoto, 2015, p. 50). Bartlett did not suggest that memory was entirely unreliable. Rather, his work countered the popular notion at the time that memory was based on unalterable traces (Ost & Costall, 2002). In a classic set of studies, Bartlett had participants read a Native North American folk tale called "War of the Ghosts". When participants were asked to recall the story after some delay, their versions included departures from the original tale. For example, details such as "canoe" became "boat". Bartlett observed that participants tended to omit and alter details in a way that was consistent with their own cultural schemas.

DOI: 10.4324/9781003308546-3

Research has shown that when memory fades, reliance on schemata increases, resulting in more stereotypical memory errors (Kleider et al., 2008). Carli (1999) offers a good example of how a schema might guide the reconstruction of a memory. In the study, participants read a story about a date that (a) ended with the male character raping the female character, (b) had no distinct ending, or (c) had a positive ending. Participants later completed a test of their memory for the story. Results showed that participants in the rape condition misremembered more details associated with common rape stereotypes (e.g., the characters consuming alcohol, the victim wearing promiscuous attire) than participants in the non-rape conditions. Hence, the memory of participants in the rape condition was influenced by a culturally salient rape schema. Other research has shown that participants remember schema-inconsistent items (e.g., a robber wearing bright clothing) better than schema-consistent items (e.g., a robber carrying a bag)—presumably due to the distinctiveness of these items. Schema-irrelevant items (e.g., the direction of the robber's escape) are the least likely to be recalled (Tuckey & Brewer, 2003). Taken together, these findings demonstrate how our schematic representations of the world influence our recollections.

Bartlett (1932) also proposed that recall is a reconstruction made primarily based on attitude, and that its effect is to justify the attitude (p. 207). Accordingly, some research has found that we tend to misremember the past in a way that brings it in line with our present knowledge, opinions, and beliefs. This has been termed *consistency bias* (Schachter, 2021). In one study, participants were presented with scientific evidence on climate change. Participants who were experimentally induced or dispositionally inclined to justify the economic system later misremembered the evidence for climate change as weak (Hennes et al., 2016). However, it is important to note that research on consistency bias has been somewhat mixed, with the effect depending heavily on factors like the length of delay between encoding and recall of a memory (Roberts, 1985).

Forgetting

Memories are thought to become inaccessible over time as the result of decay or disuse (Bjork & Bjork, 1992; Hardt et al., 2013). The acquisition of new information (especially if it is highly similar) can also cause us to forget old information. *Retroactive interference* occurs when new information causes a person to forget older information. *Proactive inhibition* occurs when old information interferes with the acquisition of new information. Interference effects are especially relevant for memories of repeated events. For example, children and adults who experience repeated sexual abuse may struggle to accurately attribute certain details to a specific instance of abuse (Brubacher et al., 2011; Deck & Paterson, 2020).

The passage of time also affects the level of detail and accuracy with which we recall memories. In a classic study, the philosopher and psychologist Hermann Ebbinghaus (1850–1909) learned lists of nonsense syllables and then relearned them after varying intervals. He measured forgetting in terms of how long it took him to relearn the lists and found that a stable pattern emerged: forgetting occurred rapidly at first but then slowed and eventually levelled off (Ebbinghaus, 1885). The pattern identified by Ebbinghaus also applies to episodic memories. Hirst and colleagues (2015) conducted a longitudinal study of people's memory for the September 11th attacks on the World Trade Centre in New York City. Such major public events are thought to evoke what are known as *"flashbulb" memories* (Brown & Kulik, 1977). People often report a high degree of confidence in the accuracy of their recall for these memories (Talarico & Rubin, 2003). Hirst et al. (2015) asked participants to relate their memory of the 9/11 attacks one week after they occurred and then again 11, 25, and 119 months later. They found that the details of flashbulb memories were also forgotten rapidly at first and then stabilised. These results show that even confidently held memories are subject to the pattern of forgetting identified by Ebbinghaus.

Rehearsal, or retrieving and reporting a memory repeatedly, can reinforce and preserve the memory. Details that are recalled tend to be preserved and reported in subsequent retellings. Memory traces for details that are omitted from retellings weaken and decay more rapidly than those that are retold. This phenomenon is known as *retrieval induced forgetting* (Anderson et al., 1994). Selective retellings by speakers may even come to shape how listeners recall a story; this is known as *socially shared retrieval induced forgetting* (Cuc et al., 2007). Through socially shared retrieval induced forgetting, speakers and listeners come to remember and forget the same details so that their accounts of an event or story align. There is strong empirical evidence of retrieval induced forgetting in a variety of contexts (see Murayama et al., 2014 for a review). However, other researchers have found that immediate testing for a subset of learned material can facilitate later recall of material that was not initially tested—a phenomenon known as *retrieval induced facilitation* (Chan et al., 2006; Rowland & DeLosh, 2014). Early work by Saunders and MacLeod (2002) showed that having mock eyewitnesses engage in immediate guided retrieval practice 24 hours before a recall test diminished retrieval induced forgetting. Therefore, it is possible that immediate, detailed interviewing of eyewitnesses may prevent retrieval induced forgetting. However, interviewers typically elicit incomplete initial recalls from eyewitnesses, increasing the possibility that unreported details will be left out of subsequent reports due to retrieval induced forgetting (Murayama et al., 2014). Furthermore, witnesses to a crime are sometimes only interviewed after long delays (Manarin, 2009). Discussions with other witnesses or independent recall of the crime during these delays may lead to retrieval induced forgetting.

Misinformation and memory distortions

We often discuss our memories with others. Sometimes, our purpose in doing so is merely to relate an interesting story. In such instances, accuracy and completeness are not our highest priorities. Research has shown that people often selectively report, embellish, and dramatise when they are relating memories for the purpose of entertaining an audience (Dudukovic et al., 2004; Tversky & Marsh, 2000). In fact, there are many examples of high-profile individuals who have been caught exaggerating their involvement in exciting events (see Rechdan et al., 2016 for such example). However, there are times when we relate episodes of our lives for more serious reasons, and accuracy and completeness are of utmost importance. One example of this is during an eyewitness interview.

The accuracy of eyewitness testimony depends on several factors, such as the conditions in which the crime was observed (e.g., lighting, distance, arousal of the eyewitness) and events that occur in the time between witnessing the event and reporting it (e.g., discussing the crime with others, being questioned about the crime in a leading manner). The first set of factors, known as *estimator variables*, are characteristics of the witness and the context which cannot be controlled. However, the focus of this section is on a second set of variables—*system variables*, which are under the control of the criminal justice system (Wells, 1978). The length of time between the occurrence of a crime and an eyewitness' subsequent testimony is one example of a system variable. Witnesses are sometimes interviewed at the scene of a crime or within a short timeframe. However, as previously mentioned, there are also cases in which witnesses are interviewed after much longer retention periods (Manarin, 2009). Lengthy delays between encoding and recall increase the risk that a witness might be exposed to post-event information. Post-event information can be acquired through social means such as conversations with others or an interviewer's leading questions and non-verbal behaviours (Loftus, 1975; Paterson & Kemp, 2006; Gurney et al., 2013). Post-event information may also be acquired through non-social means such as written media reports (Blank et al., 2013; Gabbert et al., 2004). A witness may mistakenly attribute post-event information to the event itself, a phenomenon known as *source misattribution* (Lindsay & Johnson, 1987). The *misinformation effect* occurs when a witness incorporates post-event information—whether consistent or misleading—into their memory of the event (Loftus et al., 1978; Frenda et al., 2011).

Ost et al. (1997) investigated individual differences in suggestibility to written misinformation about experienced events. In their study, student participants provided a free recall of events they had participated in during their first week at university ("induction week"). Three weeks later, participants completed a recall questionnaire comprised of fifteen statements describing events that had supposedly occurred during the induction week. Five of the statements accurately described real events, six were distorted descriptions of events, and four described fabricated events. Participants were asked to indicate whether they recalled the events described in the statements from induction week and to rate their level of confidence on a scale from 1 (cannot remember) to 6 (clearly remember). After another three weeks had passed, participants were given negative feedback about their performance on the first questionnaire and were asked to complete it again. Participants also completed measures of memory suggestibility. The results showed that higher scores on measures of fantasy proneness and dissociation were related to greater levels of suggestibility and higher reported confidence in recall of events that did not occur.

In another study, British and Swedish participants were asked if they recalled seeing media footage of the 7/7 attacks in London. Participants in each of three conditions were asked to indicate whether they had seen (a) media footage of the aftermath of the attack, (b) non-existent CCTV footage of the attack, or (c) a non-existent computerised reconstruction of the explosion. Results showed that British participants were more likely to report having seen all three types of footage than Swedish participants. The researchers noted that it was likely that U.K. participants had been exposed to more media coverage of the attacks than Swedish participants. Exposure to similar content may have increased U.K. participants' susceptibility to misremembering the non-existent footage. Finally, in line with Ost et al. (1997), results showed that false memories of the footage were associated with higher scores on measures of dissociation and fantasy proneness (Ost et al., 2008). Taken together, the results of Ost et al. (1997) and Ost et al. (2008) suggest that familiarity with an event and individual differences can influence susceptibility to misinformation and memory distortions.

False memories

People can also produce rich *false memories* of events they have never experienced (see Loftus, 2005 for a review). Loftus and Pickrell (1995) went beyond simply altering participants' memories of an experienced event—they implanted a false memory for an event that had never occurred. In their study, participants were mailed a booklet containing four short stories of events that supposedly happened to them in childhood. Three of these were events that each participant had experienced, disclosed to the researchers by the participants' family members. A fourth, false event was fabricated by the experimenter. This false event referred to a time when the participant had gotten lost in a shopping mall at 5 years old. The participants were prompted to write as much as they could recall about each of the four events. They were later interviewed about the events on two occasions. Participants were asked to rate the clarity of their memory for each event, as well as how confident they were that they would be able to recall additional details about the event later. Participants recalled most of the true events. A quarter of the participants also recalled the false event either fully or partially. However, these participants used more words to describe true events than the false event and gave higher clarity and confidence ratings for the true events than they did the false event. The latter finding indicates that while some participants did report false memories, these memories were qualitatively different from their true memories.

The experimental approach used by Loftus and Pickrell (1995) is referred to as the "lost in the shopping mall" or "parental misinformation" paradigm. Ost et al. (2005) used this paradigm to investigate whether participants would report false memories in appropriately conducted (non-coercive) interviews.

To ensure they were using appropriate methods, all interviewers received training. Furthermore, an independent rater coded all interviews for perceived "social pressure" tactics exerted by interviewers. Participants were interviewed three times (at one-week intervals) about two events. One of the events was a true event reported by the interviewee's parents; the second event was one that the interviewee had not experienced. Interviewers were kept blind as to the veracity of the events. Results showed that even when interviewed appropriately, with low levels of social influence reported by an independent rater, nearly a quarter of participants still reported details of childhood events that did not occur. One participant produced what could be described as a "full" report of the false event, while six others produced "partial" reports. Ost et al. (2005) also found a positive correlation between participants' scores on the Dissociative Experiences Scale and their levels of recall for the false event. It is important to note that participants who partially or fully recalled the false event reported higher confidence in the accuracy of their memories for the true event—indicating there was some distinction between the two types of memories.

Research on rich false memories has practical implications for the criminal legal system. In fact, much of the research in this area was inspired by cases of alleged child sexual abuse in the 1980s and 1990s, in which the accuser "recovered" memories of abuse in adulthood. Many accusers recovered memories of abuse after undergoing some form of therapy (Ost & Tully, 2016). Forensic assessors in cases involving recovered memories face a difficult task. Ost and Tully (2016) recommend that recovered memories are carefully assessed for characteristics that contrast with the way that memory is ordinarily understood to function.

Challenging the veracity of memories

False memories are common enough to merit the attention of scholars and practitioners (Nash et al., 2017). Furthermore, research has shown that such memories may persist after their veracity has been challenged and their inaccuracy accepted by the rememberer (Clark et al., 2012; Mazzoni, Clark et al., 2014; Mazzoni, Scoboria et al., 2010). When we share our memories with other people, there is the possibility that they will challenge them. For example, imagine recounting with your sibling a time you won a mini-golf trophy while on holiday. As you describe this cherished memory, you see the look of confusion on your sibling's face. They then insist that you didn't win the trophy—they did. Such a situation is not uncommon. These memories of shared ownership, known as *disputed memories*, have been reported between siblings, twins, and even friends (Sheen et al., 2006). It is therefore interesting to consider what happens to a memory once it has been challenged.

Compared to research showing the implantation of false memories and the distortion of existing memories (Loftus, 2005), there is relatively little research on the consequences of challenging memories. Perhaps one reason for this is that research has shown that when people are given the opportunity to discuss a co-witnessed event, the implantation of new memories or the distortion of existing memories are both more likely to occur than the omission of remembered details. In one study by Gabbert et al. (2006), pairs of participants watched what they thought was the same video of a crime. In actuality, a different version of the video was shown to each participant in the pair. After having an opportunity to discuss the video, the participants were interviewed individually. The findings showed that participants were more likely to include new details mentioned by their co-witness (that they themselves had not seen) than contradictory details (where each witness had seen different objects). Furthermore, when one participant failed to mention a detail that was present in their co-witness' version of the crime video, the co-witness very rarely withheld this information from their subsequent memory reports. These findings demonstrate that it is easier to implant new memories and change existing memories than it is to remove existing memories.

Conversely, some research has shown that it is easier to get participants to omit memories for certain details than it is to change or implant new details. Merckelbach et al. (2007) showed participants a series of images of rooms from around a home (e.g., a bedroom) in the presence of a confederate. Next, both the participants and confederate engaged in collaborative recall, taking turns recalling items that were presented in each scene. In one condition, during collaborative recall, the confederate intentionally reported seeing a detail that was not present in the scenes. In a second condition, the confederate challenged the participant when they reported an item. In a third condition, the confederate reported correct items only. After the collaborative recall, participants were given a free recall task where they recalled items from the scenes in the absence of the confederate. The results showed that nearly three-quarters of participants withheld at least one of the items challenged by the confederate, compared with only a third of participants in the control condition. In the condition where the confederate reported a new item, just over half of participants reported at least one of the false items reported by the confederate, compared with none of the participants in the control condition. These results suggest that challenging participants' memories for certain details can lead them to withhold these details in subsequent memory tasks.

Challenging the accuracy of an individual's recall for some details of an event may even affect how they report other, non-challenged details. In one study, participants watched a mock crime video alongside a confederate. They then verbally reported their answers to "practice task" questions about the crime. In one condition, the confederate corroborated the participant's answers with high confidence. In a second condition, the confederate gave responses that contradicted the participant's, also with high confidence. In a third control condition, the participant and the confederate did not report their answers to the practice task verbally. The participant then privately answered a different set of questions about the same event. Results showed that participants who heard contradictory answers from the confederate in the practice task exercise reported less detailed (more coarse-grained) information in the second recall task than participants in the other two conditions. The researchers proposed that having one's memory challenged may weaken their sense of memory self-efficacy, thus leading them to give more conservative responses to subsequent questions about the same event (Rechdan et al., 2018).

Non-believed memories

To understand the impact that challenges can have on our memory, it is important to consider some of the components of memory. Mazzoni and Kirsch (2002) distinguished between false *memories* and false *beliefs*. According to these authors, it is possible for a person to believe an event occurred in their past even though they do not clearly recall it. For example, you might see a photograph of an event you do not remember attending, but seeing the photograph could be sufficient for you to believe you experienced the event. Similarly, it has been established that people may hold vivid recollections of events that they no longer believe happened, or *nonbelieved memories* (Mazzoni et al., 2010).

Mazzoni et al. (2010) found that almost one-in-five people reported having a nonbelieved memory. Nonbelieved memories shared many of the phenomenological characteristics (e.g., visual details, intensity of emotions, and feelings of reliving the event) of memories that people still believed had occurred. When the researchers asked participants why they had stopped believing the event occurred, a leading reason was being told by someone else that it had not. These findings suggest that when other people challenge our memories, we retain the memory, but our belief that the event occurred is reduced.

To further understand nonbelieved memories, researchers have tried to elicit them in laboratory settings by challenging participants' memories. Clark et al. (2012) used doctored video evidence to implant false memories that participants had performed actions that they had not performed. In the first part of that research, participants were video recorded as they sat opposite a researcher who performed an action (e.g., clapping their hands), which the participant then performed themselves. This process was followed until 28 actions had been performed. The participant then left the room, and the researcher returned to the table to perform two additional actions. The researchers then created a video which showed the participant watching the researcher perform a series of actions, predominantly those that the participant themselves had also performed in the initial session. However, using video editing software, the researchers doctored two new videos which showed the participants watching the researcher performing the two additional actions that had been performed after the participants had left—these were the fake actions. When participants returned two days later, they saw these videos. The intention was that by seeing themselves in the video, watching the researcher performing the action, they would then "remember" performing the action themselves. Indeed, after seeing the videos, participants reported remembering and believing that they had performed the actions, including the false actions. Thus, participants had falsely remembered performing actions they had not performed. A few hours after the second session, participants returned for a third session. During this session, the participants' memory was challenged when the researchers provided details about how the videos had been doctored. Participants were then asked to provide ratings of their recollection and belief for performing each action. This time, participants' memory ratings were similar to their initial ratings, but their belief ratings for the false action decreased significantly. Thus, by challenging the participants' memories, the researchers managed to create nonbelieved memories (see Otgaar et al., 2013 for similar results).

Challenging false memories could be considered similar to correcting someone who misremembers a past event, such as in the mini-golf example above. However, what happens when the challenge is directed towards a true memory of something that did happen? Adopting the procedure used by Clark et al. (2012), Mazzoni et al. (2014) examined what happens when true memories are challenged. Instead of implanting false memories, participants were told that they had been exposed to doctored videos, although this was not the case. Participants provided belief and memory ratings before and after being told about the "doctored" videos. The results showed that challenging these true memories decreased participants' belief that they had performed the actions but not their memory. These findings demonstrate that challenging the memory of others might have a larger impact on their belief than their memory.

The enduring influence of belief

While our memories are often assumed to influence our behaviour (Nelson, 1993), recent research has shown that belief is more influential than memory (Bernstein et al., 2015). Scoboria et al. (2008) suggested to participants that they had become ill after eating peach yoghurt as a child. After being exposed to this suggestion, participants were less likely to eat peach yoghurt in a subsequent taste-testing session. Similarly, Laney et al. (2008) suggested to participants that they had had a positive experience with asparagus as a child. This resulted in the participants saying they would be more willing to order asparagus and pay more for it. It is unclear whether the behaviour changes reported in these two studies were motivated by a false memory or a false belief. However, Bernstein et al. (2005) specifically examined the development of beliefs and memories and their impact on behaviour by suggesting to participants that they had either become ill after eating hard-boiled eggs or dill pickles. Participants were then asked to state whether they actually remembered becoming ill, whether they believed they had become ill, or whether they did not believe they had experienced the illness. The results showed that those who reported believing they had become ill showed the greatest avoidance towards the foods. This finding demonstrates the influence that false beliefs can have on our behaviour.

The distinction between memory and belief is important for our understanding of false memories. Not all misremembering can be attributed to people falsely remembering events. In some cases, people may not remember an event but instead come to believe that it occurred. This was highlighted in the recent re-analysis of a study in which the authors reported that over two-thirds of their participants falsely remembered committing a crime (Shaw & Porter, 2015). When Wade et al. (2018) looked at these data, they considered that some of the participants might not have developed a false memory, but a false belief about committing the crime. Indeed, they found that nearly a third of participants met the criteria for false memories, and almost half met the criteria for false beliefs. What we don't yet know is whether these false memories or false beliefs could have behavioural consequences. Further research is needed in this area to examine how challenging the memory of a witness might impact their willingness to report information to investigators.

Concluding remarks

Inaccuracies in the recall of victims and eyewitnesses, whether they arise as the result of normal memory processes or through external sources of influence, continue to present a challenge for the criminal legal system. It is imperative that investigators follow research-based protocols to ensure that eyewitness memory is not contaminated and to elicit reports that are as detailed and accurate as possible. Research in this domain has come a long way in the space of nearly 40 years (see Meissner, 2021). Notably, in many countries, investigative interviews are now recorded, and body-worn cameras are used by police (though the latter have produced mixed results; Blaskovitz & Bennell, 2020; Christodoulou et al., 2019). Furthermore, the United Nations recently introduced *Principles on Effective Interviewing for Investigations and Information Gathering* (Méndez et al., 2021). Such developments will have the potential to greatly influence outcomes in criminal cases. However, real-world progress remains heavily dependent on the willingness of legal professionals to apply science in practice.

References

Anderson, M. C., Bjork, R. A., & Bjork, E. L. (1994). Remembering can cause forgetting: Retrieval dynamics in long-term memory. *Journal of Experimental Psychology: Learning, Memory, and Cognition, 20*(5), 1063–1087.

Bartlett, F. C. (1932). *Remembering: A study in experimental and social psychology.* Cambridge University Press.

Bernstein, D., Laney, C., Morris, E., & Loftus, E. (2005). False memories about food can lead to food avoidance. *Social Cognition, 23*(1), 11–34.

Bernstein, D., Scoboria, A., & Arnold, R. (2015). The consequences of suggesting false childhood food events. *Acta Psychologica, 156*, 1–7.

Bjork, R. A., & Bjork, E. L. (1992). A new theory of disuse and an old theory of stimulus fluctuation. In A. Healy, S. Kosslyn, & R. Shiffrin (Eds.), *From learning processes to cognitive processes: Essays in honor of William K. Estes* (Vol. 2, pp. 35–67). Earlbaum.

Blank, H., Ost, J., Davies, J., Jones, G., Lambert, K., & Salmon, K. (2013). Comparing the influence of directly vs. indirectly encountered post-event misinformation on eyewitness remembering. *Acta Psychologica, 144*(3), 635–641.

Blaskovitz, B., & Bennell, C. (2020). Exploring the potential impact of body worn cameras on memory in officer-involved critical incidents: A literature review. *Journal of Police and Criminal Psychology, 35*(3), 251–262.

Brown, R., & Kulik, J. (1977). Flashbulb memories. *Cognition, 5*(1), 73–99.

Brubacher, S. P., Glisic, U., Roberts, K. P., & Powell, M. (2011). Children's ability to recall unique aspects of one occurrence of a repeated event. *Applied Cognitive Psychology, 25*(3), 351–358.

Carli, L. L. (1999). Cognitive reconstruction, hindsight, and reactions to victims and perpetrators. *Personality and Social Psychology Bulletin, 25*(8), 966–979.

Chan, J. C. K., McDermott, K. B., & Roediger, H. L. III. (2006). Retrieval-induced facilitation: Initially nontested material can benefit from prior testing of related material. *Journal of Experimental Psychology: General, 135*(4), 553–571.

Christodoulou, C., Paterson, H., & Kemp, R. (2019). Body-worn cameras: Evidence-base and implications. *Current Issues in Criminal Justice, 31*(4), 513–524.

Clark, A., Nash, R. A., Fincham, G., & Mazzoni, G. (2012). Creating non-believed memories for recent autobiographical events. *PLoS One, 7*(3), e32998.

Cuc, A., Koppel, J., & Hirst, W. (2007). Silence is not golden: A case for socially shared retrieval-induced forgetting. *Psychological Science, 18*(8), 727–733.

Deck, S. L., & Paterson, H. M. (2020). Adults also have difficulty recalling one instance of a repeated event. *Applied Cognitive Psychology, 35*, 286–292.

Dudukovic, N. M., Marsh, E. J., & Tversky, B. (2004). Telling a story or telling it straight: The effects of entertaining versus accurate retellings on memory. *Applied Cognitive Psychology, 18*(2), 125–143.

Ebbinghaus, H. (1885). *Über das gedächtnis: untersuchungen zur experimentellen psychologie.* Duncker & Humblot.

Frenda, S. J., Nichols, R. M., & Loftus, E. F. (2011). Current issues and advances in misinformation research. *Current Directions in Psychological Science, 20*(1), 20–23.

Gabbert, F., Memon, A., Allan, K., & Wright, D. B. (2004). Say it to my face: Examining the effects of socially encountered misinformation. *Legal and Criminological Psychology, 9*(2), 215–227.

Gabbert, F., Memon, A., & Wright, D. (2006). Memory conformity: Disentangling the steps toward influence during a discussion. *Psychonomic Bulletin & Review, 13*(3), 480–485.

Gould, J. B., & Leo, R. A. (2010). One hundred years later: Wrongful convictions after a century of research. *The Journal of Criminal Law and Criminology*, 825–868.

Gurney, D. J., Pine, K. J., & Wiseman, R. (2013). The gestural misinformation effect: Skewing eyewitness testimony through gesture. *The American Journal of Psychology, 126*(3), 301–314.

Hardt, O., Nader, K., & Nadel, L. (2013). Decay happens: The role of active forgetting in memory. *Trends in Cognitive Sciences, 17*(3), 111–120.

Hennes, E. P., Ruisch, B. C., Feygina, I., Monteiro, C. A., & Jost, J. T. (2016). Motivated recall in the service of the economic system: The case of anthropogenic climate change. *Journal of Experimental Psychology: General, 145*(6), 755–771.

Hirst, W., Phelps, E. A., Meksin, R., Vaidya, C. J., Johnson, M. K., Mitchell, K. J., Buckner, R. L., Budson, A. E., Gabrieli, J. D., Lustig, C., Mather, M., Ochsner, K. N., Schacter, D., Simons, J. S., Lyle, K. B., Cuc, K. F., & Olsson, A. (2015). A ten-year follow-up of a study of memory for the attack of September 11, 2001: Flashbulb memories and memories for flashbulb events. *Journal of Experimental Psychology, General, 144*(3), 604–623.

Kleider, H. M., Pezdek, K., Goldinger, S. D., & Kirk, A. (2008). Schema-driven source misattribution errors: Remembering the expected from a witnessed event. *Applied Cognitive Psychology, 22*(1), 1–20.

Laney, C., Morris, E. K., Bernstein, D. M., Wakefield, B. M., & Loftus, E. F. (2008). Asparagus, a love story: Healthier eating could be just a false memory away. *Experimental Psychology*, *55*(5), 291–300.

Lindsay, D. S., & Johnson, M. K. (1987). Reality monitoring and suggestibility: Children's ability to discriminate among memories from different sources. In *Children's eyewitness memory* (pp. 92–121). Springer.

Loftus, E. F. (1975). Leading questions and the eyewitness report. *Cognitive Psychology*, *7*(4), 560–572.

Loftus, E. F. (2005). Planting misinformation in the human mind: A 30-year investigation of the malleability of memory. *Learning & Memory*, *12*(4), 361–366.

Loftus, E. F., Miller, D. G., & Burns, H. J. (1978). Semantic integration of verbal information into a visual memory. *Journal of Experimental Psychology: Human Learning and Memory*, *4*(1), 19–31.

Loftus, E. F., & Pickrell, J. E. (1995). The formation of false memories. *Psychiatric Annals*, *25*(12), 720–725.

Manarin, B. (2009). Bedeviled by delay: Straight talk about memory loss, procedural manipulation and the myth of swift justice. *Windsor Review of Legal and Social Issues*, *27*, 117.

Mazzoni, G., Clark, A., & Nash, R. (2014). Disowned recollections: Denying true experiences undermines belief in occurrence but not judgments of remembering. *Acta Psychologica*, *145*, 139–146.

Mazzoni, G., & Kirsch, I. (2002). Autobiographical memories and beliefs: A preliminary metacognitive model. In T. J. Perfect & B. L. Schwartz (Eds.), *Applied metacognition* (pp. 121–145). Cambridge University Press.

Mazzoni, G., Scoboria, A., & Harvey, L. (2010). Nonbelieved memories. *Psychological Science*, *21*(9), 1334–1340.

Meissner, C. A. (2021). "What works?" Systematic reviews and meta-analyses of the investigative interviewing research literature. *Applied Cognitive Psychology*, *35*(2), 322–328.

Méndez, J. E., et al. (2021). *Principles on effective interviewing for investigations and information gathering*. Retrieved July 5, 2022, from https://interviewingprinciples.com/

Merckelbach, H., Van Roermund, H., & Candel, I. (2007). Effects of collaborative recall: Denying true information is as powerful as suggesting misinformation. *Psychology, Crime & Law*, *13*(6), 573–581.

Murayama, K., Miyatsu, T., Buchli, D., & Storm, B. C. (2014). Forgetting as a consequence of retrieval: A meta-analytic review of retrieval-induced forgetting. *Psychological Bulletin*, *140*(5), 1383–1409.

Nash, R. A., Wade, K. A., Garry, M., Loftus, E. F., & Ost, J. (2017). Misrepresentations and flawed logic about the prevalence of false memories. *Applied Cognitive Psychology*, *31*(1), 31–33.

Nelson, K. (1993). The psychological and social origins of autobiographical memory. *Psychological Science*, *4*(1), 7–14.

Ost, J., & Costall, A. (2002). Misremembering Bartlett: A study in serial reproduction. *British Journal of Psychology*, *93*(2), 243–255.

Ost, J., Fellows, B., & Bull, R. (1997). Individual differences and the suggestibility of human memory. *Contemporary Hypnosis*, *14*(2), 132–137.

Ost, J., Foster, S., Costall, A., & Bull, R. (2005). False reports of childhood events in appropriate interviews. *Memory*, *13*(7), 700–710.

Ost, J., Granhag, P. A., Udell, J., & Roos af Hjelmsäter, E. (2008). Familiarity breeds distortion: The effects of media exposure on false reports concerning media coverage of the terrorist attacks in London on 7 July 2005. *Memory*, *16*(1), 76–85.

Ost, J., & Tully, B. (2016). Recovered memory. In *Encyclopedia of forensic and legal medicine* (pp. 77–82). Elsevier.

Otgaar, H., Scoboria, A., & Smeets, T. (2013). Experimentally evoking nonbelieved memories for childhood events. *Journal of Experimental Psychology: Learning, Memory, and Cognition*, *39*(3), 717–730.

Paterson, H. M., & Kemp, R. I. (2006). Comparing methods of encountering post-event information: The power of co-witness suggestion. *Applied Cognitive Psychology*, *20*(8), 1083–1099.

Rechdan, J., Hope, L., Sauer, J. D., Sauerland, M., Ost, J., & Merckelbach, H. (2018). The effects of co-witness discussion and misinformation on confidence and precision in eyewitness memory reports. *Memory*, *26*(7), 904–912.

Rechdan, J., Saurland, M., Hope, L., & Ost, J. (2016). Was that how it happened? Shaping our memory for personal experiences in conversation with others. *The Inquisitive Mind*, *7*(31).

Roberts, J. V. (1985). The attitude-memory relationship after 40 years: A meta-analysis of the literature. *Basic and Applied Social Psychology*, *6*(3), 221–241.

Roediger III, H. L., & DeSoto, K. A. (2015). Psychology of reconstructive memory. In *International encyclopedia of the social and behavioral sciences* (2nd ed., pp. 50–55). Elsevier.

Rowland, C. A., & DeLosh, E. L. (2014). Benefits of testing for nontested information: Retrieval-induced facilitation of episodically bound material. *Psychonomic Bulletin & Review*, *21*(6), 1516–1523.

Saunders, J., & MacLeod, M. D. (2002). New evidence on the suggestibility of memory: The role of retrieval-induced forgetting in misinformation effects. *Journal of Experimental Psychology: Applied*, *8*(2), 127–142.

Schachter, D. L. (2021). The seven sins of memory: An update. *Memory*, 1–6.

Scoboria, A., Mazzoni, G., & Jarry, J. (2008). Suggesting childhood food illness results in reduced eating behavior. *Acta Psychologica*, *128*(2), 304–309.

Semmler, C., Brewer, N., & Bradfield Douglass, A. (2012). Jurors believe eyewitnesses. In B. L. Cutler (Ed.), *Conviction of the innocent: Lessons from psychological research* (pp. 185–209). American Psychological Association.

Shaw, J., & Porter, S. (2015). Constructing rich false memories of committing crime. *Psychological Science*, *26*(3), 291–301.

Sheen, M., Kemp, S., & Rubin, D. (2006). Disputes over memory ownership: What memories are disputed? *Genes, Brain and Behavior*, *5*(S1), 9–13.

Talarico, J. M., & Rubin, D. C. (2003). Confidence, not consistency, characterizes flashbulb memories. *Psychological Science*, *14*(5), 455–461.

Tuckey, M. R., & Brewer, N. (2003). The influence of schemas, stimulus ambiguity, and interview schedule on eyewitness memory over time. *Journal of Experimental Psychology: Applied*, *9*(2), 101–118.

Tversky, B., & Marsh, E. J. (2000). Biased retellings of events yield biased memories. *Cognitive Psychology*, *40*(1), 1–38.

Wade, K. A., Garry, M., & Pezdek, K. (2018). Deconstructing rich false memories of committing crime: Commentary on Shaw and Porter (2015). *Psychological Science*, *29*(3), 471–476.

Wells, G. L. (1978). Applied eyewitness-testimony research: System variables and estimator variables. *Journal of Personality and Social Psychology*, *36*(12), 1546–1557.

West, E., & Meterko, V. (2015). Innocence project: DNA exonerations, 1989–2014: Review of data and findings from the first 25 years. *Albany Law Review*, *79*, 717.

2 Intersections between metamemory and eyewitness testimony

Renan Benigno Saraiva

Erroneous eyewitness testimony can have very influential costs for society and the criminal justice system all over the world. That is because eyewitness testimony errors can motivate useless lines of investigation, or in more severe cases, contribute to the conviction of innocent suspects. Further additional crimes committed by actual perpetrators are only one of the many devastating impacts of wrongful testimony, in addition to severe negative consequences facing innocent convicts. On the other hand, eyewitnesses' correct accounts play an essential role in the prosecution of actual perpetrators, especially when other physical evidence is lacking. So, as with other types of evidence, eyewitness testimony can be both a crucial lead to solving criminal cases or a remarkably harmful piece of evidence if it is poorly handled or poorly understood. Psychological research has greatly contributed to that matter by advancing our understanding of human memory functioning, which has helped establish, for example, better guidelines for interviewing witnesses and conducting more effective lineup identification procedures. This chapter will summarize a new research line in the field of eyewitness testimony which examines the role of metamemory in how individuals remember and report criminal events. Metamemory is a construct used to describe the knowledge, perceptions, and beliefs individuals have about their own memory and the memory system in more general terms. Several important elements of eyewitness testimony settings are closely related to metamemory factors, such as witnesses' judgements about whether they can remember certain aspects of the crime or judgements of confidence for specific suspect identifications. This chapter will present some of the key links between eyewitness testimony and metamemory research, including whether metamemory assessments can be used to estimate eyewitness memory performance and the role of metamemory as an underlying mechanism that gives rise to confidence statements.

Theoretical frameworks of metamemory

We all need to make judgements about the likely accuracy of our memories from time to time. An interviewer relying on his or her notes must make this judgement, as must an eyewitness sworn to tell the truth in court. The ability

DOI: 10.4324/9781003308546-4

to examine one's own memory performance is a critical feature of normal metacognitive functioning. Metamemory, an aspect of metacognition, is a latent construct that was formulated from the early developmental psychology literature to describe the knowledge, perceptions, and beliefs individuals have about their own memory and the memory system in more general terms (Dunlosky & Bjork, 2008). These beliefs and judgements greatly influence behaviour because they are used to monitor and control how we deploy cognitive resources. For example, if students believe some important material was not properly learned, they may spend more time studying that material or employ strategies to better memorize its content. Thus, metamnemonic judgements indicate how well target items are either available or accessible in memory. For instance, an individual may be able to retrieve an online password now, but metamnemonic judgements assess whether the same password will be retrievable at some future date. Similarly, at test, an individual may decide that even though she or he may not know the password now, she or he has a high "feeling of knowing" for the item, so the individual chooses to spend more time trying to retrieve the password.

Both memory monitoring and control play an important role in a variety of everyday life situations. For instance, depending on monitoring results, non-mastered materials can be further studied, a more effective learning strategy can be adopted, or external cues can be used to improve remembering. The efficacy of this metacognitive system requires a feedback system between monitoring and control mechanisms, which is provided by metamemory judgements. Several types of metamemory judgements have been investigated, including reality and source monitoring, retrospective confidence judgements, "don't know" judgements, hindsight judgements, and judgements of subjective experience (Metcalfe, 2000).

Metamemory judgements can be divided into those made during the acquisition of knowledge (judgements of learning) and judgements made at the time of retrieval (feelings of knowing; Nelson & Narens, 1994). Judgements of learning can be defined as prospective confidence judgements of encoding efficiency made after exposure to an item but prior to a recall test. In forensic settings, judgements of learning can be observed when eyewitnesses of a crime are asked whether they would be able to recognize the perpetrator or produce a facial composite. In this scenario, the eyewitness needs to reflect on their memory ability, their internal state, and the encoding conditions when deciding whether a recognition would be possible. In contrast, a feeling of knowing can be defined as a retrospective confidence judgement of encoding efficiency made during the time of retrieval. After making a lineup identification, for example, eyewitnesses may express how confident they are in their decision. Confidence judgements are one commonly used method for determining an individual's belief that the information retrieved from memory is accurate.

A common assumption across metamemory theories is that the processes underlying memory confidence judgements fall into two broad categories: target-based sources and cue-based sources. That is, confidence judgements are based on many different characteristics of memory retrieval processes, such as memory vividness and completeness, response latency, and the quantity and intensity of retrieved information. Target-based sources include the ease of stimuli processing, the amount of information encoded, or interference from distractors. In direct-access theories, for example, there is an emphasis on target-based information so that people monitor the specific memory representation of an item when making metamnemonic judgements. Cue-based sources include information that is not intrinsic to the target, such as familiarity with the stimuli, domain knowledge, and social desirability (Metcalfe, 2000). Cue-based sources play an important role in familiarity-based theories and accessibility theories, positing that people draw on information other than the specific representation to form a confidence judgement.

One influential theoretical framework proposed by Koriat (2000) extends on the processes leading to metacognitive judgements just outlined. In this framework, metacognitive judgements can be based on information (or theory-based) and experience (or affect-based). That is, monitoring memory processes can be based on an explicitly inferential process or on a sheer subjective feeling. Consider, for example, an eyewitness who fails to recall a specific fact of a crime or a characteristic of the perpetrator. The witness may still be able to make an educated guess about the plausibility that the solicited information will be subsequently recalled or recognized. Such judgement may be based on domain-specific memories and beliefs and can take the form of "there is little chance that I would know the answer" or "I ought to know the answer".

Judgements of confidence and memory self-efficacy

The degree of confidence that an individual expresses in a memory plays a critical role in how an outsider evaluates the verity of that memory. In many applied areas, such as jury decisions and medical diagnoses, confidence in one's judgements determines the likelihood of translating these judgements to action. But the functional value of confidence depends on whether people are generally accurate in monitoring their memories or knowledge. Results of many studies have demonstrated positive correlations across items between subjective confidence and objective accuracy in knowledge tests, suggesting that people have good insights into the relative accuracy of their knowledge. This has been found to be the case across a variety of metacognitive judgements. Judgements of learning made about different items during study are moderately predictive of the relative future recall or recognition of these items (Narens et al., 2008). Similarly, feelings of knowing judgements following a recall failure are predictive of the likelihood of recalling the target at some later time. Finally, confidence judgements in general knowledge answers are generally diagnostic of the answer's correctness (Koriat et al., 2008).

A specific dimension of metamemory that is relevant to everyday memory functioning is memory self-efficacy, defined as the self-evaluation of one's general competence and ability across many different memory domains and tasks.

Hertzog and Dixon (1994) propose a hierarchical structure for this construct, including global beliefs about memory ability, "I have a good memory", and situational beliefs, "I can remember this address, so I will go there without looking it up". Unlike situational beliefs, global memory self-efficacy beliefs are enduring and have been constructed on the basis of previous experiences and implicit theories and schemas about memory. Global memory self-efficacy beliefs may also be defined in relation to an individual's appraisal of his or her ability in a specific memory domain, such as semantic memory, memory for faces, or episodic memory. Some evidence points to a positive relation between memory self-efficacy and memory performance in different tasks. However, the outcomes of studies focusing specifically on face recognition show that individuals have limited insight into their ability to recognize unfamiliar faces (Bindemann et al., 2012).

Metamemory in eyewitness testimony contexts

Metamemory processes are implicated at various stages of memory formation, and those operating during remembering are particularly crucial in determining memory accuracy and error. These processes have several functions that are notably relevant in eyewitness testimony contexts, such as: specifying the origin of mental experience, avoiding suggestibility effects and memory contamination by attributing them to their proper source, adopting appropriate strategies to enhance memory for the task at hand, formulating a comprehensive and informative account of a past event, monitoring the accuracy of remembered information, and regulating the reporting of information according to the incentive for accuracy.

Metacognitive monitoring has been studied in many different contexts, such as education, language learning, problem-solving, and teaching, offering an integrated theoretical framework to explain how people evaluate and judge their own memories. Trace access theory, for example, postulates that both confidence and accuracy are dependent on memory trace strength. Stronger memory traces, or information with a higher number of associated stimuli, is more likely to be remembered and receive higher confidence ratings. Findings regarding the optimality hypothesis reported by Deffenbacher (1980) are consistent with trace access theory so that witnesses with better encoding conditions are more capable of making correct identifications and accurate judgements about their performance. However, studies focusing on understanding why optimal conditions increase the confidence-accuracy (CA) relationship seem sparse. Better viewing conditions provide witnesses with better memory traces, leading to higher accuracy rates. But why optimal conditions lead to a higher CA relationship is a more challenging question. Leippe and Eisenstadt (2014) argue that better access to memory evaluation may allow witnesses to correctly reduce their confidence when they are inaccurate. They also propose that witnesses with an overall weak memory would have weaker memory traces despite optimal conditions and would use other sources of information—including their weak memory traces—to make confidence judgements. In both cases, inaccurate information would be more likely to be followed by low confidence decisions, increasing the CA relationship.

Despite its contribution, trace access theory ignores many important aspects of memory confidence judgements. Information derived from a memory trace is just one of many sources of information that influence witnesses' metamemory and beliefs. Witnesses making a self-evaluation to gauge confidence can take into account many intrinsic, heuristic, and self-credibility cues, especially when the memory trace is weak (Leippe & Eisenstadt, 2014). Intrinsic cues include self-reflections on memory processes, from which people identify information that they learned to associate with accurate or inaccurate memory. For example, Kebbell et al. (1996) found that witnesses showed less confidence in their correct answers to hard questions when compared to their correct answers to easy questions, possibly because question difficulty is used as a heuristic to judge confidence. Furthermore, witnesses usually rely on recognition speed to make inferences about their confidence, showing greater confidence when they are able to make rapid judgements.

Heuristic cues comprise one's beliefs about external factors that can help or impair memory encoding and retrieval. It may be the case, for example, that witnesses feel more confident when they put more effort into recalling tasks, even when this does not lead to changes in accuracy. People also usually believe that their memory will be stronger with prolonged exposure duration, consequently showing higher confidence for stimuli they have been exposed to longer (Memon et al., 2003). Finally, self-credibility cues derive from people's self-evaluation of their overall memory performance. Some could overestimate their ability to recall events, being overconfident on identification and recall tasks; others may underestimate their memory ability and show underconfidence (Olsson & Juslin, 1999). If confidence statements and memory traces are partially based on heuristic cues, it can be expected that self-ratings of memory capacity are predictive of performance in eyewitness memory tasks. That is, an individual's self-evaluations of their own memory performance may be related to their accuracy, confidence, and over/underconfidence in identification and free recall settings.

Eyewitness confidence–accuracy relationship

Criminal justice systems may rely on eyewitnesses' confidence when evaluating the likely guilty of a defendant or a suspect. The U.S. Supreme Court, for instance, endorses eyewitnesses' confidence as one criterion for assessing their accuracy (Neil v. Biggers, 1972). Literature also shows that eyewitnesses' confidence influences decisions made by police officers, lawyers, and jurors. For example, jurors are more likely to believe testimony when it is provided by a confident, rather than uncertain, witness. So, although confidence measures can be central to criminal investigations, they may lead to undesirable consequences for justice if eyewitnesses are overconfident or underconfident.

Overconfident witnesses may lead investigators to follow incorrect leads or—more severely—incriminate an innocent person. Underconfident witnesses may withhold relevant information or be insufficiently confident even when a perpetrator is correctly identified.

Results from most of the earliest studies on the witness' confidence-accuracy (CA) relationship showed that confidence and accuracy were often poorly correlated. A few years later, Bothwell et al. (1987) conducted a meta-analysis of 35 staged-event studies and found a small effect size for the confidence-accuracy relationship, recommending caution when using confidence to predict identification accuracy in actual cases. At the turn of the millennium, the majority of experts in eyewitness memory interviewed by Kassin et al. (2001) agreed that confidence is not a good marker of accuracy. However, new approaches to statistical inference in the field of eyewitness testimony revealed two important aspects that challenged the previously negative conclusions about the CA relationship: the role of calibration approaches and the likely impact of moderator variables.

Calibration approaches draw on the principle that there are multiple ways of calculating the relationship between confidence and accuracy. The most conventional method, for example, simply compares the accuracy of individuals who differ in confidence. This calculation is basically a point-biserial correlation between confidence and accuracy across the witnesses, usually used in studies where many witnesses testify about a single event. This approach is suitable for answering the question of whether a more confident witness is also likely to be a more accurate witness or vice versa. However, some researchers have argued that the point-biserial correlation is not the most informative measure of the CA relationship because it does not express the extent to which confidence corresponds to the actual probability of accuracy (e.g., Juslin et al., 1996). An alternative approach is the use of calibration, which aims to verify if a witness is more accurate about the information for which they show the greatest confidence. In this approach, the confidence-accuracy relationship is computed across every level of confidence, typically in 10% increments (e.g., a scale that ranges from 0%—"not at all certain"—to 100%—"totally certain"). A perfect calibration occurs when the group's confidence level equals the percentage of accurate answers for that group (e.g., 90% of accurate witnesses in the group with 90% confidence). The calibration levels can be expressed visually by plotting accuracy rates as a function of confidence grouping; in this case, a diagonal line would represent perfect calibration on all confidence groups (see Figure 2.1). Usually, a confidence index (CI) is computed, comprising the average squared discrepancy for each witness in a given confidence level and the actual proportion of witnesses who were correct in the same confidence group. Values of CI near zero indicate a stronger confidence-accuracy relation. Another related statistic is over/underconfidence (O/U), which is computed by subtracting the mean accuracy from mean confidence for the entire witness sample, with scores that range from -1 (underconfidence) to +1 (overconfidence).

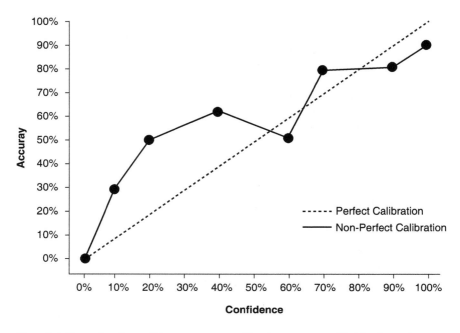

Figure 2.1 Example of a confidence-accuracy calibration curve provided by the author.

Research adopting calibration techniques shows that good calibration might exist for eyewitness confidence-accuracy in identification tasks even if the data yield low correlations values. Olsson (2000), for example, has found that although confidence-accuracy correlations were small to moderate, the calibration indices were found to be more valid indicators of accuracy. Also, Brewer et al. (2002) conducted a study using a videotaped theft and found good calibration indices for eyewitness identifications, even though the correlation indices for this same experiment were rather low ($r = 0.14$). These and other findings show that the CA relationship is stronger when expressed in terms of calibration computations than when expressed using conventional r indices. The practical implication of this discussion is that, at first sight, calibration measures may have more substantial forensic application because they are often better predictors of the identification accuracy of individuals.

Calibration approaches may have some limitations, though. Leippe and Eisenstadt (2014) identify five reasons to be cautious when evaluating the usefulness of calibration methods, even though this approach seems to show a higher level of a CA relationship correspondence than r. The first is that the small literature on CA calibration comprises studies that have not found good calibration in identification tasks. Second, CI values present the same diagnosticity problem that modest CA r values do. In other words, the interpretation of a witness CI score is dependent on multiple-assessment comparisons. Of course, the comparison of multiple assessments is not likely to be present in real cases where single assessments of witness confidence for the identification of a single target predominate. The third one is that percentage scales, commonly used in experiments to assess confidence, are not used by practitioners, raising doubts about comparisons between calibration and the open-ended questions adopted by police (i.e., question: "How confident are you?" answer: "Very confident"). However, it is worth noting that this third limitation is of an applied practice nature, and it is not specifically related to a problem with calibration itself. Fourth, subjective probabilities such as CI values might not be useful in actual cases where the parties want to know for sure if a witness is correct or not. Finally, confidence and accuracy are highly malleable. This means that any type of CA relationship might still present imperfections when given other social and cognitive factors that influence either confidence or accuracy.

A more complete picture of the usefulness of confidence measures can only be achieved when considering the necessary conditions for a CA relation to be stronger. In other words, CA effects are not fixed but vary depending on many other variables that can reduce or increase the CA relationship (see Wixted & Wells, 2017). The first studies on the role of moderator variables showed that eyewitnesses with optimal viewing conditions often show higher CA relationships (Deffenbacher, 1980), which was later confirmed by further studies on exposure duration (Memon et al., 2003). Characteristics of the identification target, such as attractiveness and distinctiveness, also affect the CA relation. Eyewitnesses that take longer intervals to give a testimony are often more overconfident than those that give accounts or identifications shortly after the event, an effect possibly associated with memory contamination (Sauer et al., 2010). A meta-analytic review by Sporer et al. (1995) on target-present and target-absent line-ups also showed that the CA relationship was dependent on choice, with choosers (positive identifications) often having a higher CA relation than non-choosers.

Metamemory traits as predictors of eyewitness performance

Some recent research has focused on whether eyewitnesses' expressions of confidence are influenced by individual differences related to memory self-efficacy and endorsement of memory strategies. It was posited that if confidence judgements are partly based on individual differences and intrinsic cues, then witnesses could tend to be underconfident or overconfident depending on their metamemory traits (Leippe & Eisenstadt, 2014). One new line of research aims to elucidate whether metamemory assessments could be useful to distinguish overconfident from underconfident witnesses.

In the context of eyewitness identifications, one specific scale has been developed to assess witnesses' memory self-efficacy for identifying persons and faces. The Eyewitness Metamemory Scale (Saraiva et al., 2019a, 2020b) was tailored specifically for use in face memory and eyewitness identification settings, containing 23 items assessing memory contentment ("I am confident with my ability to remember faces in a stressful situation"), memory discontentment ("Compared to other people, I think I would be a much worse eyewitness"), and memory strategies ("I often create a visual image in my mind of a face that I want to remember"). The scale has shown adequate psychometric properties, although its predictive value of eyewitness identification performance has shown some mixed results. In Saraiva et al. (2020a), for example, it was found that the discontentment factor of the Eyewitness Metamemory Scale (EMS) was predictive of identification accuracy among choosers for both biased and unbiased lineups. That is, the more discontent witnesses were with their general ability to remember faces and persons, the less accurate they were in identification tasks. However, in a similar study by Saraiva et al. (2019b), it was found that the EMS-contentment factor was predictive of identification performance but not EMS-discontentment. Therefore, the current findings on this research line seem to suggest that memory self-efficacy may indeed be a predictor of identification performance, although the exact memory self-efficacy factors that are better predictors of accuracy still warrant further research.

Although still incipient, some research lines have focused on determining whether individual differences can provide diagnostic information for lineup identifications. In this context, it is argued that the outcome of lineup identifications may be dependent on eyewitnesses' ability to process and recognize unfamiliar faces. In fact, a growing literature supports the idea that performance on standardized tests of face recognition can provide a more informative assessment of eyewitness identification performance. Other studies have focused on individual differences that may predispose eyewitnesses to choose someone from a lineup. Baldassari et al. (2019), for example, found that individuals who have a higher proclivity to choose in a lineup skills test are more likely to choose someone from a mock witness lineup identification. Knowing whether some eyewitnesses are more inclined to choose someone from a lineup is important as this information can be used to better weigh the probative value of suspect identifications.

Concluding remarks

This chapter was focused towards elucidating the relation between metamemory and eyewitness identification accuracy, confidence, and confidence-accuracy relation. The overview of studies in this area suggests that to improve or better estimate eyewitness memory accuracy, it is crucial to understand how people monitor and evaluate their own memory cognitive processes. Specifically, this research line contributes to our understanding of the relation between self-assessments of memory-efficacy and eyewitnesses' performance. This new knowledge can provide a solid foundation for research investigating the relation between metamemory assessments and eyewitness memory accuracy and confidence in the future. Although still in its infancy, this line of research has important implications for the understanding and application of postdictors of eyewitness accuracy, ultimately contributing to a better evaluation of eyewitness evidence in the criminal justice system.

References

Baldassari, M. J., Kantner, J., & Lindsay, D. S. (2019). The importance of decision bias for predicting eyewitness lineup choices: Toward a Lineup Skills Test. *Cognitive Research: Principles and Implications*, *4*(1), 2.

Bindemann, M., Avetisyan, M., & Rakow, T. (2012). Who can recognize unfamiliar faces? Individual differences and observer consistency in person identification. *Journal of Experimental Psychology. Applied*, *18*(3), 277–291.

Bothwell, R. K., Deffenbacher, K. A., & Brigham, J. C. (1987). Correlation of eyewitness accuracy and confidence: Optimality hypothesis revisited. *Journal of Applied Psychology*, *72*(4), 691.

Brewer, N., Keast, A., & Rishworth, A. (2002). The confidence-accuracy relationship in eyewitness identification: The effects of reflection and disconfirmation on correlation and calibration. *Journal of Experimental Psychology: Applied*, *8*(1), 44–56.

Deffenbacher, K. A. (1980). Eyewitness accuracy and confidence. *Law and Human Behavior*, *4*(4), 243–260.

Dunlosky, J., & Bjork, R. A. (2008). *Handbook of metamemory and memory*. Psychology Press.

Hertzog, C., & Dixon, R. A. (1994). *Metacognitive development in adulthood and old age*. In J. Metcalfe & A. P. Shimamura (Eds.), *Metacognition: Knowing about knowing* (pp. 227–251). MIT Press.

Juslin, P., Olsson, N., & Winman, A. (1996). Calibration and diagnosticity of confidence in eyewitness identification: Comments on what can be inferred from the low confidence—accuracy correlation. *Journal of Experimental Psychology: Learning, Memory, and Cognition*, *22*(5), 1304.

Kassin, S. M., Tubb, V. A., Hosch, H. M., & Memon, A. (2001). On the "general acceptance" of eyewitness testimony research: A new survey of the experts. *American Psychologist*, *56*(5), 405.

Kebbell, M. R., Wagstaff, G. F., & Covey, J. A. (1996). The influence of item difficulty on the relationship between eyewitness confidence and accuracy. *British Journal of Psychology*, *87*, 653–662.

Koriat, A. (2000). The feeling of knowing: Some metatheoretical implications for consciousness and control. *Consciousness and Cognition*, *9*(2), 149–171.

Koriat, A., Nussinson, R., Bless, H., & Shaked, N. (2008). In J. Dunlosky & R. Bjork (Eds.), *Handbook of metamemory and memory* (pp. 117–136). Psychology Press.

Leippe, M. R., & Eisenstadt, D. (2014). Eyewitness confidence and the confidence-accuracy relationship in memory for people. In R. C. Lindsay, D. F. Ross, J. D. Read, & M. M. P. Toglia (Eds.), *The handbook of eyewitness psychology: Volume II: Memory for people* (pp. 377–425). Psychology Press.

Memon, A., Hope, L., & Bull, R. (2003). Exposure duration: Effects on eyewitness accuracy and confidence. *British Journal of Psychology*, *94*(3), 339–354.

Metcalfe, J. (2000). Metamemory: Theory and data. In E. Tulving & F. I. M. Craik (Eds.), *The Oxford handbook of memory* (pp. 197–211). Oxford University Press.

Narens, L., Nelson, T. O., & Scheck, P. (2008). Memory monitoring and the delayed JOL effect. In J. Dunlosky & R. Bjork (Eds.), *Handbook of metamemory and memory* (pp. 137–153). Psychology Press.

Neil v. Biggers. (1972). *Oyez*. Retrieved July 5, 2022, from www.oyez.org/cases/1972/71-586

Nelson, T. O., & Narens, L. (1994). Why investigate metacognition. Metacognition: Knowing about knowing, 1–25. In J. Metcalfe & A. P. Shimamura (Eds.), *Metacognition: Knowing about knowing* (pp. 1–26). MIT Press.

Olsson, N. (2000). A comparison of correlation, calibration, and diagnosticity as measures of the confidence—accuracy relationship in witness identification. *Journal of Applied Psychology, 85*(4), 504–511.

Olsson, N., & Juslin, P. (1999). Can self-reported encoding strategy and recognition skill be diagnostic of performance in eyewitness identifications? *Journal of Applied Psychology, 84*(1), 42–49.

Sauer, J., Brewer, N., Zweck, T., & Weber, N. (2010). The effect of retention interval on the confidence-accuracy relationship for eyewitness identification. *Law and Human Behavior, 34*(4), 337–347.

Saraiva, R. B., Hope, L., Horselenberg, R., Ost, J., Sauer, J. D., & van Koppen, P. J. (2020b). Using metamemory measures and memory tests to estimate eyewitness free recall performance. *Memory, 28*(1), 94–106.

Saraiva, R. B., van Boeijen, I. M., Hope, L., Horselenberg, R., Sauerland, M., & van Koppen, P. J. (2019a). Development and validation of the eyewitness metamemory scale. *Applied Cognitive Psychology, 33*(5), 964–973.

Saraiva, R. B., van Boeijen, I. M., Hope, L., Horselenberg, R., Sauerland, M., & van Koppen, P. J. (2020a). Eyewitness metamemory predicts identification performance in biased and unbiased line-ups. *Legal and Criminological Psychology, 25*(2), 111–132.

Saraiva, R. B., van Boeijen, I. M., Hope, L., Horselenberg, R., & van Koppen, P. J. (2019b). *Using general and eyewitness-specific metamemory assessments to estimate performance in multiple identifications*. Retrieved March 21, 2022, from https://osf.io/pnhm3

Sporer, S. L., Penrod, S., Read, D., & Cutler, B. (1995). Choosing, confidence, and accuracy: A meta-analysis of the confidence-accuracy relation in eyewitness identification studies. *Psychological Bulletin, 118*(3), 315–327.

Wixted, J. T., & Wells, G. L. (2017). The relationship between eyewitness confidence and identification accuracy: A new synthesis. *Psychological Science in the Public Interest, 18*(1), 10–65.

3 The effects of acute stress on eyewitness memory

Carey Marr

In our everyday lives, we often experience acute stressors, such as fighting with a loved one, taking a difficult exam, or giving a public speech. Hence, most people can relate to the feeling of stress and the accompanying physiological symptoms of a racing heart, increased sweating, and a tensed body. This chapter will focus on how these ordinary stress responses affect people in extraordinary situations. In England and Wales, nearly one-third of all adults report having witnessed a crime within the past year (Willoughby, 2015). While not uncommon, witnessing a crime may cause extreme stress due to the novelty and unpredictability of such events (Dickerson & Kemeny, 2004). In addition, feelings of acute stress can emerge when eyewitnesses later give their statements at a police station or in court, situations that, for many people, are unusual and daunting. Thus, understanding how such acute stress may affect witnesses' memory performance at encoding—when the witness saw the crime—and retrieval—when the witness gave a memory report about the crime—is vital. In this chapter, I will present the current research findings regarding the effects of acute stress at encoding and retrieval on memory performance. I will then highlight some limitations of this past research that are essential to consider before applying findings to the real world. Finally, I will discuss more recent research in this area before focusing on the potential implications of the research on this topic.

Effects of acute stress experienced at encoding on memory performance

Understanding how acute stress experienced at a crime may affect eyewitnesses can be a difficult subject to research. Of course, ethical constraints reduce the situations in which researchers are able to expose participants. To understand the current state of the stress-memory literature, it is important to first be aware that two main research fields—the eyewitness memory field and the fundamental memory field—have independently studied this topic. The eyewitness memory field hopes to understand how acute stress affects memory in real-life settings, with the goal of applying this knowledge to evaluating witness accuracy. The fundamental memory field seeks more basic answers to the question,

DOI: 10.4324/9781003308546-5

studying why, when, and how acute stress affects memory performance under controlled conditions. Thus, though these fields are researching the same question, they do so from different angles and using different methods.

Findings from the two research fields have often yielded conflicting findings. On the one hand, the majority of eyewitness research suggests negative effects of encoding stress on memory performance. Many studies show impaired recall or recognition memory for participants in the stress conditions compared to participants in non-stressful control conditions, with meta-analytic results showing impairments for both identifications and crime details (Deffenbacher et al., 2004). Field studies, too, generally show that acute encoding stress impairs memory performance (e.g., Morgan et al., 2004). On the other hand, fundamental theories and experimental results suggest enhancing effects of encoding stress on memory performance (e.g., Joëls et al., 2006). These models, supported by meta-analytic findings, suggest this is particularly the case when acute stress occurs within the same context as the encoding, that is, at the same time and space (Shields et al., 2017), as would occur in most eyewitness scenarios. Experimental results generally show that stressed participants outperform non-stressed participants on recognition tasks (e.g., Abercrombie et al., 2003; Vogel & Schwabe, 2016) as well as recall tasks (e.g., Smeets et al., 2007; Zoladz et al., 2014), though here too there are some exceptions (e.g., Goldfarb et al., 2019). Findings from a recent survey highlight this split between eyewitness and fundamental memory experts: whereas over three-quarters of fundamental memory experts agreed that experiencing stress during encoding of an event enhances memory for that event, only a third of eyewitness experts agreed (Marr et al., 2020).

So how might the differing methodologies lead to such contrasting results? The typical methodologies of each field have various strengths and weaknesses for answering the question of how acute encoding stress affects eyewitness memory. With the goal of understanding how stress may affect eyewitness memory in applied settings, the eyewitness research field typically uses ecologically valid scenarios to examine this relationship. These stressors attempt to recreate scenarios that are similar to what an eyewitness would actually experience, for example, by exposing participants to novel, negatively arousing experiences, including electric shocks, violent videos, police officer training scenarios, and military survival school programmes. In addition, most of the to-be-remembered information stems from the same situation that is causing the stress, which has been shown to be an important moderator in the relationship between acute encoding stress and memory performance (e.g., Joëls et al., 2006; Shields et al., 2017). In contrast, the fundamental memory field often invokes stress using validated laboratory stressors before or during encoding. Participants in these experiments often encode and are later asked to remember simple stimuli, for example, word lists, static pictures, or slideshows. These scenarios are less ecologically valid than those used in the eyewitness memory research field.

Nevertheless, the fundamental research memory field has its own strengths. Researchers in this area have developed several validated laboratory stressors, which reliably induce acute stress as confirmed by autonomic nervous system and hypothalamic-pituitary-adrenal (HPA) axis activity. These laboratory stressors include those elements that are known to evoke stress responses, including novelty, uncontrollability, unpredictability, and social threat (Dickerson & Kemeny, 2004). For example, in the Trier Social Stress Test (Kirschbaum et al., 1993), participants are required to give a speech and perform difficult mental arithmetic in front of a panel of critical experimenters. The reason that such laboratory stressors are frequently used is because they validly and reliably induce acute stress. That is, research shows that participants exhibit subjective and physiological stress responses to these stressors, including increased negative affect, autonomic arousal, and HPA-axis arousal, as demonstrated with increases in cortisol levels (e.g., Dickerson & Kemeny, 2004). In addition, fundamental researchers use manipulation checks to ensure successful stress inductions by collecting measures like blood pressure, heart rate, and cortisol. In contrast, stressors in the eyewitness field are typically not validated: in most experiments, there are no physiological stress checks. Subjective reports of stress do not always correlate with physiological acute stress responses (Hellhammer & Schubert, 2012) and are thus not alone sufficient. Research suggests that some of the methods used by eyewitness researchers, including showing arousing videos, do not produce cortisol responses (e.g., Peterson et al., 2014). Thus, although these eyewitness stressors better reflect reality, they may not sufficiently induce acute stress, a vital element to confirm when investigating this topic.

Certain methodological timing considerations may also help explain conflicting findings between the research disciplines. Importantly, stress has distinct effects on the different memory phases: whereas stress at encoding and consolidation can enhance memory, stress experienced at retrieval has been shown to impair memory (e.g., Shields et al., 2017; Wolf, 2017). Physiological stress responses are long-lasting, such that increased genomic glucocorticoids after a stressful experience can remain elevated for hours (Quaedflieg & Schwabe, 2018). Eyewitness experiments often use single session designs, with the encoding and retrieval portions of a task taking place within minutes of each other. This design can be problematic for isolating the effects of encoding stress on memory (see Sauerland et al., 2016). Fundamental memory researchers typically overcome this confound by separating encoding and retrieval by at least 24 hours. Also relevant is the relative timing of the stressor and encoding. For eyewitness researchers, it is often important for the stress and encoding to occur simultaneously, as would happen in a real crime scenario. However, fundamental memory experiments sometimes include a delay between the stressor and the encoding to await peak cortisol responses (i.e., around 15 min poststressor, e.g., Wolf, 2012). Though they may seem minor, these differences in timing could contribute to conflicting findings. Some research suggests that enhancing effects of encoding stress on memory performance are mostly seen with stressors experienced immediately before or during encoding, whereas stress induced prior to (i.e., 25 minutes or more) encoding may impair memory performance (e.g., Schwabe et al., 2012; Zoladz et al., 2011, 2018).

Some recent work has sought to combine the strengths of the disciplines when investigating encoding stress effects on memory performance. For example, findings from two studies using validated laboratory stressors and mock crime scenarios showed no effects of acute encoding stress on memory performance (Price et al., 2022; Sauerland et al., 2016). Two other recent experiments similarly revealed no effect of acute encoding stress on face recognition performance, with null results reported both during the stressor and post-stressor (Marr et al., 2021a). These experiments, along with new meta-analytic data suggesting no effects of acute psychosocial stress on memory performance (McManus et al., 2021), raise doubts about the strength and reliability of past statistically significant findings of acute stress effects on memory performance. When considering the various methodologies that have produced a plethora of different findings over the past decades, these null results seem to suggest the need for caution when translating previous laboratory studies to real-world situations. Later in this chapter, I will draw attention to what necessary additional research is needed and how it should be conducted. For now, we turn to another memory phase and examine the research on how experiences of stress during retrieval affect memory performance.

Effects of acute stress experienced at retrieval on memory performance

Eyewitnesses may also experience acute stress during retrieval, for example, when being interviewed by the police or when recounting their story in the courtroom. Even when police are sensitive to interviewees' moods and well-being, eyewitnesses will likely still find the situation stressful due to the novelty, uncontrollability, and unpredictability of such contexts, on top of the significance of the legal implications that their identifications and memory reports hold (e.g., Bornstein et al., 2013). There is more consensus regarding how acute retrieval stress affects memory performance among memory experts. In the previously mentioned survey, where eyewitness and fundamental memory experts disagreed on the broad effects of encoding stress on memory, there was far greater agreement regarding the effects of retrieval stress on memory performance. Specifically, survey results showed that nearly all memory experts agreed, "Experiencing stress while trying to remember something (i.e., at retrieval) impairs memory retrieval" (Marr et al., 2020). These beliefs are supported by a majority of findings from the fundamental memory field that suggest experiencing stress prior to or during retrieval has a negative impact on memory performance (e.g., Shields et al., 2017). Most of these experiments have been conducted in fundamental settings, for example, testing memory for basic stimuli such as word lists and static pictures (e.g., Kuhlmann et al., 2005). Still, a majority of eyewitness and fundamental memory experts seem to agree that these effects should hold in applied settings: 75% of fundamental memory experts and 81% of eyewitness memory experts agreed that "If an eyewitness is stressed during a police interview (i.e., at retrieval), his or her memory will be less accurate than if he or she were not stressed" (Marr et al., 2020).

However, only more recently has work been published on the effects of retrieval stress on memory performance in eyewitness-relevant contexts. In one recent study, participants who experienced stress during and prior to retrieval did not differ in performance from non-stressed participants on a face recognition task (Marr et al., 2021a). In a different experiment, participants who experienced acute stress prior to remembering complex images did not differ in recall or recognition performance from non-stressed participants (Marr et al., 2021b). These findings show some inconsistencies in this research topic, suggesting that the negative effects of retrieval stress are not as large or universal as often assumed.

As with research on encoding stress, understanding how methodological decisions and goals between fields could affect results is important when evaluating past findings. For example, as with encoding stress, timing matters: some experiments show no effects or even enhancements when there is little or no delay between retrieval stress and testing (e.g., Schwabe & Wolf, 2014; Smith et al., 2016). Relevantly, one study used a stressful interview-style situation to induce stress and test participant memories, a context more closely resembling a police interview experience (Schönfeld et al., 2014). Increases in participants' autonomic arousal were positively correlated with immediate memory recall under stress, suggesting memory enhancements due to stress-induced arousal. Such findings are pertinent to eyewitness settings, where the emphasis is on how stress experienced by an eyewitness *during* an identification procedure or interview may affect memory performance. Yet limited specific research has been conducted on this time period, particularly using eyewitness-relevant stimuli—such as faces or mock crimes—as well as eyewitness-relevant scenarios such as police interviews.

Other important factors to consider are how emotional the experience is and what kind of memory test is being used. Emotional valence moderates the relationship between retrieval stress and memory, with acute stress impairing retrieval to a greater extent for negative and positive information than for neutral information (e.g., Shields et al., 2017). Additionally, though research suggests that retrieval stress impairs performance on both recall (e.g., Smeets et al., 2008) and recognition tasks (e.g., Domes et al., 2004), these effects may be stronger for the recollection-based tasks than for tasks relying on familiarity, like recognition (Gagnon & Wagner, 2016). Recognition and recall memory can both be crucial to gather from an eyewitness, from recognising a perpetrator to reporting details of a crime. Thus, despite general expert consensus on the impairing effects of retrieval stress on memory performance, finding the boundaries of such effects and exploring these research questions in more applied research in eyewitness settings is essential before easy application to the real world.

The necessity of additional research

Understanding the effects of acute stress at both encoding and retrieval on memory performance in eyewitness settings requires continued research. Because of methodological limitations and mixed findings, the research on this topic at present remains inconclusive and can neither fully inform police or practitioners nor provide substantial support for policy decisions. Therefore, at the moment, the most important outcome of this program of research is assisting researchers and end-users with (1) understanding the substantial limitations of much of the past work and (2) improving future experiments that examine the stress-memory relationship in eyewitness settings.

When considering encoding stress, it would be valuable to combine the strengths of the different research disciplines to answer the applied question using contemporary methodology. In addition, future experiments could consider the role of other related factors, such as attention (Wulff & Thomas, 2021). Using eye-tracking technology, for example, may provide interesting insights into the effects of acute stress on attention, which may, in turn, affect memory performance. Most importantly, future research should use robust methodology when studying this complex topic, including properly inducing and confirming stress using physiological measures, inserting a sufficient retention interval between encoding and retrieval, and using ecologically relevant timing, stimuli, and memory tasks. If acute stress effects on memory can be examined in field studies to investigate situations of extreme stress (e.g., high fidelity training scenarios), physiological measures could help further tease apart potential differences in the effects of various stressor severities on memory performance. Similar improvements can be made when examining the relationship between retrieval stress and memory performance, for example, by adequately inducing acute stress using stressful situations that more closely mimic police interview settings (as done by Schönfeld et al., 2014). Additionally, investigating how eyewitnesses experience real police interviews and examining psychological and physiological stress levels in these applied settings would also provide better insight into how this topic plays out in the real world. From this, researchers could then work to examine ways to reduce stress levels for these eyewitnesses, to assist their wellbeing and potentially the quantity and quality of memory reports.

Finally, it is also important to note that the widespread use of open-science practices is fairly new in the psychological field. Therefore, previously published papers may be more prone to being underpowered or including questionable research practices, such as conducting numerous statistical analyses on the data but only reporting the statistically significant results. Additionally, due to publication bias, experiments showing null results may have never been published. Indeed, in a recent meta-analysis, there was evidence of publication bias for experiments examining stress effects at encoding and retrieval on memory performance (Shields et al., 2017). Specifically, the analyses suggested that there was a disproportionate amount of impairing effects reported in these publications compared with null or enhancing stress effects. This publication bias likely makes it difficult to compare the null findings in my experiments with similar findings that may exist in unpublished data. This point serves to further highlight the need for additional (and ideally preregistered) research and re-affirms the suggestion to use caution if attempting to apply previous research to legal settings.

Implications of contemporary knowledge on the stress–memory relationship

Answering these questions is of critical importance for legal situations. For police, judges, and juries to weigh the credibility of a witness, it may be essential to know how stress during a crime may have affected the memory of the eyewitness. If they believe that acute stress harms memory performance, as laypeople often assume (Marr et al., 2020), they may not value testimony from an eyewitness who says they were stressed as opposed to another non-stressed witness. Expert witnesses may be hired to share knowledge about the impact that stress may play on memory, but here too, there may be a disconnect between different experts, given that there is not a strong consensus regarding the effects of encoding stress on memory performance (e.g., Marr et al., 2020). On the other hand, legal actors may not realise that stress can have negative effects on memory, thus taking a memory report from such a witness at face value. Either course may be harmful, and before we bring this knowledge into the courtroom, we need stronger evidence and consensus on this topic. If expert witnesses do plan to discuss the stress–memory relationship in the courtroom, they should be nuanced in their presentation of these complex issues.

Relevantly, certain sub-topics relating to the stress–memory consensus show better consensus than others. For example, most experts in one recent survey generally agreed that the severity of the experienced stress matters (Marr et al., 2020). Specifically, nearly two-thirds of fundamental and eyewitness memory experts shared the belief that moderate stress may be beneficial for memory, whereas severe stress may more generally harm memory. Additionally, around 80% of both expert groups agreed that encoding stress enhances memory for central details but not peripheral details. These sub-topics, showing substantial levels of expert consensus, could already help expert witnesses who are examining stress as an estimator variable. Current experts could also use current relevant research knowledge to help counter common sense layperson beliefs such as ideas that police officers are less influenced by stress or the existence of repression (Marr et al., 2020). In such circumstances, expert testimony may help combat false preconceived beliefs, educating jurors and allowing them to make more sound, empirically-based decisions about how to interpret eyewitness evidence. That being said, recent findings have raised questions about the extent to which the current state of the field can inform practice. As such, though it may be enticing to broadly speculate or apply findings from some of the existing work in legal settings, it is imperative to show restraint when translating the current research to practice when so many limitations and knowledge gaps remain.

Understanding the effects of retrieval stress in forensic contexts may also help guide decisions about interviewing. However, as highlighted in this chapter, it is essential that we first conduct more research on this topic in applied settings. Though a considerable amount of research suggests impairing effects of retrieval stress on memory performance, other recent research shows a lack of effects of retrieval stress on memory (e.g., Marr et al., 2021a, 2021b). Better delineating the boundaries of negative effects of retrieval stress on memory will be a crucial initial step for bringing this research into reality. If, for instance, future research does suggest that acute retrieval stress experienced during an interview impairs an eyewitness' memory performance, this would be convincing evidence to advocate for ensuring that police interviews are not stressful. Reducing some of the main elements of acute stress could be a pathway to resolving such problems. For example, police officers could decrease elements of unpredictability and uncontrollability regarding the interview. For example, before coming to the police station, interviewees could be fully informed about the typical procedure and what to expect. Additionally, during the interview, allowing interviewees to be in control of the conversation could limit the experience of acute stress. Reducing any perceived feelings of judgement or evaluation could also help reduce levels of acute stress. Thus, once we understand more about *how* and *when* retrieval stress affects memory performance, we can begin better investigating what to do to reduce the negative consequences of stress. Diminishing acute stress levels in police interviews or in the courtroom may not only benefit memory performance but is also important for an eyewitness' wellbeing, an area on which there is already some research, particularly in regard to children and other vulnerable populations (e.g., Gudjonsson, 2010; Pantell, 2017). Certainly, the witness' wellbeing is essential to consider regardless of what future research shows regarding the effects of acute stress on memory performance.

Concluding remarks

Understanding the effects of acute stress on memory performance is a relevant line of research. Recent work has sought to combine the strengths of the eyewitness and fundamental research fields to examine this topic using contemporary methodology. In this chapter, I outlined some of these essential considerations and discussed areas with more established findings and areas where more work needs to be conducted. Given the recent mixed results on the stress–memory relationship, I suggest caution when bringing this issue into legal settings and highlight the need for a nuanced interpretation of findings, as well as future research using contemporary and robust methodology.

References

Abercrombie, H. C., Kalin, N. H., Thurow, M. E., Rosenkranz, M. A., & Davidson, R. J. (2003). Cortisol variation in humans affects memory for emotionally laden and neutral information. *Behavioral Neuroscience, 117*(3), 505–516.

Bornstein, B. H., Hullman, G., & Miller, M. K. (2013). Stress, trauma, and wellbeing in the legal system: Where do we go from here? In M. K. Miller & B. H. Bornstein (Eds.), *Stress, trauma, and wellbeing in the legal system* (pp. 293–309). Oxford University Press.

Deffenbacher, K. A., Bornstein, B. H., Penrod, S. D., & McGorty, E. K. (2004). A meta-analytic review of the effects of high stress on eyewitness memory. *Law and Human Behavior, 28*(6), 687–706.

Dickerson, S. S., & Kemeny, M. E. (2004). Acute stressors and cortisol responses: A theoretical integration and synthesis of laboratory research. *Psychological Bulletin, 130*(3), 355–391.

Domes, G., Heinrichs, M., Rimmele, U., Reichwald, U., & Hautzinger, M. (2004). Acute stress impairs recognition for positive words—Association with stress-induced cortisol secretion. *Stress, 7*(3), 173–181.

Gagnon, S. A., & Wagner, A. D. (2016). Acute stress and episodic memory: Neurobiological mechanisms and behavioral consequences. *Annals of The New York Academy of Sciences, 1369*(1), 55–75.

Goldfarb, E. V., Tompary, A., Davachi, L., & Phelps, E. A. (2019). Acute stress throughout the memory cycle: Diverging effects on associative and item memory. *Journal of Experimental Psychology: General, 148*(1), 13–29.

Gudjonsson, G. H. (2010). Psychological vulnerabilityies during police interviews. Why are they important? *Legal and Criminological Psychology, 15*(2), 161–175.

Hellhammer, J., & Schubert, M. (2012). The physiological response to trier social stress test relates to subjective measures of stress during but not before or after the test. *Psychoneuroendocrinology, 37*(1), 119–124.

Joëls, M., Pu, Z., Wiegert, O., Oitzl, M. S., & Krugers, H. J. (2006). Learning under stress: How does it work? *Trends in Cognitive Sciences, 10*(4), 152–158.

Kirschbaum, C., Pirke, K.-M., & Hellhammer, D. H. (1993). The 'trier social stress test': A tool for investigating psychobiological stress responses in a laboratory setting. *Neuropsychobiology, 28*(1–2), 76–81.

Kuhlmann, S., Kirschbaum, C., & Wolf, O. T. (2005). Effects of oral cortisol treatment in healthy young women on memory retrieval of negative and neutral words. *Neurobiology of Learning and Memory, 83*(2), 158–162.

Marr, C., Otgaar, H., Sauerland, M., Quaedflieg, C., & Hope, L. (2020). The effects of stress on eyewitness memory: A survey of memory experts and laypeople. *Memory & Cognition, 49*(3), 401–421.

Marr, C., Quaedflieg, C. W., Otgaar, H., Hope, L., & Sauerland, M. (2021a). Facing stress: Facing stress: No effect of acute stress at encoding or retrieval on face recognition memory. *Acta Psychologica, 219*, 103376.

Marr, C., Sauerland, M., Otgaar, H., Quaedflieg, C. W. E. M., & Hope, L. (2021b). Mitigating the negative effects of retrieval stress on memory: An arousal reappraisal intervention. *Memory, 29*(3), 330–344.

McManus, E., Talmi, D., Haroon, H., & Muhlert, N. (2021). Psychosocial stress has weaker than expected effects on episodic memory and related cognitive abilities: A meta-analysis. *Neuroscience & Biobehavioral Reviews, 132*, 1099–1113.

Morgan, C. A., Hazlett, G., Doran, A., Garrett, S., Hoyt, G., Thomas, P., Baranoski, M., & Southwick, S. M. (2004). Accuracy of eyewitness memory for persons encountered during exposure to highly intense stress. *International Journal of Law and Psychiatry, 27*(3), 265–279.

Pantell, R. H. (2017). The child witness in the courtroom. *Pediatrics, 139*(3), e20164008.

Peterson, Z. D., Janssen, E., Goodrich, D., & Heiman, J. R. (2014). Physiological reactivity in a community sample of sexually aggressive young men: A test of competing hypotheses. *Aggressive Behavior, 40*(2), 152–164.

Price, H. L., Tottenham, L. S., Hatin, B., Fitzgerald, R. J., & Rubínová, E. (2022). Effects of stress on eyewitness identification in the laboratory. *Applied Cognitive Psychology, 36*(1), 191–202.

Quaedflieg, C. W. E. M., & Schwabe, L. (2018). Memory dynamics under stress. *Memory, 26*(3), 364–376.

Sauerland, M., Raymaekers, L. H. C., Otgaar, H., Memon, A., Waltjen, T. T., Nivo, M., Slegers, C., Broers, N., & Smeets, T. (2016). Stress, stress-induced cortisol responses, and eyewitness identification performance. *Behavioral Sciences and the Law, 34*(4), 580–594.

Schönfeld, P., Ackermann, K., & Schwabe, L. (2014). Remembering under stress: Different roles of autonomic arousal and glucocorticoids in memory retrieval. *Psychoneuroendocrinology, 39*(1), 249–256.

Schwabe, L., Joëls, M., Roozendaal, B., Wolf, O. T., & Oitzl, M. S. (2012). Stress effects on memory: An update and integration. *Neuroscience & Biobehavioral Reviews, 36*(7), 1740–1749.

Schwabe, L., & Wolf, O. T. (2014). Timing matters: Temporal dynamics of stress effects on memory retrieval. *Cognitive, Affective, & Behavioral Neuroscience, 14*(3), 1041–1048.

Shields, G. S., Sazma, M. A., McCullough, A. M., & Yonelinas, A. P. (2017). The effects of acute stress on episodic memory: A meta-analysis and integrative review. *Psychological Bulletin, 143*(6), 636–675.

Smeets, T., Giesbrecht, T., Jelicic, M., & Merckelbach, H. (2007). Context-dependent enhancement of declarative memory performance following acute psychosocial stress. *Biological Psychology, 76*(1–2), 116–123.

Smeets, T., Otgaar, H., Candel, I., & Wolf, O. T. (2008). True or false? Memory is differentially affected by stress-induced cortisol elevations and sympathetic activity at consolidation and retrieval. *Psychoneuroendocrinology, 33*(10), 1378–1386.

Smith, A. M., Floerke, V. A., & Thomas, A. K. (2016). Retrieval practice protects memory against acute stress. *Science, 354*(6315), 1046–1048.

Vogel, S., & Schwabe, L. (2016). Stress in the zoo: Tracking the impact of stress on memory formation over time. *Psychoneuroendocrinology, 71*, 64–72.

Willoughby, M. (2015). Witnessing crime—findings from the crime survey for England and Wales 2013/14. In *Analytical summary prepared for the Ministry of Justice*. OGL.

Wolf, O. T. (2012). Immediate recall influences the effects of pre-encoding stress on emotional episodic long-term memory consolidation in healthy young men. *Stress, 15*(3), 272–280.

Wolf, O. T. (2017). Stress and memory retrieval: Mechanisms and consequences. *Current Opinions in Behavioral Sciences, 14*, 40–46.

Wulff, A. N., & Thomas, A. K. (2021). The dynamic and fragile nature of eyewitness memory formation: Considering stress and attention. *Frontiers in Psychology, 12*, 1–12.

Zoladz, P. R., Clark, B., Warnecke, A., Smith, L., Tabar, J., & Talbot, J. N. (2011). Prelearning stress differentially affects long-term memory for emotional words, depending on temporal proximity to the learning experience. *Physiology & Behavior, 103*(5), 467–476.

Zoladz, P. R., Duffy, T. J., Mosley, B. E., Fiely, M. K., Nagle, H. E., Scharf, A. R., Brown, C. M., Earley, M. B., Rorabaugh, B. R., & Dailey, A. M. (2018). Interactive influence of sex, stressor timing, and the BclI glucocorticoid receptor polymorphism on stress-induced alterations of long-term memory. *Brain and Cognition, 133*, 72–83.

Zoladz, P. R., Kalchik, A. E., Hoffman, M. M., Aufdenkampe, R. L., Lyle, S. M., Peters, D. M., Brown, C. M., Cadle, C. E., Scharf, A. R., Dailey, A. M., Wolters, N. E., Talbot, J. N., & Rorabaugh, B. R. (2014). ADRA2B deletion variant selectively predicts stress-induced enhancement of long-term memory in females. *Psychoneuroendocrinology, 48*, 111–122.

Part II

Investigative interviewing

4 Cross-cultural investigative interviews

Nkansah Anakwah

Eyewitnesses are a major source of evidence in criminal prosecutions (Wells et al., 2020). Witnesses may bring culturally determined reporting norms into the criminal justice context, as they have been socialised into their respective cultures. Limited insight into the role of culture in eyewitness accounts can pose a challenge to investigators interviewing witnesses in cross-cultural settings. Attending to culture is crucial to the investigative interview of witnesses, especially as recent trends in migration have made cross-cultural investigative interviews inevitable. This chapter discusses the potential role that culture may play in the investigative interview of witnesses in cross-cultural settings. The first part of the chapter provides an overview of various cultural concepts. Drawing on these concepts and previous research in cross-cultural psychology, the chapter highlights some implications for eyewitness interviews.

Attending to culture

People across the world have different histories and experiences (Brady et al., 2018). Shared norms, social practices, beliefs, and symbols have evolved from different histories and experiences of people groups over the years (Brown et al., 2020). These sets of values and beliefs shape their worldview and how they make sense of the world. It is in that regard that culture has been defined as a 'collective programming of the mind that distinguishes the members of one group or category of people from others' (Hofstede, 2011, p. 3). Hence, socialisation in different cultural contexts may lead to variations in behaviour and psychological processes.

One such cultural difference is the extent of embeddedness in social groups (Hofstede, 2001). Research in cross-cultural psychology suggests that people groups across the world differ in the extent to which they view individuals to be integrated into the social context (Minkov et al., 2017). The proposed cultural difference in the extent of embeddedness in social relationships is the key feature of the individualism-collectivism cultural framework. According to that cultural framework, individualistic cultures are cultures where individuals are viewed as separated from the social context (Hofstede, 2011). In individualistic cultures, individuals are expected to look after themselves and their immediate

DOI: 10.4324/9781003308546-7

Table 4.1 Characteristics of collectivistic and individualistic cultures by Hofstede, 2011.

Collectivistic cultures	Individualistic cultures
Individuals are born into an extended family/clan	Individuals are born into a nuclear family
Individuals are integrated into a strong, cohesive in-group	Ties between individuals are loose
Emphasis on the group (communality)	Emphasis on the individual (individuality)
Resources should be shared with relatives	Individual ownership of resources
Harmony should be maintained and direct confrontations avoided	It is healthy to speak one's mind
Communication is implicit and indirect (high-context communication)	Communication is explicit and direct (low-context communication)
More emphasis on hierarchy in social relationships (high power distance)	Less emphasis on hierarchy in social relationships (low power distance)

families. Individualistic cultures include cultures in western societies such as Australia, North America, and Western Europe.

In collectivistic cultures, on the other hand, individuals are viewed as integrated into a complex web of social relationships (Hofstede, 2011). For example, individuals in collectivistic cultures are integrated into a cohesive in-group, and the raising of a child in such cultures is considered a communal responsibility. This has been typified by the African maxim 'it takes a village to raise a child'. Consequently, individuals from collectivistic cultures are expected to remain loyal to their in-group in exchange for unquestioning loyalty. As a result, individuals socialised in collectivistic cultures strive to promote group harmony and are prone to subordinate their views, preferences, aspirations, and interests to that of the group (Wasti et al., 2007). Collectivistic cultures include cultures in non-western societies such as Latin America, East Asia, and sub-Saharan Africa. See Table 4.1 for some characteristics of individualistic and collectivistic cultures.

Depending on whether individuals are socialised in an individualistic or collectivistic culture, they tend to develop a self-construal consistent with the predominant self-construal in that cultural context. Self-construal is the meaning individuals socialised in a particular cultural context ascribe to the self in relation to others (Cross et al., 2011). Individuals socialised in individualistic cultures develop an independent self-construal, whereas those socialised in collectivistic cultures develop an interdependent self-construal (Markus & Kitayama, 1991). Individuals with the independent self-construal view the self as distinct and separate from their social context (Markus & Kitayama, 1991). For individuals with independent self-construal, life is made more meaningful and organised by emphasising one's own internal dispositions, thoughts, and feelings (Wang, 2021). As a result, individuals with an independent self-construal focus on an individual's unique dispositions and attributes than individuals with interdependent self-construal (Wang, 2004). Individuals with independent self-construal are more responsive to their social environment and often look for the best avenues to assert their unique dispositions (Markus & Kitayama, 1991).

Whereas individuals with independent self-construal view the self as unique and distinct, individuals with interdependent self-construal view the self as not separate but fundamentally connected to the social context (Wang, 2021). Thus, individuals with the interdependent self-construal view the self as less differentiated from and more connected to others in the social relationship. As a result, the behaviour of individuals with the interdependent self-construal is dependent and organised by what the individuals perceive to be the thoughts, feelings, and behaviours of others in their social relationship. Also, due to the view of the self as less differentiated from others, individuals with the interdependent construal of the self may have a tendency to fit in with others (Markus & Kitayama, 1991).

Different cultural self-construal may systematically shape cognition. Individuals with independent self-construal have been argued to develop an analytic cognition, which involves focusing more on focal objects (Wang, 2021). Individuals with an interdependent self-construal, on the other hand, have been argued to develop a holistic cognition, which involves focusing more on background objects (Masuda & Nisbett, 2006). Previous work has provided evidence consistent with the cultural differences in holistic-analytic cognition (Boduroglu et al., 2009). For example, an analysis of social media profile pictures of individuals from individualistic and collectivistic cultural backgrounds has shown cultural differences in preference for focal face and contextual details (Huang & Park, 2013). Specifically, East Asians were found to prioritise context inclusiveness in their profile pictures. Americans, on the other hand, were found to prioritise their focal face than contextual detail in their profile pictures. A similar pattern has been observed in cultural differences in aesthetic preferences (Masuda et al., 2008), where East Asians preferred photographs with more context inclusiveness than Americans. Furthermore, archival analysis of landscape drawings by East Asian and American artists demonstrates that East Asian artists are more inclined to include contextual information in their drawings than American artists, who are inclined to focus more on the focal object (Masuda et al., 2008).

Socialisation in different cultures may also shape the style of communication. Culturally determined norms of communication may come to the fore during cross-cultural interaction. Communication across cultures may either be low or high in context (Hall & Hall, 1990). In high context cultures, information is less explicitly communicated in social interactions, as the context is expected to communicate what is implied, whereas, in low context cultures, it is expected that information is communicated more explicitly (Hall, 1976). Communication in individualistic cultures tends to be low in context, whereas communication in collectivistic cultures tends to be high in context (Gao, 2019). The high-context communication style of collectivistic cultures is because individuals socialised in such cultures are integrated into the social context, hence deeply involved in each other and forming intimate relationships. Due to this embeddedness, information in such cultures may be simply shared without being explicit but contains deep meaning (Alizadeh Afrouzi, 2021). For example, a cross-cultural analysis of advertisements from low- and high-context cultures shows advertisements in high-context cultures contain fewer details than advertisements in low-context cultures, which contains explicit descriptions (Bai, 2016).

Cultures also differ in how they relate with authority figures. The power distance (PD) cultural framework has been proposed to explain cultural differences in hierarchical social relationships (Hofstede, 2011). High-PD cultures emphasise hierarchy, respect, and status in social interactions, whereas in low-PD cultures, there is less emphasis on these (Sharma, 2010). It has been observed that within organisational contexts, employees from high-PD cultural backgrounds are less willing to participate in decision-making (as decisions are made by the few at the top hierarchy) than employees with low-PD cultural backgrounds (Khatri, 2009). Employees with a high-PD cultural background also tend to mostly receive instructions from superiors compared to low-PD cultural contexts (Ghosh, 2011). Thus, whereas individuals from low-PD cultures may freely express their views to their superiors or authority, in high-PD cultures, it is difficult for individuals to freely express their views to their superiors. For example, individuals from high-PD cultures have been suggested to be less direct, are more apprehensive, and engage in mitigated speech when communicating with authority figures (Madlock, 2012). Hence, norms regarding relationships with authority figures differ across cultures.

Implications of cultural differences for investigative interviews

The cultural differences highlighted previously may have implications for investigative interviews of witnesses in cross-cultural settings. This section draws on these cultural concepts as well as empirical research to discuss potential implications for eyewitness interviews. The implications discussed in what follows may also hold for interviews with other interviewees, such as victims and suspects.

Cultural differences in detail provision

Witnesses from different cultures may differ in the elaborateness of the information they provide. Eyewitnesses socialised in individualistic cultures may be more prone to provide elaborate reports in their eyewitness accounts than eyewitnesses socialised in collectivistic cultures. That could be due to the individualistic cultural disposition to be more explicit, in line with low-context communication norms, compared to individuals with collectivistic cultures (Hall & Hall, 1990). In line with this, research in autobiographical memory shows that individuals socialised in individualistic cultures provide more detailed accounts of their experiences than individuals socialised in collectivistic cultures, who are prone to provide generic accounts (Wang, 2004). Recent work in the eyewitness memory literature shows results consistent with the autobiographical memory literature (Anakwah et al., 2020). In that study, mock witnesses from sub-Saharan Africa and Western Europe viewed stimuli scenes of mock crimes and reported what they saw. Mock witnesses with the collectivistic cultural background provided fewer details in their accounts than mock witnesses with the individualistic cultural background.

Socialisation practices in the respective cultures could play a role in elaborate memory reporting. For example, when engaging in conversations with their children, mothers from individualistic cultural backgrounds provide more richly embellished information and also elaborate on the information provided by their children, in order to provide a scaffold for their children's participation, than mothers with a collectivistic cultural background (Wang, 2006). Considering the potential role of culture in detail underreporting for witnesses with collectivistic cultural backgrounds, it would be necessary to encourage such interviewees to report as many details as possible to minimise underreporting.

In cross-cultural settings such as international criminal justice settings, recall prompts to encourage witnesses to provide as much detail may yield substantial outcomes, especially for scenes witnessed in their own cultural context. Because adjudications in such settings usually involve witnesses who have witnessed the incidents in their own cultural setting, scene elicitation about the focal event may be enhanced when they are encouraged to report whatever they saw in their own words in explicit details (i.e., free recall). In a recent work where mock witnesses viewed and reported about scenes in their own cultural setting and a non-native cultural setting, the researchers found evidence of an own-cultural-setting effect in eyewitness memory reports (Anakwah et al., 2020). Specifically, that study showed that individuals with a collectivistic cultural orientation provide more information about the focal event when a crime is witnessed in their own cultural setting rather than a different cultural setting for free recall but not for cued recall. Similarly, individuals with an individualistic cultural background reported more focal details about a crime scene witnessed in their own cultural setting than in a different cultural setting, albeit for cued recall but not for free recall. Thus, in interviewing witnesses with a collectivistic cultural orientation who might have witnessed a crime event in their own cultural setting, scene elicitation about the focal event may be enhanced when witnesses are encouraged to report in their own words, as much detail as possible.

Cultural differences and credibility assessment

The cultural difference in the elaborateness of eyewitness memory reports may have implications for credibility assessment in cross-cultural settings. Previous research shows that one of the indicators of deception is the amount of detail provided by interviewees (Vrij et al., 2007). It has been reasoned that the stories of truth-tellers may contain more details than lie-tellers because the former may have experienced a wealth of perceptual details about the event in question than the latter (Vrij et al., 2010). Hence, truth-telling interviewees may be prone to provide more details than lie-telling interviewees.

Detail provision is also used in detecting true and false intentions in intelligence gathering and asylum seeker contexts (Granhag et al., 2016; Jobson, 2009). For example, interviewees in asylum seeker contexts are required to provide memory reports of places and certain landmarks of their place of origin to verify their claim (van Veldhuizen et al., 2018). That means there is the possibility that genuine asylum seekers with a collectivistic cultural background may be wrongfully considered to be not credible if they underreport details of their experience.

It is important to note that previous research on cues to deception has largely been conducted in Western contexts, hence, problematic when such cues are used in cross-cultural situations. Indeed recent research suggests that the use of details as a cue to deception weakens in cross-cultural contexts (Taylor et al., 2017). For example, in a study with an Arab and British sample, participants were involved in a mission and later interviewed about the mission (Vrij et al., 2020). It was found that British interviewees provided more details than Arab interviewees did. It is important to make interviewers aware of this cultural difference and also exercise caution when using detail as a credibility indicator in cross-cultural settings.

It may be that there are different cues to deception in different cultures. Based on the independent-interdependent construal of the self, it can be proposed that certain characteristics may be predominant in the genuine statements of individuals from certain cultural backgrounds. For example, when American and East Asian children were asked to describe their daily events, American children made more reference to the self, personal attributes, and their internal states than the East Asian children, whose descriptions were centred on social roles and social interactions (Wang, 2004). It can be proposed, therefore, that individuals socialised in individualistic cultures may assert their individuality more in genuine statements than individuals socialised in collectivistic cultures, who may be more inclined to refer more to social roles and social interactions in genuine statements than individuals socialised in individualistic. Indeed in recent work on cross-cultural deception detection, where participants were asked to describe an experienced event and also fabricate and describe an event that never occurred, it was found that the use of first and second-person pronouns when deceiving tends to vary across cultures (Taylor et al., 2017). Specifically, whereas British participants were found to use third-person pronouns the most and first-person pronouns the least when lying, a reverse pattern was found for African participants. That study also showed that British participants used more social details and few perceptual details when lying, whereas African participants used more perceptual details and few social details when lying. This shows cues to deception could be culture-specific, hence the need not to generalise cues identified in western contexts to non-western contexts. More research is needed to examine culturally specific cues to deception to improve credibility assessments in cross-cultural interviews.

Authority and cross-cultural interviews

The mere fact of reporting to an investigator may contribute to cultural differences in detail provision. That is in view of the tendency for individuals socialised in high-power distance cultures to be more sensitive to power differentials in social interactions than individuals socialised in low-power distance cultures (Ghosh, 2011). The investigative interview context is characterised by power differentials between an interviewer and an interviewee (Abbe & Brandon, 2013). The cultural dimension of power distance may compromise the quality of investigative interviews (Sumampouw et al., 2020).

Recent work suggests that reporting to an authority figure in an investigative context may impact eyewitnesses from different cultural backgrounds differently (Anakwah et al., 2022b). Mock witnesses in that study viewed a crime event and later reported what they saw in a peer or a police context. While witnesses from a high-PD background did not differ in their reports provided in a peer and a police context, witnesses from a low-PD background provided more details to the police than in a peer context. An authority effect may have impeded the reports of high-PD mock witnesses as they did not optimise reports provided to police (compared to a peer), unlike the case for low-PD mock witnesses. Mock witnesses from the high-PD culture in that study also rated high on perceived inequality than mock witnesses from the low-PD culture. Thus, the mere fact of reporting to an investigator could impact witnesses differently depending on their cultural background. It has also been argued that there tends to be lower trust in institutions and police in high PD cultures than in low-PD cultures (Boateng et al., 2016; Doney et al., 1998). The extent to which individuals trust the police might also be a matter of historical and political experience across jurisdictions, which may systematically impact cooperation with police and detailed information provision.

The impact of authority on information elicitation may be mitigated by culturally sensitive ways of building rapport. An effective rapport may help create an atmosphere that facilitates spontaneous and free communication. As reporting to an authority figure may impede free and spontaneous communication for individuals with high-PD cultural backgrounds (Ghosh, 2011), an effective rapport is very essential. Effective rapport may facilitate cooperation, trust-building, and information elicitation (Macintosh, 2009; Vrij et al., 2014). However, research on culturally sensitive ways of building rapport is scarce. Efforts at mitigating the impact of authority in cross-cultural investigative interviews may be hampered if investigators have limited insight on how best to establish rapport in cross-cultural settings. It has been suggested that an understanding of the values and worldviews of an interviewee may be essential in establishing rapport (Abbe & Brandon, 2013). In fact, it has been shown that possessing some knowledge about the culture of the interviewee may help build an effective rapport (Goodman-Delahunty & Howes, 2016). It is, however, not clear whether such techniques may mitigate the perceived power differentials. Future research should examine culturally sensitive rapport-building techniques that could mitigate the impact of authority on informational outcomes.

Suggestibility and interrogative compliance

Cultures may also differ in suggestibility and interrogative compliance. According to the self-construal theory, individuals socialised in collectivistic cultures tend to develop an interdependent self-construal, viewing the self as not separate from the social context (Markus & Kitayama, 1991). Individuals socialised in individualistic cultures, on the other hand, develop an independent self-construal, viewing the self as inherently distinct and separate from the social context (Markus & Kitayama, 1991). Previous research has shown that independent self-construal is associated with co-witness suggestibility (Petterson & Paterson, 2012). Specifically, individuals with independent self-construal were less susceptible to misleading suggestions from co-witnesses. However, Petterson and Paterson (2012) did not find the interdependent self-construal to be associated with co-witness suggestibility. It is important to bear in mind, however, that participants for that study were recruited in a western context, hence the association of independent self-construal (but not interdependent self-construal) with co-witness suggestibility. Thus, that study does not give a clear picture of the role of the interdependent self-construal on misinformation acceptance.

Because individuals socialised in collectivistic cultures view the self as embedded within the social context (interdependent self-construal), it has been reasoned that they may be more prone to accepting misinformation from social sources (Wiafe-Akenten, 2020). In recent research using a mock witness paradigm, participants sampled from two cultures representing the individualistic (independent self-construal) and collectivistic (interdependent self-construal) cultures, respectively, were exposed to misleading post-event information (Anakwah et al., 2022a). It was found that mock witnesses socialised in collectivistic cultures were more prone to accepting misleading post-event information than mock witnesses socialised in individualistic cultures. Nevertheless, across cultures, memory was impaired to the same extent after exposure to misleading post-event information. The observed cultural differences in misinformation acceptance show the need to avoid suggestive questions, especially in cross-cultural investigative interviews.

The role of the independent-interdependent self-construal in suggestibility may also have implications for false confessions. Suggestibility and compliance have been identified to be among the risk factors for false confessions (Otgaar et al., 2021). Individuals with a collectivistic cultural background (interdependent self-construal) seem to score higher on measures of conformity than individuals socialised in individualistic cultures (Bond & Smith, 1996). Consequently, acquiescence response patterns tend to be stronger in collectivistic cultures (De Bruïne et al., 2018). Hence, it is likely that interviewees from cultures where the interdependent self-construal is emphasised may be more prone to false confessions. In fact, in previous research where participants completed measures of self-construal and interrogative compliance, it was found that participants from cultures where the interdependent self-construal is predominant were more likely to score higher on interrogative compliance than participants from cultures where the independent self-construal is predominant (Oeberst & Wu, 2015). In view of the potential role of self-construal and interrogative compliance in false confessions, caution should be exercised when interviewing interviewees from cultures where the interdependent self-construal is predominant.

Concluding remarks

The culture of an interviewee is an important factor to be considered in cross-cultural investigative interviews. This chapter provides an overview of some cultural concepts. Drawing on these concepts and previous research, the chapter evaluates the implications of investigative interviews in cross-cultural settings and proposes directions for future research. In an increasingly multicultural society, legal psychological research should pay attention to the role of culture in witness interviews. Investigative interviewers in cross-cultural settings must be cognisant that the interviewee's cultural background may shape their accounts.

References

Abbe, A., & Brandon, S. (2013). The role of rapport in investigative interviewing: A review. *Journal of Investigative Psychology and Offender Profilinf, 10*(3), 237–249.

Alizadeh Afrouzi, O. (2021). Humanitarian behavior across high-/low-context cultures: a comparative analysis between Switzerland and Colombia. *Journal of International Humanitarian Action, 6*(2).

Anakwah, N., Horselenberg, R., Hope, L., Amankwah-Poku, M., & van Koppen, P. J. (2020). Cross-cultural differences in eyewitness memory reports. *Applied Cognitive Psychology, 34*(2), 504–515.

Anakwah, N., Horselenberg, R., Hope, L., Amankwah-Poku, M., & van Koppen, P. J. (2022a). *The misinformation effect and eyewitness memory reports: A cross-cultural investigation.* Manuscript.

Anakwah, N., Horselenberg, R., Hope, L., Amankwah-Poku, M., & van Koppen, P. J. (2022b). *The authority effect and eyewitness memory reports across cultures.* Manuscript.

Bai, H. (2016). A Cross-cultural analysis of advertisements from high-context cultures and low-context cultures. *English Language Teaching, 9*(8), 21.

Boateng, F. D., Lee, H. D., & Abess, G. (2016). Analyzing citizens' reported levels of confidence in the police: A Cross-national study of public attitudes toward the police in the United States and South Korea. *Asian Journal of Criminology, 11*, 289–308.

Boduroglu, A., Priti, S., & Nisbett, R. E. (2009). Cultural differences in allocation of attention in visual information processing. *Journal of Cross-Cultural Psychology, 40*(3), 349–360.

Bond, R., & Smith, P. B. (1996). Culture and conformity: A meta-analysis of studies using asch's (1952b, 1956) line judgment task. *Psychological Bulletin, 119*(1), 111–137.

Brady, L. M., Fryberg, S. A., & Shoda, Y. (2018). Expanding the interpretive power of psychological science by attending to culture. *Proceedings of the National Academy of Sciences of the United States of America, 115*(45), 11406–11413.

Brown, N., Mcilwraith, T., & Tubelle De González, L. (2020). Perspectives: An open introduction to cultural anthropology. In *An open introduction to cultural anthropology* (2nd ed., pp. 382–406). The American Anthropological Association.

Cross, S. E., Hardin, E. E., & Gercek-Swing, B. (2011). The what, how, why, and where of self-construal. *Personality and Social Psychology Review, 15*(2), 142–179.

De Bruïne, G., Vredeveldt, A., & van Koppen, P. J. (2018). Cross-cultural differences in object recognition: Comparing asylum seekers from Sub-Saharan Africa and a matched Western European control group. *Applied Cognitive Psychology, 32*(4), 463–473.

Doney, P. M., Cannon, J. P., & Mullen, M. R. (1998). Understanding the influence of national culture on the development of trust. *Academy of Management Review, 23*(3), 601–620.

Gao, Y. (2019). Differences and strategies of high and low context cultures from the perspective of Burberry's advertisement. *Advances in Social Science, Education and Humanities Research, 309*, 317–320.

Ghosh, A. (2011). Power distance in organizational contexts-A review of collectivist cultures. *Indian Journal of Industrial Relations, 47*(1), 89–101.

Goodman-Delahunty, J., & Howes, L. M. (2016). Social persuasion to develop rapport in high-stakes interviews: Qualitative analyses of Asian-Pacific practices. *Policing and Society, 26*(3), 270–290.

Granhag, P. A., Mac Giolla, E., Sooniste, T., Strömwall, L., & Liu-Jonsson, M. (2016). Discriminating between statements of true and false intent: The impact of repeated interviews and strategic questioning. *Journal of Applied Security Research, 11*(1), 1–17.

Hall, E. T. (1976). *Beyond culture*. Anchor Press.

Hall, E. T., & Hall, M. R. (1990). *Understanding cultural difference*. Intercultural Press.

Hofstede, G. (2001). *Culture's consequences: Comparing values, behaviors, institutions and organisations* (2nd ed.). Sage.

Hofstede, G. (2011). Dimensionalizing cultures: The Hofstede model in context. *Online Readings in Psychology and Culture, 2*(1), 1–26.

Huang, C. M., & Park, D. (2013). Cultural influences on Facebook photographs. *International Journal of Psychology, 48*(3), 334–343.

Jobson, L. (2009). Cultural differences in specificity of autobiographical memories: Implications for asylum decisions. *Psychiatry, Psychology and Law, 16*(3), 453–457.

Khatri, N. (2009). Consequences of power distance. *Vision, 13*(1), 1–9.

Macintosh, G. (2009). Examining the antecedents of trust and rapport in services: Discovering new interrelationships. *Journal of Retailing and Consumer Services, 16*(4), 298–305.

Madlock, P. E. (2012). The influence of power distance and communication on Mexican workers. *Journal of Business Communication, 49*(2), 169–184.

Markus, H. R., & Kitayama, S. (1991). Culture and the self: Implications for cognition, emotion, and motivation. *Psychological Review, 98*(2), 224–253.

Masuda, T., Gonzalez, R., Kwan, L., & Nisbett, R. E. (2008). Culture and aesthetic preference: Comparing the attention to context of East Asians and Americans. *Personality and Social Psychology Bulletin, 34*(9), 1260–1275.

Masuda, T., & Nisbett, R. E. (2006). Culture and change blindness. *Cognitive Science, 30*(2), 381–399.

Minkov, M., Dutt, P., Schachner, M., Morales, O., Sanchez, C., Jandosova, J., . . . Mudd, B. (2017). A revision of Hofstede's individualism-collectivism dimension. *Cross Cultural & Strategic Management, 24*, 386–404.

Oeberst, A., & Wu, S. (2015). Independent vs. interdependent self construal and interrogative compliance: Intra-and cross-cultural evidence. *Journal of Personality Differences*, *85*, 50–55.

Otgaar, H., Schell-Leugers, J. M., Howe, M. L., Vilar, A. D. L. F., Houben, S. T. L., & Merckelbach, H. (2021). The link between suggestibility, compliance, and false confessions: A review using experimental and field studies. *Applied Cognitive Psychology*, *35*(2), 445–455.

Petterson, B., & Paterson, H. M. (2012). Culture and conformity: The effects of independent and interdependent self-construal on witness memory. *Psychiatry, Psychology and Law*, *19*(5), 735–744.

Sharma, P. (2010). Measuring personal cultural orientations: Scale development and validation. *Journal of the Academy of Marketing Science*, *38*, 787–806.

Sumampouw, N. E. J., Otgaar, H., La Rooy, D., & De Ruiter, C. (2020). The quality of forensic child interviewing in child sexual abuse cases in Indonesia. *Journal of Police and Criminal Psychology*, *35*(2), 170–181.

Taylor, P. J., Larner, S., Conchie, S. M., & Menacere, T. (2017). Culture moderates changes in linguistic self-presentation and detail provision when deceiving others. *Royal Society Open Science*, *4*(6), 170128.

van Veldhuizen, T. S., Maas, R. P. A. E., Horselenberg, R., & van Koppen, P. J. (2018). Establishing origin: Analysing the questions asked in asylum interviews. *Psychiatry, Psychology and Law*, *25*(2), 283–302.

Vrij, A., Granhag, P. A., & Porter, S. (2010). Pitfalls and opportunities in nonverbal and verbal lie detection. *Psychological Science in the Public Interest*, *11*(3), 89–121.

Vrij, A., Hope, L., & Fisher, R. P. (2014). Eliciting reliable information in investigative interviews. *Policy Insights from the Behavioral and Brain Sciences*, *1*(1), 129–136.

Vrij, A., Leal, S., Mann, S., Vernham, Z., Dalton, G., Serok-jeppa, O., . . . Vernham, Z. (2020). 'Please tell me all you remember': A comparison between British and Arab interviewees' free narrative performance and its implications for lie detection. *Psychiatry, Psychology and Law*, 1–14.

Vrij, A., Mann, S., Kristen, S., & Fisher, R. P. (2007). Cues to deception and ability to detect lies as a function of police interview styles. *Law and Human Behavior*, *31*(5), 499–518.

Wang, Q. (2004). The emergence of cultural self-constructs: Autobiographical memory and self-description in European American and Chinese children. *Developmental Psychology*, *40*(1), 3–15.

Wang, Q. (2006). Relations of maternal style and child self-concept to autobiographical memories in Chinese, Chinese immigrant, and European American 3-year-olds. *Child Development*, *77*, 1794–1809.

Wang, Q. (2021). The cultural foundation of human memory. *Annual Review of Psychology*, *72*(1), 151–179.

Wasti, S. A., Tan, H. H., Brower, H. H., & Önder, Ç. (2007). Cross-cultural measurement of supervisor trustworthiness: An assessment of measurement invariance across three cultures. *Leadership Quarterly*, *18*(5), 477–489.

Wells, G. L., Kovera, M. B., Douglass, A. B., Brewer, N., Meissner, C. A., & Wixted, J. T. (2020). Policy and procedure recommendations for the collection and preservation of eyewitness identification evidence. *Law and Human Behavior*, *44*(1), 3–36.

Wiafe-Akenten, C. B. (2020, May 1). COVID-19 fight: Misinformation and unfounded beliefs (part 1). *Citi Newsroom*.

5 Cognitive barriers to obtaining information during investigative interviews

Nicole Adams-Quackenbush

The investigative interview is the most important tool used by investigators and law enforcement personnel. Victims, witnesses, and suspects of wrongdoing often hold investigation-relevant information (IRI) that can be used to close cases and generate evidence for court. Most public knowledge about investigative interviewing and interrogation practices comes from true-crime stories or accounts within our favourite fictional crime dramas. While aspects of these dramatisations have some basis of truth, these representations of the investigative interview are over-simplistic. Sure, they convey some of the tactics used to obtain information from witnesses and suspects. Some of the better ones even convey how frustrating and difficult it can be to get humans to disclose accurate and reliable information. But what these dramatisations do not convey is that several of the more aggressive and interrogative tactics are ineffective in obtaining investigation relevant information. The dramas do not accurately depict the plethora of psychological factors at play during an investigative interview, and they certainly do not tell you that several of the behaviours exhibited by your favourite detectives are the result of flawed rationalisation and biased thinking.

Decades of research have demonstrated that a skilled interviewer can easily obtain information by using a variety of evidence-based techniques. However, interviewers often depart from their training and sometimes rely on biased thinking and instinctive tactics to elicit the information they seek. Those types of interviewing behaviours can introduce doubt regarding the truthfulness and validity of the information gathered. This can lead to cases being left unsolved, statements rendered inadmissible for court, as well as miscarriages of justice. One of the main challenges with addressing biased and prejudicial thinking in police interviewing is the difficulty in proving it occurred. Research in the area relies mainly on experimental studies with mock or non-police interviewers in highly controlled environments. Even if a research team has the connections to access police interview recordings or transcripts, bias can only be inferred through behaviour.

Applied researchers and evaluators of investigative interview techniques can only assume bias may be present by analysing the interviewer's behaviour or language to make educated assumptions about the underlying thinking or cognitions behind the activity. For example, by analysing the linguistic patterns,

DOI: 10.4324/9781003308546-8

word choices, and questions posed by interviewers, some assumptions can be made regarding their decision-making process—including the influence of biases or beliefs. Although these types of studies offer no guarantee that bias occurred, recommendations can be made to suggest alternative approaches to avoid negatively influencing the interview. Despite the efforts of researchers and practitioners to advise against biased and unprofessional interview practices, these problems persist with sometimes detrimental effects on information elicitation and disclosure. In this chapter, some of the more common issues with information elicitation are examined through the lens of cognitive psychology. Specifically, the phenomenon of cognitive load and cognitive biases in the context of interviewing behaviours are discussed.

Interviewer behaviour as a barrier to information disclosure

Cognition and behaviour are causally linked through a process of systems that involves obtaining information from the surroundings, understanding that information, deciding on how to act, and then executing that behaviour. An investigative interview is an organised interaction that occurs within a complex set of circumstances. Thus, it requires a large amount of attention from the interviewer and the interviewee to make the best decisions and behave accordingly. Both the interviewer and the interviewee can influence the dynamic of the interaction, but the interviewer arguably exerts the most influence on the overall outcome of the interview (Hudson et al., 2018). For example, an interviewer can manipulate the tone, topic, direction, and questioning techniques of the interview through their behaviour or by using certain questioning techniques to elicit information (Haworth, 2017). The interviewer can also influence an interviewee's responses and behaviour through the questions they choose to ask (Oxburgh et al., 2010).

The investigative interviewing literature is wrought with experimental and applied findings that demonstrate what behaviours, tactics, and techniques should be avoided so as not to erect barriers to information disclosure by engaging in counterproductive interviewing practices. These are behaviours that originate in confirmation bias, and they seem to be the largest concern in obtaining investigation relevant information. The underlying cognitions and processes associated with behaving in a confirmatory manner create barriers for the interviewer to effectively elicit information. The interviewers' behaviour can also create barriers to information disclosure from the interviewee. For example, in a previous study, I attempted to make connections between interviewer behaviour and potential cognitions using content analysis and linguistic techniques in a series of police-suspect interviews (see Adams-Quackenbush et al., 2019). The study explored the assumption that confirmation bias within the interview manifests as guilt-presumptive questioning and behaviours in the interviewers. By analysing the questions and other utterances made by the interviewers, I found several instances where the language was accusatory and guilt presumptive. It was clear that the interviewers believed they had their suspect and decided he was guilty. As a result, the interviewer's behaviour and questioning were focused on gaining a confession, refusing to hear denials of involvement, and framing any explanations or exonerating details as lies or twisted facts.

While analysing the interview transcripts and video, it was incredibly clear that the interviewers were closed to alternative scenarios that may explain the evidence they collected. It was evident that they were not picking up on reasonable explanations provided by the suspect. Subsequent questioning around disclosed information was designed to lead the response to conform to some established beliefs about the case. In essence, the information-gathering interview that had been promised to the suspect quickly turned into an interrogation with a confession-seeking motive. When I turned my attention to how these behaviours influenced information disclosure, interesting findings emerged. Within the very first interview, the chatty and cooperative suspect became uncooperative and started to disclose less information. This occurred immediately after the first guilt-presumptive utterance. As the interviews progressed, an inverse relationship between guilt presumptive interview behaviour and interviewee information disclosure persisted. Although the study produced some interesting findings, causal links between the interviewer's behaviour, their underlying beliefs, and cognitive processes cannot be made. Instead, researchers must often deconstruct the behaviour to make assumptions about the underlying cognitions. In this case, the behaviour of the interviewers also suggests they were engaged in *tunnel vision*.

Tunnel vision is used to describe the behaviour of an individual who is focused on a particular person, thing, or outcome. However, within the psycho-legal literature, the meaning of tunnel vision has been expanded to include confirmatory behaviours within that intent focus (Findley, 2012). Tunnel vision is often used to describe behaviour directed towards a prime suspect, and only information that seems to incriminate that suspect is gathered. Information gathered prior to identifying a prime suspect is also interpreted in a manner that implicates the suspect. Moreover, researchers have demonstrated that tunnel vision influences the decision-making process by limiting the amount of information an individual may naturally attempt to gather and the type of information sought. Any disconfirming information is ignored or explained away.

It can also be argued that the police interviewers from the Adams-Quackenbush et al. (2019) study formed *expectancy effects* either prior to or during the interview. Expectancy is not often used within the psycho-legal literature to describe behaviour based in confirmation bias; however, a strong argument can be made that expectancy is the best term to describe some of the confirmatory behaviours found within investigative interview settings. For example, when an interviewer enters an investigative interview with a presumption of guilt, they have created an expectancy regarding culpability. There may also be an expectation that the suspect will deny guilt and engage in deceptive behaviour. Moreover, the interviewer may hold an expectation of resistance to the "truth" by the suspect. All these expectations held by the interviewer influence the interviewer's behaviour regarding question types and their verbal and nonverbal behaviour. The interviewer's expectations can also influence the suspect's behaviour and the interview outcomes by creating expectancy effects within the interviewee that are exhibited through the *self-fulfilling prophecy* phenomenon (Darley & Fazio, 1980).

Other research in this area has demonstrated that obtaining prior information about a case can influence the behaviour of police investigators and interviewers. This can create an *anchoring bias*, which is the tendency to base final judgements on information obtained early in the decision-making process. Anchoring bias is particularly problematic when investigators must assess case information. Psycho-legal researchers have demonstrated that officers who form theories early in an investigation are more likely to dismiss information that disconfirms their beliefs as less reliable (Ask et al., 2008). Researchers have also found that police investigators are more likely to engage in confirmatory thinking because identifying a prime suspect requires a belief that the suspect is involved in the crime (O'Brien, 2009).

Cognitive factors as barriers to information elicitation

Just as interviewer behaviour can prevent interviewees from disclosing important information, it can also prevent the interviewer from eliciting valuable information. Little is known about the influence of an investigative interviewer's behaviour in terms of cognitive processes and how they may influence the interview outcome. Understanding the cognitive mechanisms that underpin interviewer behaviour is important to improve investigative interviewing but also to address enduring questions around poor interview practices in question formulation and eliciting investigation relevant information.

Cognitive load in the interview room

Within the investigative interviewing literature, it is widely accepted that interviewing is a cognitively demanding activity for both the interviewer and interviewee (Hanaway et al., 2018). Cognition involves a multitude of processes involved with how we think, know, remember, judge, problem-solve, and decision-make. An important component of cognition includes the working memory, which is involved in memory formation, decision-making, and behaviour. Working memory has a limited capacity and is directly related to the volume of information that needs to be processed. The amount of information held within the working memory is referred to as cognitive load, and there are three types: intrinsic, extraneous, and germane (Sweller, 2010).

Normal attentional demands on working memory capacity are called *intrinsic load* because they are essential to the demands of cognition (e.g., memory, thought, communication). Intrinsic load is a base load that is always present and varies by individual. It cannot be reduced further than its natural baseline; however, this type of load can increase with the demands of a task or process. Once the task is simplified or removed, the intrinsic load will return to baseline. *Germane load* is defined in terms of intrinsic load as it is responsible for knowledge acquisition and the storage of learned information. External demands in the environment create *extraneous load*. This involves processing information that is presented to us so we can respond accordingly or perform tasks. Extraneous load increases as information becomes more complex or the tasks become more challenging, and a higher skillset is needed (e.g., difficult questioning, increased distraction, multiple tasks, or tasks beyond expertise). As a result, attentional demands increase exponentially, and baseline loads also increase. The ability to successfully perform tasks and respond to the environment when extraneous load is high also depends on levels of germane load. This type of load works to create permanent storage for the extraneous information we receive by creating schema or mental shortcuts that allow for a quick interpretation of that information.

Although cognitive load is a normal and naturally occurring product of being a sentient human, it can become problematic when present in an investigative interview. Within an investigative interview, interviewers must actively listen, execute their interview plan, maintain control, remember information, connect information, seek additional information, and employ other decision-making strategies. The interviewer has little control over how the information is presented or the amount of relevant information received at once. This means that the capacity for germane load to process the information and create schema is reduced as resources in working memory are devoted to the extraneous load (Sweller, 2010). Thus, the need to rely on pre-existing schema and employ heuristics may increase. This, in turn, can increase the presence of cognitive biases.

The demand of cognitive load on interviewer performance was recently demonstrated in a mock interview study conducted by Hanaway and colleagues (2021). The researchers evaluated the mental workload of 102 mock interviewers across three conditions: high, moderate, and low. Mock interviewers were instructed to listen attentively to a witness statement and to develop additional questions for the witness whilst making decisions about the order the questions would be asked. The participant's perception of their cognitive load was measured, and then they completed a cognitively taxing task based on their assigned condition. Participants were then tested on their recollection of the information provided in the witness statement with both a free narrative and a cued recall task. Hanaway found that participants in the high and moderate conditions perceived their cognitive load to be high and performed more poorly on the free narrative recall task. Participants in the high cognitive load condition also performed more poorly on the cued recall task.

The findings from Hanaway et al. (2021) illustrate the effects of cognitive load on attending and processing statement information. The ability to attend to and retain information is crucial for developing additional questions to obtain more information disclosure. Although Hanaway's study was conducted on a non-policing sample, the findings can be generalised to an investigative or law enforcement population because this process occurs in all humans. That is, Hanaway was able to demonstrate a known phenomenon (cognitive load) on a specialised task (investigative interview) that is relevant to a specific demographic (interviewers). What remains unknown is whether the effects of cognitive load present differently in trained interview professionals versus mock interviewers. It is also unknown what other factors are present in the interview that can increase or decrease the effects of cognitive load (e.g., interviewer characteristics, interviewee characteristics, external pressures, crime type, or interview type). Whilst individual differences in working memory capacity may account for many aspects of individual performance, understanding the influence of cognitive load on the interview can help improve interview practices overall. For example, processes for formulating additional questions and gathering more investigation-relevant information could be improved.

Cognitive bias in the interview room

Another essential part of the cognitive process involves schema formation. A schema is a cognitive framework that organises information and helps to interpret it and is an element of germane cognitive load. Schemas are useful because they organise information into categories and relationships for easy and quick retrieval. However, this process also contributes to stereotype formation and makes it difficult to retain information that does not conform to our world views, which creates a host of cognitive biases (Nickerson, 1998). The presence of cognitive biases within the investigative interview is difficult to overcome. Over 180 cognitive biases have been identified and categorised (Manoogian & Benson, 2017). Cognitive biases permeate many types of information processing, and the most common type for investigative interviewers is likely confirmation bias due to the analysis of prior information in decision-making and question formulation. This bias involves seeking out what we already believe to be true to confirm those beliefs and can influence a person to interpret new information so it also conforms to the belief.

Some researchers argue that confirmation bias is an adaptive cognitive strategy that uses heuristics. A heuristic is an approach to problem-solving or decision-making that uses a practical method but makes no guarantee of being rational or optimal. Heuristics are sufficient to handle decision-making for an immediate situation and could be necessary for the successful completion of tasks that require focus and dedication under high-pressure (see Gigerenzer, 2008). Notwithstanding the decision-making benefits of some heuristics, belief-based heuristics can act as a barrier to objective and logical thinking and lead to biased behaviour. For example, during an investigative interview, the belief in a suspect's guilt may be based on heuristics about how guilty or deceptive people behave during questioning. An interviewer who believes that only guilty people confess, and holds a guilty judgement about a suspect, may be more likely to push for a confession (Kassin et al., 2003). In sum, reliance on instinct and an intense focus on a prime suspect is not appropriate for the investigative interview because that is the part of the job where skills such as strategic questioning and an ability to process large amounts of information are more likely to assist with the task of information-gathering.

When making decisions in high stress/high cognitive load situations, individuals are more likely to come to their conclusions quickly and use very little of the information available to them (see Findley, 2012). If an interviewer is under a lot of pressure to gather quality information or to gain a confession, it can influence their decision-making abilities and their performance as an interviewer (Adams-Quackenbush et al., 2019). Researchers have found that interviewers who are engaged in focused and confirmatory thinking are more apt to use coercive tactics (Narchet et al., 2011), ask more accusatory questions (Adams-Quackenbush et al., 2020), and rely more heavily on nonverbal behaviour when assessing the truthfulness of the information.

Overcoming cognitive barriers to information elicitation

Many of the issues that surround information elicitation and disclosure stem from underlying cognitive processes and biases. It can be difficult to modify one's cognitive processes and subsequent behaviours, but it is not impossible. Modifying cognitive strategies and behaviour involves three main steps: (1) identify the behaviour, (2) acknowledge its detriment, and (3) engage in conscious behaviour modification (Berkman, 2018). The first step in this process is the most important. It requires acknowledging there may be a problem with certain behaviours that may have historically resulted in perceived success (e.g., case closure, obtaining a confession, handling increased workload). A helpful approach may be to acknowledge past accomplishments but dedicate the future to incorporating some strategies into your practice that will make for better interviews and more successful investigations.

Due to the lack of research on cognitive load in investigative settings, there are no suggestions on how interviewers may address this. Most explorations into strategies for reducing load are aimed at trainers and educators. Although there are strategies suggested for educators to reduce cognitive load in learning environments, many cannot be applied to the task of interviewing. However, Mugford and colleagues (2013) found that general police training informed by cognitive load theory can improve learning and promote skill transferability in recruits. When learning is designed with cognitive load theory in mind, it incorporates strategies that facilitate informed schema creation. It could be argued that creating and reinforcing fully informed schemas during interview training would create a better information base for use with heuristics when cognitive load is high. It should be noted that it is not an easy task to simply change counterproductive behaviours by being trained in new techniques and interview models. Training knowledge fades, and if new skills are not maintained through practice, constructive feedback, and evaluation, the newly acquired schema may degrade over time.

Conversely, lessening the presence of confirmation bias during the interview may be within the interviewer's control. For example, improving techniques for information elicitation and disclosure through alternative scenario creation can be beneficial. When we generate and consider several possibilities for why something may be as it is, we must suspend our beliefs and focus on the information at hand. Within investigative contexts, the ability to assess information from a variety of perspectives is known as *generating alternative scenarios*. This involves analysing each piece of known information on its own merits and then within the context of additional information, generating as many plausible explanations for the piece of information as possible. This strategy requires the interviewer to focus on information gathering as opposed to theory confirmation.

It should be noted that generating alternative hypotheses is not immune to the effects of confirmation bias (see Ask & Granhag, 2005). When people are required to imagine or explain a possible scenario, there is a moment when they must believe the scenario is true. Confidence in the truthfulness of the scenario may increase, and the likelihood that confirmatory information searches will also increase. There is also the possibility that the belief of suspect guilt is more plausible than a scenario where they are not guilty. Thus, the motivation to be accurate in the guilty scenario may rise, increasing the likelihood of seeking information that confirms the guilt presumption. To address this, recent research has suggested that weighting criminal evidence using pencil and paper to make notes, whilst considering alternative scenarios, helps to reduce confirmation bias in criminal investigation contexts (Rassin, 2018). The researchers concluded that creating a schematic overview of the known information can combat the effects of confirmation bias that can occur when generating alternative scenarios.

Interviewers who use alternative scenario generation must also be vigilant for the illusion of being thorough. O'Brien (2009) found that despite engaging in alternative hypothesis generation, participants who formed multiple scenarios exhibited the same amount of bias as those who considered only one scenario. The researcher concluded that participants who created several scenarios may have believed that they considered all the evidence and then moved on to make their case for a primary suspect. This behaviour may also be further exacerbated if there is high pressure or time constraints (Alison et al., 2013).

Concluding remarks

The issues associated with cognitive processes and investigative interviewing are complex. The presence of cognitive load can alter how an interviewer behaves and the questions they ask, and it can increase the likelihood of engaging in cognitive biases. In high-stress and complex task situations, information processing becomes automated to rely on schema, and the behaviour is often a result of heuristics. Whilst the expansive literature on investigative interviewing continues to grow, explorations into the cognitive mechanisms underpinning potentially detrimental interviewer behaviour are rare. Researchers interested in questions involving the cognitively complex task of investigative interviewing need to create studies rooted in cognitive theory and consider the cognitive load experienced by interviewers. Until more evidence is produced around the cognitive mechanisms that hinder investigative information elicitation and disclosure, we cannot fully understand why issues in question formulation, guilt-presumption, and confession-seeking persist. In the meantime, interviewers interested in ensuring they behave in a way that facilitates interviewee disclosure can adopt strategies dedicated to objective thinking. It may be that the best defence against detrimental interview behaviours is the acceptance that instinctive judgements may be biased, and initial theories may not be correct.

References

Adams-Quackenbush, N. M., Horselenberg, R., Tomas, F., & van Koppen, P. J. (2019). Detecting guilt presumption in a police-suspect interview. An evaluation of the questions asked in a Dutch murder case. *Investigative Interviewing Research and Practice*, *10*(1), 37–60.

Adams-Quackenbush, N. M., Vrij, A., Horselenberg, R., Satchell, L. P., & van Koppen, P. J. (2020). Articulating guilt? The influence of guilt presumption of interviewer and interview behaviour. *Current Psychology*, 1–13.

Alison, L., Doran, B., Long, M. L., Power, N., & Humphrey, A. (2013). The effects of subjective time pressure and individual differences on hypotheses generation and action prioritization in police investigations. *Journal of Experimental Psychology: Applied*, *19*(1), 83–93.

Ask, K., & Granhag, P. A. (2005). Motivational sources of confirmation bias in criminal investigations: The need for cognitive closure. *Journal of Investigative Psychology and Offender Profiling*, *2*(1), 43–63.

Ask, K., Rebelius, A., & Granhag, P. A. (2008). The 'elasticity' of criminal evidence: A moderator of investigator bias. *Applied Cognitive Psychology: The Official Journal of the Society for Applied Research in Memory and Cognition, 22*(9), 1245–1259.

Berkman, E. T. (2018). The neuroscience of goals and behavior change. *Consulting Psychology Journal: Practice and Research*, *70*(1), 28–44.

Darley, J. M., & Fazio, R. H. (1980). Expectancy confirmation process arising in the social interaction sequence. *American Psychologist*, *35*(10), 867–881.

Findley, K. A. (2012). Tunnel vision. In B. L. Cutler (Ed.), *Conviction of the innocent: Lessons from psychological research* (pp. 303–323). American Psychological Association.

Gigerenzer, G. (2008). Why heuristics work. *Perspectives on Psychological Science, 3*(1), 20–29.

Hanaway, P., & Akehurst, L. (2018). Voices from the front line: Police officers' perceptions of real-world interviewing with vulnerable witnesses. *Investigative Interviewing: Research and Practice*, *9*(1), 14–33.

Hanaway, P., Akehurst, L., Vernham, Z., & Hope, L. (2021). The effects of cognitive load during an investigative interviewing task on mock interviewers' recall of information. *Legal and Criminological Psychology*, *26*(1), 25–41.

Haworth, K. (2017). The discursive construction of evidence in police interviews: Case study of a rape suspect. *Applied Linguistics, 38*(2), 194–214.

Hudson, C. A., Satchell, L. P., & Adams-Quackenbush, N. M. (2018). It takes two: the round-robin methodology for investigative interviewing research. *Frontiers in Psychology, 9*, 2181.

Kassin, S. M., Goldstein, C. C., & Savitsky, K. (2003). Behavioral confirmation in the interrogation room: On the dangers of presuming guilt. *Law and Human Behavior, 27*(2), 187–203.

Manoogian, J., & Benson, B. (2017). *Cognitive bias codex* [Online]. [Retrieved March 22, 2022].

Mugford, R., Corey, S., & Bennell, C. (2013). Improving police training from a cognitive load perspective. *Policing: An International Journal of Police Strategies & Management, 36*(2), 312–337.

Narchet, F. M., Meissner, C. A., & Russano, M. B. (2011). Modeling the influence of investigator bias on the elicitation of true and false confessions. *Law and Human Behavior, 35*(6), 452–465.

Nickerson, R. (1998). Confirmation bias: A ubiquitous phenomenon in many guises. *Review of General Psychology, 2*(2), 175–220.

O'Brien, B. (2009). Prime suspect: An examination of factors that aggravate and counter-act confirmation bias in criminal investigations. *Psychology, Public Policy, and Law, 15*(4), 315–334.

Oxburgh, G. E., Myklebust, T., & Grant, T. (2010). The question of question types in police interviews: A review of the literature from a psychological and linguistic perspective. *The International Journal of Speech, Language and the Law, 17*(1), 45–66.

Rassin, E. (2018). Reducing tunnel vision with a pen-and-paper tool for the weighting of criminal evidence. *Journal of Investigative Psychology and Offender Profiling, 15*(2), 227–233.

Sweller, J. (2010). Element interactivity and intrinsic, extraneous, and germane cognitive load. *Educational Psychological Review, 22*(2), 123–138.

6 Lack of cooperation in witness interviews

Alejandra De La Fuente Vilar

In this chapter, I discuss psycho-legal issues related to crime witnesses who are not willing to cooperate with the investigation, specifically those unwilling to provide valid information to assist the police during an interview. First, I refer you to a recent Dutch case that illustrates some of the perils of lack of witness cooperation for crime management in general. Second, I introduce a cost-benefit model to understand individuals' decisions on whether to cooperate with the police in general. I then propose the application of this model to understand witness cooperation and information disclosure in a police investigative interview. Third, I present a brief empirical overview of some of the effects of lack of witness cooperation on the interviewee and the interviewer affecting overall information elicitation. Lastly, I present evidence-based interviewing recommendations to promote cooperation and reflect on the real-life implications of lack of witness cooperation for police practitioners in the interview room and in the criminal justice system more broadly.

Lack of witness cooperation in criminal investigations

Police rely on witness cooperation to gather accurate and detailed accounts about crimes that inform lines of investigations and impact their success. Those witness statements can later be used as evidence in criminal proceedings, which also makes them relevant for the administration of justice. Therefore, witnesses who cooperate in criminal investigations fulfil a role of assistance to the police. As such, witnesses contribute directly to the police's task of fighting crime and maintaining public order in the community. However, witness cooperation is not always granted, and there are some witnesses who are not willing to cooperate with the police, which negatively affects effective crime management (Tyler & Fagan, 2008).

DOI: 10.4324/9781003308546-9

Case box 6.1   A summary of a public violence case in the Netherlands that illustrates the consequences of lack of witness cooperation in criminal investigations

In May 2019, in the Dutch city of Enschede, a father allegedly intervened in a children's quarrel. In reaction, a group of 15–20 neighbours visited his home. After an argument, they dragged him and his wife out of their home and beat them with sticks in front of their children and a large crowd of 'silent as a grave' witnesses (Rohmensen, 2019). Reportedly, the assaulted family were Syrian refugees, and the alleged perpetrators were Dutch citizens. The police immediately investigated this incident and relocated the refugee family for safety reasons. A month later, the police still did not have any major leads in the investigation. Despite having called witnesses to come forward using an 'SMS-blast' (i.e., a simultaneous and automated mass text messaging based on information from mobile antennas) to a large number of citizens present, around the time when, and in the vicinity of where, the incident took place (Politie, 2019), and despite having invested many resources in the investigation with the neighbourhood police (Timmers, 2019), the investigation stood still. The mayor of the city declared that the investigation had stalled as 'too many people do not dare to speak up' (Lindeman, 2020). In the following month, an eighteen-year-old woman was arrested for public violence. She lived in the house next to the alleged victims' house and was accused of facilitating the entrance of the 'mob' of neighbours into the Syrian family's home. The media reported that the suspect's mother was advised to encourage the perpetrators to come forward for the release of her daughter, who reported feeling used as 'bait' (Timmers, 2019). As a result, three individuals turned themselves in and the suspect was released. Soon after, the case was closed with three convictions (Lindeman, 2020).

The Enschede case (see Case box 6.1) illustrates how necessary public cooperation is for policing crime. It highlights the need for cooperation from witnesses in the absence of other types of evidence. Some of the detrimental consequences that lack of witness cooperation can have on an investigation are obstruction and delays in justice. Overall, the relevance of this topic to the policing context concerns the impediment that lack of witness cooperation represents to investigative goals. Such lack of witness cooperation can more specifically negatively affect interviewing of crime witnesses, a core task in criminal investigations. Recent research indicates a high prevalence of uncooperative witnesses; that is, individuals who are unwilling to become involved in a criminal investigation and refuse to provide accurate and detailed information during police witness interviews (De La Fuente Vilar et al., 2022b; Wheeler et al., 2017). Therefore, it is necessary to better understand how to effectively promote witness cooperation.

Towards a cost-benefit model of witness cooperation in the interview room

Kidd (1979) proposed a rational decision-making processing model in which witnesses consider material and psychological costs and benefits to decide whether to report or not a witnessed crime to the authorities. I propose to expand this model to understand witness cooperation during a police witness interview. The basic tenet is that witnesses engage in a similar cost-benefit analysis to regulate the extent of disclosing or withholding units of information about the witnessed crime in the interview room. Information disclosure thus results from a positive subjective appraisal of the associated benefits outweighing the costs of cooperation. Conversely, perceived high costs with perceived low benefits can lead to the decision to not cooperate with the police, which in turn negatively affects information disclosure. Below I outline the model proposing witness cooperation and lack thereof as determinants of information disclosure in police interviews.

Previous cognitive processes

Initially, an individual who witnesses an illegal act needs to have paid sufficient attention to it and have identified it as a crime. Witnessing criminal activity, according to Kidd (1979), triggers a state of internal arousal in the individual, which motivates the individual to act in response to it. The individual then may initiate a prosocial action such as reporting crime details to the police or may engage in cognitively restructuring the interpretation of the witnessed event to justify inaction on their part.

Cost-benefit analysis

Subsequently, the individual who became a crime witness will engage in an analysis of the perceived costs and benefits associated with cooperating or not with the police to guide their behaviour. Previous research has identified different factors that compromise or motivate the decision to cooperate with the police in general, of which some are relevant for the decision to cooperate in an investigative interview in particular. Specifically, the initial decision to cooperate is influenced by one or many of the characteristics and context of the crime, the individual characteristics of the perpetrator, and the witness themselves (see De La Fuente Vilar, 2020 for a review).

Table 6.1 Some factors that compromise or motivate an individual's initial decision to cooperate with the police in a witness interview.

Situational factors	Individual factors
— Type and severity of the crime.	— Characteristics of the witness, including criminal history.
— Characteristics of the offender.	
— Influence of (absence of) other witnesses.	— Personal beliefs, moral ideas, and social norms.
— Material costs (e.g., time and money spent in attending legal proceedings).	— Previous experience and personal perceptions of the police and criminal justice system.
— Material rewards (e.g., money, leniency).	— Relationship between witness and perpetrator.
— Subjective rewards (e.g., local recognition).	— Relationship between witness and victim.
— Fear or threats of retaliation.	— Cultural differences and language barriers between witnesses and police.
— Lack of information about role as a witness.	
— Concerns about legal proceedings and the unpredictability of legal outcomes.	

Additionally, an international survey of experienced criminal investigators reports that lack of witness cooperation in police interviews can be motivated by witnesses' fear of negative consequences—for example, if a witness fears retaliation from the perpetrator. Further, some witnesses' unwillingness to cooperate is based on previous negative experiences with the police or due to holding negative perceptions of the police. Alternatively, if a witness has a criminal history, they may also be afraid of self-incrimination. Lack of witness cooperation can also be motivated by the fear of negative consequences for someone else—for instance, in cases in which the witness has a relationship with the perpetrator and wishes to protect them (De La Fuente Vilar et al., 2022b). See Table 6.1 for an overview of the situational and individual factors that can affect initial witness cooperativeness in the interview room.

Witness cooperativeness decisions

After weighing the different factors that compromise or motivate cooperation, witnesses reach an initial decision that oscillates in a *continuum of cooperativeness-uncooperativeness*. That initial stance guides witness behaviour in the interview room to fluctuate between a *willingness-unwillingness to report* (and withhold) the remembered information about the witnessed crime (Shepherd, 1993). The initial decision to cooperate may be revised throughout the duration of an interview due to the dynamic nature of the interaction between the interviewer and the witness. Therefore, both actors in the interview need to work in tandem for effective information elicitation. At this stage, the proposed model provides the opportunity to conceptualise the interviewing approach as

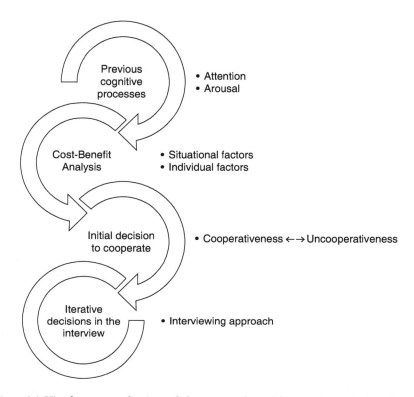

Figure 6.1 Visual conceptualisation of the proposed model to understand the effect of witness cooperation on information elicitation in an investigative interview provided by the author.

an external component which can modulate the subjective evaluation of costs and benefits associated with cooperation.

This second tenet in the proposed model is that the interviewing approach used can influence the witness' cooperativeness-uncooperativeness stance resulting in information elicitation. Previous research demonstrates that an information-gathering approach, including rapport-based techniques, can foster cooperation and reduce resistance, which, in turn, maximises information disclosure (Gabbert et al., 2020; Vrij et al., 2014). Conversely, a direct, controlling, and accusatorial interviewing approach can provoke or exacerbate resistance and decrease information elicitation and accuracy (Vrij et al., 2017). Therefore, in investigative interviewing practice, the onus is on the interviewer to use interviewing techniques that promote cooperation and effective information elicitation. A visual conceptualisation of the model proposed to understand the effects of witness cooperation on information elicitation is presented in Figure 6.1.

Effects of lack of witness cooperation

The cost-benefit model outlined previously posits that uncooperativeness regulates information disclosure and the interviewing approach, which has been empirically supported. In an experimental study, we manipulated high costs of cooperation by simulating a mock-witness scenario in which participants risked negative consequences from the disclosure of information. We found evidence that instructions to not cooperate decrease the amount of information disclosed by mock-witnesses, and the accuracy to a lesser extent (De La Fuente Vilar et al., 2020). Moreover, participants instructed to not cooperate self-reported an inclination to disclose less accurate information, and to disclose a combination of accurate and inaccurate information in their accounts (De La Fuente Vilar et al., 2020). These findings, taken together, provided initial evidence for detrimental effects on the quantity, and to a lesser extent on the quality, of the information disclosed that lack of witness cooperation can provoke in an investigative interview.

The negative effects of lack of witness cooperation on the interviewee's disclosure are somewhat similar to the effects of it on the interviewer's approach in the sense that they jeopardise effective information elicitation. Specifically, lack of witness cooperation challenges the interviewer's task of obtaining information from the witness. Using a non-police sample of participants in a mock-investigation paradigm, we found preliminary evidence that lack of witness cooperation can affect mock-interviewers' behaviour. Specifically, facing uncooperative behaviour, in combination with a lack of interviewing training, can lead to a shift from an information-gathering to a direct approach to interviewing (De La Fuente Vilar et al., 2022a). Such interviewing approach over-relies on the use of direct and closed questions that reduces the amount of information reported and its accuracy (Vrij et al., 2014). In contrast, following an information-gathering interviewing approach can lead to more effective information elicitation and promotes cooperation (Gabbert et al., 2020).

Evidence-based interviewing of cooperative and uncooperative witnesses

The Cognitive Interview (CI; Fisher & Geiselman, 1992) is an evidence-based tool for interviewing cooperative witnesses that I consider also offers a foundation for how to interview uncooperative witnesses (De La Fuente Vilar, 2020). For the latter group of interviewees, developing rapport and a positive relationship between the interviewer and the interviewee is a prerequisite before facilitating recall. In practice, this means prioritising the use of the relational components before administering the memory-enhancing techniques of the CI. That is, using rapport-building techniques and focusing on transferring control to the witness. Therefore, the aim in interviews of uncooperative witnesses needs to be to first increase the witness' *willingness to report* before facilitating the *ability to remember* (i.e., accurately recall).

Rapport-building techniques are recommended to build trust and facilitate communication and recall (Abbe & Brandon, 2013). Relevantly for interviewing uncooperative witnesses, rapport can allow for the exploration of the reasons why the witness is unmotivated to cooperate. In addition, interviewers who transfer control to the witness can promote cooperation by setting expectations about the active role of the witness. The witness must understand that they are responsible for generating information based on their memory of the crime during the interview. A detailed and complete free witness narrative can then be elicited using open and non-suggestive prompts, by respecting the witness' pace, and by avoiding interruptions (Fisher, 2010).

While the best-practice interviewing guidelines outlined previously promote cooperation, they may be insufficient to overcome a lack of witness cooperation. Evidence of validated specialised interviewing techniques that overcome a lack of witness cooperation is lacking. The proposed model of witness cooperation and information elicitation in this chapter provides a basic theoretical consideration for the endeavour of developing and testing techniques recommended for interviewing uncooperative witnesses. Future techniques should be designed to reduce costs associated with reporting crime information or increase its benefits. In that way, interviewers can be more equipped to decrease any uncooperativeness and initial unwillingness to report information.

Most importantly, interviewers must not take witness cooperation for granted. The onus is on them to gain, maintain, and recover witness cooperation to elicit information. This mindset can serve as a starting point to avoid interviewers reverting to intuitive ineffective interviewing in the face of challenging uncooperativeness. The interviewer's success at maximising information disclosure is dependent on the witness' willingness to report information. Interviewers, therefore, must adapt their approach according to the witness' stance. Overall, the aim of the information elicitation techniques used to interview uncooperative witnesses ought to be producing gradual movements towards cooperation or at least not exacerbating any initial uncooperativeness (Alison et al., 2013). Police interviewing practice, however, regrettably shows that ineffective interviewing techniques are commonly in use (see De La Fuente Vilar, 2020 for a review), in particular in interviews of uncooperative witnesses (Davis & Leo, 2017).

Implications of lack of witness cooperation in the criminal justice system

The cases of wrongful convictions based on erroneous and false witness testimony are the epitome of the much-needed reform in witness interviewing. Currently (to February 25th, 2022), there are 2991 exonerations in the United States, and in 61% of those cases, perjury or a false accusation were the factors contributing to the wrongful conviction, followed by police and prosecutorial misconduct (The National Registry of Exonerations, 2022). An analysis of recantation cases conducted by Gross and Gross (2013) suggests that the incidence of perjury results from coercion, undue pressure, and threats to witnesses from the police during the investigations. Furthermore, Davis and Leo (2017) noted that witnesses who are less willing to cooperate with the police are more likely to be targets of an accusatorial interviewing approach (e.g., the Reid Technique, Inbau et al., 2013; Meissner et al., 2012). It warrants concern, however, that the application of accusatorial and coercive interviewing techniques in laboratory and real-life witness interviews increases false accusations (Loney & Cutler, 2016; Moore et al., 2014).

Considering that witness statements serve as a legal basis in the adjudication of justice, the quality and integrity of witness statements obtained by the police following an accusatorial interviewing approach should be called into question. A relevant evidence-based recommendation to improve interviewing practice and witness evidence is the mandatory audio-visual recording of witness interviews. This measure can inhibit the use of ineffective interviewing techniques and protects the integrity of the witness statement. Furthermore, the recordings not only facilitate the reproduction of the witness statement, but they also inform on how it was obtained, thereby enriching its evidential value (Milne & Shaw, 1999). Importantly, admitting a video-recorded police interview as evidence is crucial in criminal cases in which uncooperative witnesses are unwilling to provide their testimony in court.

Concluding remarks

While the current state-of-the-art does not provide definite responses on how to overcome some of the obstacles that lack of witness cooperation represents in the interview room, this chapter discussed key aspects relevant to promoting witness cooperation and effectively eliciting information. The beacon in interviewing uncooperative witnesses is not to take cooperation for granted and to consider the costs and benefits associated with cooperation for each witness. The aim is to produce movements towards cooperativeness to influence the witnesses' willingness to report crime information. An effective interview thus follows an information-gathering approach that prioritises the use of rapport-based techniques before the use of cognitive interviewing techniques that facilitate memory recall.

References

Abbe, A., & Brandon, S. E. (2013). The role of rapport in investigative interviewing: A review. *Journal of Investigative Psychology and Offender Profiling, 10*(3), 237–249.

Alison, L. J., Alison, E., Noone, G., Elntib, S., & Christiansen, P. (2013). Why tough tactics fail and rapport gets results: Observing Rapport-Based Interpersonal Techniques (ORBIT) to generate useful information from terrorists. *Psychology, Public Policy, and Law, 19*(4), 411–431.

Davis, D., & Leo, R. (2017). A damning cascade of investigative errors: Flaws in homicide investigation in the USA. In F. Brookman, E. R. Maguire, & M. Maguire (Eds.), *The handbook on homicide* (pp. 578–598). Wiley-Blackwell.

De La Fuente Vilar, A. (2020). *A broken tandem: Understanding lack of witness cooperation in the interview room* (Doctoral dissertation). Maastricht University & University of Gothenburg.

De La Fuente Vilar, A., Horselenberg, R., Hope, L., Strömwall, L. A., & van Koppen, P. J. (2022a). *Unfulfilled expectations of cooperation in witness interviews*. Manuscript.

De La Fuente Vilar, A., Horselenberg, R., Landström, S., & van Koppen, P. J. (2022b). *Lack of witness cooperation in investigative interviews: An international survey of criminal investigators*. Manuscript.

De La Fuente Vilar, A., Horselenberg, R., Strömwall, L. A., Landström, S., Hope, L., & van Koppen, P. J. (2020). Effects of cooperation on information disclosure in mock-witness interviews. *Legal and Criminological Psychology, 25*(2), 133–149.

Fisher, R. P. (2010). Interviewing cooperative witnesses. *Legal and Criminological Psychology, 15*(1), 25–38.

Fisher, R. P., & Geiselman, R. (1992). *Memory-enhancing techniques for investigative interviewing: The cognitive interview*. Charles C. Thomas, Publisher.

Gabbert, F., Hope, L., Luther, K., Wright, G., Ng, M., & Oxburgh, G. (2020). Exploring the use of rapport in professional information-gathering contexts by systematically mapping the evidence base. *Applied Cognitive Psychology, 35*(2), 329–341.

Gross, A., & Gross, S. (2013). *Witness recantation study: Preliminary findings*. The National Registry of Exonerations.

Inbau, F. E., Reid, J. E., Buckley, J. P., & Jayne, B. C. (2013). *Criminal interrogation and confessions*. Jones & Bartlett Learning.

Kidd, R. F. (1979). Crime reporting: Toward a social psychological model. *Criminology, 17*(3), 380–394.

Lindeman, P. (2020). Racisme? Nee, gewone woede bij mishandeling vluchtelingen in Enschedese volkswijk Dolphia [Racism? No, ordinary anger with mistreatment of refugees in the Dolphia neighborhood of Enschede]. *Tubantia*. Retrieved March 22, 2022, from www.tubantia.nl/enschede/racisme-nee-gewone-woede-bij-mishandelingv luchtelingen-in-enschedese-volkswijk-dolphia~af5a181a/

Loney, D. M., & Cutler, B. L. (2016). Coercive interrogation of eyewitnesses can produce false accusations. *Journal of Police and Criminal Psychology, 31*(1), 29–36.

Meissner, C. A., Redlich, A. D., Bhatt, S., & Brandon, S. (2012). Interview and interrogation methods and their effects on true and false confessions. *Campbell Systematic Reviews, 8*(1), 1–53.

Milne, R., & Shaw, G. (1999). Obtaining witness statements: the psychology, best practice and proposals for innovation. *Medicine, Science and the Law, 39*(2), 127–138.

Moore, T. E., Cutler, B. L., & Shulman, D. (2014). Shaping eyewitness and alibi testimony with coercive interview practices. *The Champion, 8*, 34–40.

The National Registry of Exonerations. (2022). *Percentage of exonerations by contributing factor*. Newkirk Center for Science & Society at University of California Irvine, the University of Michigan Law School, & Michigan State University College of Law.

Politie. (2019, June 3). Politie verstuurt SMS-bom in onderzoek naar incident in wijk Dolphia [Police send SMS bomb in investigation of incident in Dolphia district]. *Politie*.

Rohmensen, G. J. (2019, May 12). Hoe die ruzie met een Syrisch gezin ontspoorde? De Enschedese omwonenden zwijgen als het graf [How did that fight with a Syrian family derail? The residents of Enschede are silent as the grave]. *Trouw*.

Shepherd, E. (1993). Resistance in interviews: The contribution of police perceptions and behaviour. *Issues in Criminological & Legal Psychology*, *18*, 5–12.

Timmers, F. (2019, June 19). Romy (18) aangehouden na mishandeling Syrisch gezin in Enschede: 'Politie gebruikte mijn dochter als lokaas' [Romy (18) arrested after mistreatment of Syrian family in Enschede: 'Police used my daughter as bait']. *Tubantia*.

Tyler, T. R., & Fagan, J. (2008). Legitimacy and cooperation: Why do people help the police fight crime in their communities. *Ohio State Journal of Criminal Law*, *6*, 231–275.

Vrij, A., Hope, L., & Fisher, R. P. (2014). Eliciting reliable information in investigative interviews. *Policy Insights from Behavioral and Brain Sciences*, *1*(1), 129–136.

Vrij, A., Meissner, C. A., Fisher, R. P., Kassin, S. M., Morgan III, A., & Kleinman, S. M. (2017). Psychological perspectives on interrogation. *Perspectives on Psychological Science*, *12*(6), 927–955.

Wheeler, R., Gabbert, F., Clayman, S., & Jones, S. (2017). *Information gathering with reluctant witnesses: A practitioner survey* [Paper presentation]. 2017 Conference of the International Investigative Interviewing Research Group, Monterey Bay, CA, United States.

7 Priming in investigative interviewing

A critical review

David A. Neequaye

This chapter is a critical review of the idea that priming people's motivations to share information may be a viable way to enhance disclosures in investigative interviews. Investigative interviews are social interactions where interviewers solicit information about topics on which an interviewee may be knowledgeable. These topics include security concerns or other interests not necessarily related to security. Priming is a social psychological phenomenon that exponents claim occurs when individuals become internally motivated to perform certain behaviours due to the nudge of an external influence. Importantly, proponents of priming claim that such effects occur outside of awareness. The qualities of priming, just described, make the phenomenon a suitable psychological tool to utilize in investigative interviews. For various reasons, interviewees are not always forthcoming with the information interviewers need. Therefore, social influence methods that facilitate disclosure are useful to interviewers. Pragmatically, such techniques are preferable if they exert the required influence subtly. People may negatively react if they become aware that one is actively trying to influence their behaviour.

So, is priming a viable tool when it comes to facilitating disclosure in investigative interviews? If the answer to this question is yes, it behoves researchers and their funders to devote more resources to studying the phenomenon. Practitioners can rely on the insights produced from the research. If priming holds little promise for the enterprise of investigative interviewing, then one can invest resources elsewhere. Suppose you are a stakeholder contending whether priming is a viable option. This chapter is an attempt to help you decide. I will explore the viability of priming by answering the following questions: (a) What is priming in social psychology, and how reliable is the phenomenon? (b) Have researchers examined priming influences in investigative interviews, and what have they found? (c) To what extent can the existing research on priming in investigative interviewing inform practitioners' work in the field? In the remainder of this chapter, I discuss answers to these questions in the order listed here.

Priming in social psychology

Broadly speaking, social psychologists define priming or social priming as temporarily increasing the mental accessibility of meaningful concepts to influence

DOI: 10.4324/9781003308546-10

thoughts and behaviour in a manner consistent with the prime (Dijksterhuis & Bargh, 2001). Those primes can be motivations, mindsets, stereotypes, social situations, et cetera. Researchers have examined a broad range of social priming effects. However, there is a consensus that such priming influences occur unconsciously or outside of conscious awareness. A person may or may not be objectively aware of a prime stimulus. Yet, one can say that a priming effect has manifested when the stimulus impacts how a person thinks or behaves, and the person does not intentionally link the prime to their behaviour.

The origins of priming research

The idea of social priming was borne from a proposal by Karl Lashley (see Bargh, 2014). That is, humans perform behaviours effortlessly because when one plans to enact behaviour, the intention readies or primes the needed behavioural sequence (Lashley, 1951). The seminal priming research centred on primes affecting people's impressions of others. Notably, in a study by Srull and Wyer (1979, Experiment 1), participants were primed with high or low levels of the concept hostility. The authors introduced the prime somewhat covertly by having the participants unscramble a high or low number of sentences describing hostility. After, in an ostensibly unrelated study, participants rated the personality of a man called Donald, who exhibited ambiguously hostile behaviours. The results revealed that those who received higher levels of the hostility prime rated Donald as more hostile.

Subsequent research extended the boundaries of priming effects beyond impression formation. Later studies indicated that priming could lead people to perform observable behaviours unconsciously. The seminal works here include studies by Bargh et al. (1996) and Dijksterhuis and van Knippenberg (1998). But there is no shortage of social psychology research demonstrating various priming effects on behaviour (see Bargh, 2006). Bargh and colleagues (1996) primed participants with the concept of rudeness or politeness. Those who received the rudeness prime tended to be more interruptive than their counterparts, whom the authors primed to be polite. In a second experiment, participants who had the elderly stereotype called to mind walked more slowly when exiting the premises of the experiment than those who did not undergo the prime. Dijksterhuis and van Knippenberg's (1998) research demonstrated that it may be possible to prime intelligence. The researchers primed some participants by asking them to list the attributes of a professor or a secretary. In a subsequent supposedly unrelated experiment, those who had the professor stereotype called to mind performed better on a general knowledge test.

How does priming work?

There are several explanations for the mechanisms underlying priming effects. I will attempt to provide a broad summary here. The interested reader can consult other texts for more in-depth discussions of priming theories (e.g., Neequaye, 2018). Early theoretical models proposed that priming effects derive from a perception-behaviour link (Dijksterhuis & Bargh, 2001). The notion stems from the evolutionary idea that humans' perceptual abilities evolved to enable humans to respond to what they perceive. That process aided humans' adaptation. When one perceives a meaningful stimulus, that is, a prime; the stimulus prompts one to act. Such readiness is what induces the unconscious influence of priming. Indeed, people typically draw on what they can easily remember when making decisions instead of conducting an exhaustive memory search (Tversky & Kahneman, 1973).

Later theories of priming concur with the proposal that mental accessibility, namely readiness, is a critical driver of priming. But they note that human behaviour is flexible enough such that several factors can inhibit the perception-behaviour link. Thus, the influence of primes has boundaries and not uncontrollable reign over thoughts and behaviour. For example, one is unlikely to yield to the suggestion a prime calls to mind if the suggestion is undesirable or conflicts with current motivations (e.g., Macrae & Johnston, 1998). Such inhibition may also occur when the prime does not sufficiently induce mental accessibility (e.g., Loersch & Payne, 2011). Moreover, a prime may fail to impact behaviour if one's current situation does not allow a person to enact the primed action (Loersch & Payne, 2011). However, suppose a prime elicits sufficient mental accessibility, and one's goals or situation allows the primed behaviour. In that case, a person will likely unconsciously behave in a prime-consistent way.

Debating the reliability of priming

An essential aspect of establishing the robustness of scientific findings—in this case, priming effects—is to replicate them (Simons, 2014). Generally, replications involve repeating a previous study's procedures to examine whether one can obtain the same results (Zwaan et al., 2018). Suppose a replication reveals findings similar to the initial research. In that case, the replication increases confidence that the initial finding is reliable. Conversely, if a replication fails to obtain similar results as a study in question, the failed replication decreases confidence in the original research findings.

Recently, several failures to replicate priming effects have surfaced, notably the seminal ones. A direct replication of Srull and Wyer's (1979, Experiment 1) failed to obtain the hostile priming effect described earlier (see McCarthy et al., 2018). Doyen et al.'s (2012) replication of the elderly stereotype priming effect also did not replicate the original study (i.e., Bargh et al., 1996). Additionally, Shanks and colleagues (2013) conducted nine experiments, exploring conditions under which one may observe the intelligence priming effect reported by Dijksterhuis and van Knippenberg (1998). All their attempts failed (see also Harris et al., 2013).

These failed replications do not necessarily indicate that priming effects are altogether spurious. However, such consistent failures to replicate give pause about the reliability of priming. Some schools of thought have questioned the role of unconscious processes on behaviour, specifically, the perception-behaviour link (Newell & Shanks, 2014). These critics believe that the abundance of replication failures demonstrate that priming effects are short-lived at best and elusive at worst (Shanks et al., 2013). It is worth mentioning that proponents of priming have presented evidence indicating that although some priming research may fail to replicate, priming remains a reliable phenomenon (Payne et al., 2016). However, a critic has rebutted the claims and conclusions Payne and colleagues offered (see Shanks, 2017).

Priming in investigative interviewing

Imagine one agrees that priming effects are short-lived. In that case, can one conclude that the potential benefit of priming in investigative interviewing is not worth exploring? Not necessarily. Such small effects may still exert consequential influence in the field or the real world. See Lakens (2013) on the importance of interpreting effect sizes contextually. Possibly, a short-lived priming effect may lead an interviewee to disclose useful information within the priming influence's limited span. Thus, investigative interviewing researchers have explored the possibility of priming concepts and motivations that facilitate disclosure. In this research paradigm, authors examine priming's *viability* as a useful tool by testing whether it elicits *more* information than no priming or priming an antithetical concept to the one hypothesized to promote disclosure.

Additionally, this research paradigm implements direct questions to inquire about a topic of interest in interviews—during experiments. Direct questioning is arguably devoid of social influence. It allows the experimental control needed to assess the effect of priming against a comparison condition. Moreover, law enforcement interviewers frequently employ direct questioning in the field (Kelly et al., 2016).

Priming a secure attachment

Dawson et al. (2015) hypothesized that priming attachment security would influence individuals to be forthcoming with information. Essentially, a secure attachment is the support, trust, and comfort one shares with others in significant interpersonal relationships (Bowlby, 1982) for a comprehensive discussion on secure attachment. The attachment security hypothesis emerged from two important premises: (a) One's store of attachment security from existing relationships can spill over to new interactions (Andersen & Chen, 2002), and (b) Activating secure attachment enhances prosocial behaviour (Mikulincer & Shaver, 2016).

Dawson et al. (2015) invited participants to assume the role of an interviewee with information about a mock terror plot. Next, in what participants believed was a concentration exercise, the researchers covertly primed attachment security. The primed participants reflected on their relationship with a confidant. The comparison group received no prime. After, an interviewer questioned all the participants about the terror plot.

The results indicated that those primed with attachment security revealed more information than their non-primed counterparts did. However, that difference was not statistically significant by conventional standards, and the study's replicability remains unclear. Hence, the idea that priming attachment security may be a viable means to facilitate the amount of disclosure is tenuous and inconclusive.

Priming interviewees to be open with information

Dawson et al. (2017) drew on the common conceptual metaphor whereby people describe others' communication as *open* if one is forthcoming with information. Conversely, a person may be characterized as *closed* off if they hold back information. It was hypothesized that priming openness would lead people to disclose more information. The researchers conducted two experiments to examine the prediction.

Participants took on the role of an interviewee with information about a mock terror threat. In the first study, the researchers covertly introduced the openness prime using the spaciousness of the interview room. Primed participants underwent the questioning in a relatively large room containing various features depicting the metaphor openness; for example, 'a picture of open water and an open sky' (Dawson et al., 2017). The interviewer questioned the non-primed participants in a substantially smaller room than the one used to prime openness. The results indicated that the priming led participants to disclose more information, as Dawson et al. (2017) predicted.

The second study had a similar design as the first one. The researchers explored the influence of openness priming using objects illustrating the metaphor compared to no priming. Participants underwent interviewing in one of four conditions: a spacious room that either contained objects depicting openness or (b) did not include such objects; less spacious rooms were also set up with these two conditions. The findings revealed that priming openness via the spaciousness of a room facilitated the amount of information participants disclosed. Taken together, the two studies by Dawson et al. (2017) indicate that room spaciousness may be a viable priming method in investigative interviews.

Recently, others have attempted to conceptually replicate the openness priming effect on information disclosure just described. Conceptual replication is when researchers use essentially different methods to examine the same hypothesis as a previous study in question (Nosek & Errington, 2017). These conceptual replications have generally failed to obtain similar results as Dawson et al. (2017). The findings of Dianiska et al. (2019) indicated that priming openness via objects depicting the metaphor did not necessarily increase disclosure. In this study, the comparison groups either received neutral primes or ones intended to activate being closed off and holding back information. Hoogesteyn et al. (2019) found that manipulating room size and interpersonal sitting distance had little impact on the amount of information people disclosed.

In all, the body of work examining the viability of openness priming has produced largely inconclusive evidence. The method does not reliably lead people to reveal more information than no priming or activating the antithetical motivation of being closed off with information.

Priming helpfulness motivations

Neequaye (2018) hypothesized that activating people's motivations to be helpful via priming would enhance the amount of information disclosure. The prediction emerged from two premises. Helpfulness tendencies boost cooperation in social dilemmas (e.g., Van Lange, 1999). Helpfulness priming promotes cooperation (Arieli et al., 2014; Capraro et al., 2014).

Researchers conducted two identical studies to examine the viability of helpfulness priming in investigative interviews (Neequaye et al., 2018, 2019). Participants assumed the role of an informant with information about an imminent mock terror attack. Next, in what participants believed was an unrelated reflection exercise, they covertly underwent priming. The helpfulness prime consisted of participants reflecting on and writing about engaging in helpfulness behaviour. Those in the comparison condition reflected on and wrote about their morning routine. An interviewer then questioned participants about the terror plot. The studies framed the interview style in two ways to align with the priming or not. The interviewer either explicitly asked for participants' *help* while posing direct questions—or the interviewer did not expressly call on participants to help by providing information. The results of both experiments did not support Neequaye's (2018) working hypothesis. The helpfulness priming nor the helpfulness-focused interview elicited more information than the neutral prime or direct questions, respectively (Neequaye et al., 2018, 2019). The differences in disclosure between those who received the prime and those who were not primed failed to reach statistical significance by conventional standards.

Taken together, the existing research provides little support for the notion that priming is a viable tool to utilize in investigative interviews. That is, priming attachment security, openness, or helpfulness does not seem to reliably enhance the amount of information interviewees disclose.

Priming effects and interviews in the field

One may argue that perhaps priming attachment security or helpfulness does not reliably facilitate the amount of disclosure. However, Dawson et al.'s (2017) research indicates that priming openness enhances such disclosure. Despite the failed conceptual replications (Dianiska et al., 2019; Hoogesteyn et al., 2019), openness priming could still be a viable tool. After all, the present discussion is a narrative review, not a meta-analysis. Moreover, researchers may yet discover disclosure motivations that, when primed, could reliably enhance the amount of disclosure. It is worth reminding the reader that replications of basic priming research have also largely failed (e.g., Doyen et al., 2012; Harris et al., 2013; Shanks et al., 2013). These results give pause about the reliability of priming effects in general. Nonetheless, the potential objection just described raises a vital question. Suppose one grants that openness priming or some yet-to-be-discovered priming promotes the amount of disclosure. In that case, what is the practical applicability of research examining how to promote the amount of disclosure? Next, I explore this question.

Let us conceptualize an interviewer's inquiries in terms of the scope. In this conceptualization, an interviewer may be seeking a narrower range of information on a topic, say a single detail. Or the interviewer may want a broader range of information, for example, the sequence of events that transpired over a period. Irrespective of the scope, interviewers typically have specified objectives regarding what they want to know (see, e.g., Soufan, 2011; Toliver, 1997). Thus, I contend that examining the amount of information a method, in this case, priming, elicits is impoverished. This efficacy benchmark hardly informs interviewers about the specific type of information that priming methods can elicit more of—as opposed to less. It might generally be better to know more about some *x-topic* of interest. My objection is that examining the amount of information priming elicits offers little insight about *which x-topic* suits priming. To be fair, this limitation is pervasive across the literature on psychological investigative interviewing techniques, not priming alone.

To enhance the practical applicability of research, it behooves stakeholders to theorize about interviewees' mental representation of information. The goal being to determine the generic features of the information that interviewers may want interviewees to reveal. Put differently, researchers must model comprehensive theories predicting the generic situations interviewers are likely to encounter when soliciting information from interviewees (see Neequaye et al. (2022) for an attempt to model such a theory). Such theories will allow an interviewer to hypothesize about how an interviewee (i) may respond to an inquiry about *x-topic*. By extension, the theory will enable researchers to design studies that better mimic the goals interviewers typically pursue. They usually have specific inquiries that vary in scope. Suppose a theory of interviewees' mental representation predicts that i is likely to reveal *x-topic*. The next puzzle to solve is to determine whether an elicitation method, say priming, can facilitate the disclosure. Conversely, the theory could indicate that i may resist disclosing *x-topic*. In that case, a practical approach would be one that can elicit i's cooperativeness. There are, of course, other considerations to be mindful of when assessing the practicality of some elicitation methods. For example, one might also consider whether the approach is ethical. Facilitating disclosure is only one aspect of such a determination.

As discussed, the openness priming effect is tenuous. But let us grant for argument's sake that the method may facilitate the amount of disclosure. There is still no theorizing and concomitant testing on the conditions where openness priming increases disclosure. Hence, in my view, the method is hardly practically applicable given the nature of interviewers' inquiries. Should interviewers use the method to increase the disclosure of information an interviewee is *more* or *less* likely to disclose? It remains unclear what *x-topic* interviewers should use openness priming to elicit.

One can issue important rebuttals to the practical limitations just described. Perhaps theorizing about the generic situations interviewers are likely to encounter is irrelevant. Researchers might be unable to model generic features to comprehensively predict the encounters in investigative interviews. Moreover, openness priming, or some yet-to-be-discovered priming, may elicit *any* information under *any* condition. We may well find in the future that priming reliably facilitates the amount of disclosure. These points beg an essential question. Can one expect future research to discover that priming some motivation leads interviewees to disclose any information an interviewer could want? If the answer is yes, it behoves future work to persist in pursuing priming research. If the answer is no, stakeholders may invest resources elsewhere.

It is useful to reiterate that the evidence supporting the reliability of priming is generally tenuous. Also, recall that primes do not have an unbridled influence on behaviour. Unsuitable situations, disincentives, or conflicting goals can inhibit priming (Macrae & Johnston, 1998). Priming can hardly override an intent that inhibits the primed behaviour. Theorists argue that the body of work on priming indicates that the phenomenon may facilitate what a person has formed a clear intention to do (Di Nucci, 2012). Thus, priming a disclosure motivation may elicit what an interviewee wants to disclose. If the information an interviewer seeks is something an interviewee has decided to withhold, priming is unlikely to elicit it. In this view, openness priming, or some yet-to-be-discovered priming, cannot elicit *any* information under *any* condition. The method is unlikely to change what an interviewee has determined to withhold.

Concluding remarks

In this chapter, I discussed priming in investigative interviewing. I explored the idea that priming motivations to share information may be a viable way to enhance disclosure. Incidentally, exposing people to meaningful concepts or motivations (i.e., primes) lead people to behave in a prime-consistent manner. Theorists argue that such priming effects occur outside awareness. Because of priming's subtlety, researchers have examined whether interviewers can use the method to boost the amount of information interviewees disclose.

Several failures to replicate priming effects have sparked debate about priming's reliability and validity. Critics argue that the phenomenon is short-lived and elusive. Additionally, there is little cumulative evidence that priming reliably increases the amount of information interviewees disclose. At best, priming a disclosure motivation may elicit what an interviewee is already likely to disclose. Asking direct questions can arguably achieve such a goal. Suppose an interviewer's aim is to elicit what an interviewee intends to withhold. In that case, priming is *not* a viable option.

References

Andersen, S. M., & Chen, S. (2002). The relational self: An interpersonal social-cognitive theory. *Psychological Review, 109*(4), 619–645.

Arieli, S., Grant, A. M., & Sagiv, L. (2014). Convincing yourself to care about others: An intervention for enhancing benevolence values. *Journal of Personality, 82*(1), 15–24.

Bargh, J. A. (2006). What have we been priming all these years? On the development, mechanisms, and ecology of nonconscious social behavior. *European Journal of Social Psychology, 36*(2), 147–168.

Bargh, J. A. (2014). The historical origins of priming as the preparation of behavioural responses: Unconscious carryover and contextual influences of real-world importance. *Social Cognition, 32*(Supplement), 209–224.

Bargh, J. A., Chen, M., & Burrows, L. (1996). Automaticity of social behaviour: Direct effects of trait construct and stereotype activation on action. *Journal of Personality and Social Psychology, 71*(2), 230–244.

Bowlby, J. (1982). Attachment and loss: Retrospect and prospect. *American Journal of Orthopsychiatry, 52*(4), 664–678.

Capraro, V., Smyth, C., Mylona, K., & Niblo, G. A. (2014). Benevolent characteristics promote cooperative behaviour among humans. *PLoS One, 9*(8), e102881.

Dawson, E., Hartwig, M., & Brimbal, L. (2015). Interviewing to elicit information: Using priming to promote disclosure. *Law and Human Behaviour, 39*(5), 443–450.

Dawson, E., Hartwig, M., Brimbal, L., & Denisenkov, P. (2017). A room with a view: Setting influences information disclosure in investigative interviews. *Law and Human Behaviour, 41*(4), 333–343.

Di Nucci, E. (2012). Priming effects and free will. *International Journal of Philosophical Studies, 20*(5), 725–734.

Dianiska, R. E., Swanner, J. K., Brimbal, L., & Meissner, C. A. (2019). Conceptual priming and context reinstatement: A test of direct and indirect interview techniques. *Law and Human Behaviour, 43*(2), 131–143.

Dijksterhuis, A., & Bargh, J. A. (2001). The perception-behaviour expressway: Automatic effects of social perception on social behaviour. In *Advances in Experimental Social Psychology* (Vol. 33, pp. 1–40). Academic Press.

Dijksterhuis, A., & van Knippenberg, A. (1998). The relation between perception and behaviour, or how to win a game of Trivial Pursuit. *Journal of Personality and Social Psychology; Washington, 74*(4), 865–877.

Doyen, S., Klein, O., Pichon, C. L., & Cleeremans, A. (2012). Behavioural priming: It's all in the mind, but whose mind? *PLoS One, 7*(1), e29081.

Harris, C. R., Coburn, N., Rohrer, D., & Pashler, H. (2013). Two failures to replicate high-performance-goal priming effects. *PLoS One, 8*(8), e72467.

Hoogesteyn, K., Meijer, E., & Vrij, A. (2019). The influence of room spaciousness on investigative interviews. *Legal and Criminological Psychology, 24*(2), 215–228.

Kelly, C. E., Miller, J. C., & Redlich, A. D. (2016). The dynamic nature of interrogation. *Law and Human Behaviour, 40*(3), 295–309.

Lakens, D. (2013). Calculating and reporting effect sizes to facilitate cumulative science: A practical primer for t-tests and ANOVAs. *Frontiers in Psychology, 4*.

Lashley, K. S. (1951). The problem of serial order in behaviour. In L. A. Jeffress (Ed.), *Cerebral mechanisms in behaviour* (pp. 112–131). Wiley.

Loersch, C., & Payne, B. K. (2011). The situated inference model: An integrative account of the effects of primes on perception, behaviour, and motivation. *Perspectives on Psychological Science, 6*(3), 234–252.

Macrae, C. N., & Johnston, L. (1998). Help, I need somebody: Automatic action and inaction. *Social Cognition, 16*(4), 400–417.

McCarthy, R. J., Skowronski, J. J., Verschuere, B., Meijer, E. H., Jim, A., Hoogesteyn, K., Orthey, R., Acar, O. A., Aczel, B., Bakos, B. E., Barbosa, F., Baskin, E., Bègue, L., Ben-Shakhar, G., Birt, A. R., Blatz, L., Charman, S. D., Claesen, A., Clay, S. L., . . . Yıldız, E. (2018). Registered replication report on Srull and Wyer (1979). *Advances in Methods and Practices in Psychological Science, 1*(3), 321–336.

Mikulincer, M., & Shaver, P. R. (2016). Attachment security, compassion, and altruism. *Current Directions in Psychological Science, 14*(1), 34–38.

Neequaye, D. A. (2018). *Eliciting information in intelligence interviews through priming: An examination of underlying mechanisms* (Doctoral dissertation). University of Gothenburg & University of Portsmouth.

Neequaye, D. A., Ask, K., Granhag, P. A., & Vrij, A. (2018). Facilitating disclosure in intelligence interviews: The joint influence of helpfulness priming and interpersonal approach. *Journal of Investigative Psychology and Offender Profiling, 15*(3), 319–334.

Neequaye, D. A., Ask, K., Granhag, P. A., & Vrij, A. (2019). Eliciting information in intelligence contexts: The joint influence of helpfulness priming and interview style. *Investigative Interviewing: Research and Practice, 10*(1), 19.

Neequaye, D. A., Luke, T. J., & Kollback, K. (2022). *Managing disclosure-outcomes in intelligence interviews.* Manuscript.

Newell, B. R., & Shanks, D. R. (2014). Unconscious influences on decision making: A critical review. *Behavioural and Brain Sciences, 37*(1), 1–19.

Nosek, B. A., & Errington, T. M. (2017). Making sense of replications. *ELife, 6*, e23383.

Payne, B. K., Brown-Iannuzzi, J. L., & Loersch, C. (2016). Replicable effects of primes on human behaviour. *Journal of Experimental Psychology: General, 145*(10), 1269–1279.

Shanks, D. R. (2017). Misunderstanding the behaviour priming controversy: Comment on Payne, Brown-Iannuzzi, and Loersch (2016). *Journal of Experimental Psychology: General, 146*(8), 1216–1222.

Shanks, D. R., Newell, B. R., Lee, E. H., Balakrishnan, D., Ekelund, L., Cenac, Z., Kavvadia, F., & Moore, C. (2013). Priming intelligent behaviour: An elusive phenomenon. *PLoS One, 8*(4), e56515.

Simons, D. J. (2014). The value of direct replication. *Perspectives on Psychological Science, 9*(1), 76–80.

Soufan, A. (2011). *The black banners: The inside story of 9/11 and the war against al-qaeda.* W. W. Norton & Company.

Srull, T. K., & Wyer, R. S. (1979). The role of category accessibility in the interpretation of information about persons: Some determinants and implications. *Journal of Personality and Social Psychology, 37*(10), 1660–1672.

Toliver, R. F. (1997). *The interrogator: The story of Hans-Joachim Scharff, master interrogator of the Luftwaffe.* Schiffer Pub.

Tversky, A., & Kahneman, D. (1973). Availability: A heuristic for judging frequency and probability. *Cognitive Psychology, 5*(2), 207–232.

Van Lange, P. A. M. (1999). The pursuit of joint outcomes and equality in outcomes: An integrative model of social value orientation. *Journal of Personality and Social Psychology, 77*(2), 337–349.

Zwaan, R. A., Etz, A., Lucas, R. E., & Donnellan, M. B. (2018). Making replication mainstream. *Behavioural and Brain Sciences, 41*.

8 Pragmatic inferences in investigative interviewing

Meghana Srivatsav

Imagine that you are at work on a Friday afternoon and have an important meeting scheduled at 1900hrs that evening. A colleague knocks on your door and asks, "We are heading for drinks and dinner at 1800hrs to the usual place. Will you join us?" From this short exchange, you could most likely draw the following inferences: (a) your colleague does not know that you have a meeting later, (b) your colleague assumes that you know the location, (c) your colleague has invited others who you are friends with, (d) your colleague does not know if you can join or not, and (e) your colleague does not know if you have any other prior appointments for the evening.

These inferences may seem unsurprising and obvious to you but notice how easily we can draw these conclusions and gather unsaid information with such a short exchange. Human communication heavily relies on such "filling up the blanks" to draw meaningful conclusions without having to verbalize everything. We have effective communication on a regular basis without stating every detail, usually without any serious loss of understanding. How do we engage in this seamless communication and inferential process?

For several decades, psycholinguists have tried to answer that question (e.g., Grice, 1975). That area of psycholinguistics, concerned with human communication and drawing inferences, is referred to as *pragmatic implicature*. While researchers in that area of study have explored human communication in general, this chapter focuses on a more specific field where inferential and implied information can be of high value: suspect interviews and interrogations.

Previously, the idea of pragmatic implicatures has been subtly explored within a suspect interview context. For example, Kassin and McNall (1991) have challenged a common interrogation tactic called minimization, wherein the investigator, reducing the seriousness of the offence committed, can lead to pragmatically implying a less serious consequence if the suspect were to confess to the crime, even though the investigator never explicitly states the lenient treatment (also see Kassin et al., 2010; Luke & Alceste, 2020). More recently, Brimbal and her colleagues (2017) carried out an extensive literature review on how the content of investigative questions can influence suspects' inferences regarding the prior crime-related information or evidence held by the interviewer against the suspect. In this chapter, the author explores the first set of

DOI: 10.4324/9781003308546-11

studies that were conducted to empirically examine how suspects draw inferences regarding the prior information held by the interviewer through pragmatic implicature—which is referred to as *perceived interviewer knowledge* (PIK).

Perceived interviewer knowledge is posited to be an important construct for suspects' strategies and behaviour in police interviews (Granhag & Hartwig, 2015). Specifically, the idea is that PIK allows a suspect to make decisions regarding what is the best strategy to employ to appear innocent in the eyes of the interviewer. That is, based on how much prior incriminating information the suspect thinks the interviewer holds against them, the suspect decides whether to reveal or withhold critical information related to the crime (Granhag, Hartwig et al., 2015; Granhag, Rangmar et al., 2015). Most existing research is on how suspects' PIK can be influenced as a function of various evidence-disclosure tactics—that is, the interviewer informing the suspect through various strategies that she/he holds certain evidence against the suspect (Granhag & Hartwig, 2015). However, as illustrated in the beginning of this chapter, people easily draw inferences about others' prior knowledge and intent based on the communicated information. It is, therefore, highly likely that suspects draw inferences about the interviewer's prior knowledge or intent based on the mere content of the investigative questions without evidence-disclosure. To explore that possibility, the psycholinguistic concepts of *relevance theory* (Sperber & Wilson, 1996) were employed to base the predictions and design the specific question content variables in the studies explored in this chapter.

Relevance theory

Sperber and Wilson (1996) proposed relevance theory to understand how people understand communicated information and draw pragmatic inferences. The theory was based on Paul Grice's (1975) work that postulated that all communicated information is based on an implied rule that the information is relevant. While Grice did not further specify the meaning of "relevant" in his theory, Sperber and Wilson bridged that gap with relevance theory.

According to relevance theory, we draw inferences under the assumption that people are communicating the most straightforward information in the simplest way possible. That is, the easiest interpretation is the most informative and the correct one. That means that we assume that the information communicated to us is informative and then fill in the blanks about what surrounding information must also be true in order for the statement to be true. For instance, in the example at the beginning of this chapter, the colleague's statement "we are going for drinks and dinner at the usual place" does not contain the specific information about the place. But to make this statement meaningful and informative, you would think of the place that your colleagues and you would go to more often than any other place. That is, we inherently work backwards with the assumption that the communicated information, in fact, contains some relevant information even though it is not explicitly stated.

Another important assumption is that the communicated information not only depends on an established context but also for whom the question is relevant. That is, when your colleague asks if you are joining for dinner, it could imply that the dinner includes people known to you in a familiar place, and that is why the question is relevant to you. Your colleague has already assumed that the invitation is of relevance to you and your response to your colleague is of relevance to them. Your colleague has also indicated their level of prior knowledge regarding your plans for the evening. That is, your colleague is not aware of your plans for the evening, and a relevant response would be to inform him of your prior appointment, which will imply that you will not be able to make it to dinner or that you will join post the meeting. Thus, relevance theory posits that we draw inferences about the prior information known to the speaker and what new information the speaker intends to learn based on the content of the questions asked. Based on these inferences, we decide on what would be an appropriate and relevant response to give (for a more thorough treatment of interrogatives in relevance theory, see Clark, 1991; Jacobssen, 2010).

Pragmatic inferences by suspects

Based on our understanding of how people draw inferences in everyday human communication contexts, we can now apply these ideas to suspects drawing inferences in police interviews. For the specific studies reviewed in this chapter, the author focused specifically on guilty suspects and excluded innocent suspects. The rationale for this exclusion was that the variables explored and the behaviours hypothesized are more easily observable in guilty suspects in comparison to innocent suspects. Drawing from the concepts of relevance theory, four specific factors were identified related to investigative question content that could influence guilty suspects' inferences regarding what prior information the interviewer already holds about the suspects' role in crime. These factors were empirically tested in two studies. They are: (a) *topic-discussion*—questioning about a specific crime-related topic, (b) *level of specificity*—including specific crime-related details, (c) *stressor*—emphasizing on a specific crime-related detail, and (d) *level of suspicion*—whether the question implies high suspicion or low suspicion on the suspect.

In the earlier illustration, the context was an office set-up where your colleague asks you to join for dinner later that evening. Let us now change the context and imagine the following: A theft has taken place in your office on Friday night and a detective is interviewing possible suspects in the office. You had a meeting that evening and were one of the last ones to leave work, and therefore you are one of the main suspects.

Topic discussion

When a person merely mentions a specific topic, it indicates that the speaker has some prior knowledge of this topic. For example, if the detective asks you,

"Were you working late on Friday evening?" the question indicates that the detective has some knowledge about (a) your presence at the office on the day of the theft and (b) some probable evidence showing that you were at the office. Just the fact that the detective is talking to you about the time of leaving work indicates that they hold some prior information.

Level of specificity

The detective asks you, "Were you working late on Friday evening?" This question may seem more *general*—that the detective is requesting more information. You can draw the following inferences: (a) the detective probably knows that you left the office late or needs confirmative information, (b) the detective may not know about the meeting you had scheduled on Friday, and (c) the detective may hold some evidence regarding your presence at the office late that evening. However, if the detective asks you a more *specific* question, such as "Were you working late after your meeting on Friday evening?" it implies more prior knowledge of the detective, and you may infer (a) that the detective knows of your meeting, (b) may hold information that you stayed back after your meeting ended, and (c) probably holds some evidence that you stayed after your meeting. That type of a specific question may require a more specific response for it to be informative and relevant.

Stressor

Let us consider how an emphasis on specific crime-related information could influence our inferences. If the detective were to ask you, "This information is critical. Were you working late after your meeting on Friday evening?" Adding emphasis on the importance of the specific information could indicate that that information is of most relevance to the detective. You could draw the inference that confirming or denying would be relevant.

Level of suspicion

Imagine if the detective asks: "We have information that you could be involved in the theft that took place on Friday evening. Could you tell me if you were working late after your meeting that day?" Adding a degree of suspicion to the question could imply that the detective may hold a higher amount of information regarding the theft. On the other hand, if the detective asked, "There was a theft on Friday evening at the office and I am questioning all the employees who were present that day at work. Were you working late on Friday evening?" This indicates less suspicion and more of a request for information scenario and therefore indicates low prior knowledge of the detective.

The previously illustrated factors were tested across two individual studies (Srivatsav et al., 2019, 2020) based on the idea that these factors could influence suspects' inferences. In both the studies, a significant main effect of topic discussion was found on PIK such that guilty suspects inferred that the interviewer had more knowledge about a crime-related topic that was questioned, which seemed to increase PIK of other topics that were not questioned. Stressors seemed to reduce the PIK of the suspect, while more specific crime-related details in the questions also seemed to indicate an increase in PIK. On the other hand, the level of suspicion content within questions did not seem to influence the suspects' PIK. This was interpreted as indicating a weak manipulation of the level of suspicion variable rather than the actual lack of influence of the variable on PIK.

Implications on research and practice

While building "techniques" and models for investigative interviewing is important, delving deeper into how the building blocks of these techniques would help researchers and practitioners to extend the scope of existing tactics (Alison et al., 2013). For instance, knowing when and how to alter a specific construct in an interview could optimize interview outcomes. Interviewers can employ strategies that will, in turn, result in the suspects engaging in identifiable and predictable behaviours in relation to the interviewer. That is, interviewers can understand more easily the perspective of the suspect and predict outcomes.

Another important contribution of the current research findings is the integration of two different areas of research—i.e. psycholinguistics and police interviewing. The research brings to light the need for collaboration between academicians of diverse research areas as this would be beneficial in expanding the scope of research and practice beyond existing boundaries of individual subjects of study.

Moving towards the specific theoretical construct that was the focus of this chapter, namely PIK, to the best of the author's knowledge, this was the first attempt at empirically testing the influence of psycholinguistic factors on PIK. As mentioned earlier, PIK had only been studied as a function of evidence disclosure; therefore, the findings from this study are an important step forward within the investigative interviewing framework. One might question why it is necessary to broaden our perspectives as researchers and practitioners regarding PIK beyond evidence-disclosure. To articulate the importance of the findings, we need to acknowledge that only using evidence-disclosure tactics to influence the important and influential construct of PIK would limit its scope of use to only in the presence of evidence.

In certain investigative scenarios, there may not be strong or substantial evidence held by the interviewer. In these situations, the interviewer may not benefit from disclosing the trivial information held by them to gather more critical information from the suspect. In such situations, an interviewer could influence the PIK of the suspect by merely asking a specific question regarding a certain activity. For instance, if the interviewer revealed that they held eyewitness evidence placing the suspect at the crime scene, the suspect could explain this with an alibi. Instead, if the interviewer did not mention the evidence but instead used this information to question the suspect's activities at the crime scene, the suspect might infer that the interviewer has more prior knowledge regarding their activities.

Another scenario where psycholinguistics could be employed is when there could be a threat to the informant's life if existing evidence is revealed. For instance, if the informant is the only one who could possibly have the knowledge or the evidence to convict the suspect, the informant might hesitate to provide a statement due to fear for one's life. In such a scenario, the interviewer could utilize the knowledge of this evidence to tactically phrase questions to influence the suspect's PIK and gather the evidence from the suspect directly. The use of existing evidence could also be deemed unlawful in specific situations where this information is considered classified, such as during national security or military engagements. In such scenarios as well, the interviewer can utilize the knowledge of evidence to question the suspect tactically and gather more information.

Concluding remarks

Over the last few decades, research within the suspect interviewing frameworks has focused on developing techniques that employ strategic tactics to capture the complex cognitive strategies of suspects. However, there is a need for understanding the theoretical constructs that ground the techniques with a strong foundation. The current chapter is an overview of studies conducted to explore one such instrumental construct, PIK, that directly impacts the outcome of the interview by influencing the suspects' decision-making processes. The need for such research is to strengthen existing theory and provide a larger scope for practice and new research. Understanding the dynamic environment that exists between the suspect and the interviewer, along with the complex decision-making processes that suspects engage in, will benefit researchers and practitioners in optimizing interview outcomes. Also, a collaborative environment between different research areas could be beneficial in expanding the scope to other applied contexts.

References

Alison, L. J., Alison, E., Noone, G., Elntib, S., & Christiansen, P. (2013). Why tough tactics fail, and rapport gets results: Observing rapport-based interpersonal techniques (ORBIT) to generate useful information from terrorists. *Psychology, Public Policy, and Law, 19*(4), 411.

Brimbal, L., Hartwig, M., & Crossman, A. M. (2017). The effect of questions on suspects' perception of evidence in investigative interviews: What can we infer from the basic literature? *Polygraph & Forensic Credibility Assessment, 46*(1), 10–39.

Clark, W. (1991). *Relevance theory and the semantics of non-declarative sentences* (Doctoral dissertation). University College London.

Granhag, P. A., & Hartwig, M. (2015). The strategic use of evidence (SUE) technique: A conceptual overview. In P. A. Granhag, A. Vrij, & B. Verschuere (Eds.), *Deception detection: Current challenges and new approaches* (pp. 231–251). Wiley-Blackwell.

Granhag, P. A., Hartwig, M., Giolla, E. M., & Clemens, F. (2015). Suspects' verbal counter-interrogation strategies: Towards an integrative model. In P. A. Granhag, A. Vrij, & B. Verschuere (Eds.), *Detecting deception: Current challenges and cognitive approaches* (pp. 293–313). Wiley-Blackwell.

Granhag, P. A., Rangmar, J., & Strömwall, L. A. (2015). Small cells of suspects: Eliciting cues to deception by strategic interviewing. *Journal of Investigative Psychology and Offender Profiling, 12*(2), 127–141.

Grice, H. P. (1975). Logic and conversation. In P. Cole & J. L. Morgan (Eds.), *Syntax and semantics, vol. 3, speech acts* (pp. 41–58). Academic Press.

Jacobssen, R. R. (2010). The interpretation of indirect speech acts in relevance theory. *The Journal of Linguistic and Intercultural Education, 3*, 7–24.

Kassin, S. M., Drizin, S. A., Grisso, T., Gudjonsson, G. H., Leo, R. A., & Redlich, A. D. (2010). Police-induced confessions: Risk factors and recommendations. *Law and Human Behavior, 34*(1), 3–38.

Kassin, S. M., & McNall, K. (1991). Police interrogations and confessions: Communicating promises and threats by pragmatic implication. *Law and Human Behavior, 15*(3), 233–251.

Luke, T. J., & Alceste, F. (2020). The mechanisms of minimization: How interrogation tactics suggest lenient sentencing through pragmatic implication. *Law and Human Behavior, 44*(4), 266–285.

Sperber, D., & Wilson, D. (1996). *Relevance: Communication and cognition* (2nd ed.). Wiley-Blackwell.

Srivatsav, M., Luke, T. J., Granhag, P. A., & Vrij, A. (2019). *How does question content influence guilty suspects' inferences about what the interviewer knows?* PsyArXiv.

Srivatsav, M., Luke, T. J., Granhag, P. A., & Vrij, A. (2020). How do the questions asked affect suspects' perceptions of the interviewer's prior knowledge? *Journal of Investigative Psychology and Offender Profiling, 17*(2), 160–172.

9 The discouraging past and promising future of research on innocent suspects' alibis

Shiri Portnoy

Imagine sitting in a police station, being asked to explain what you were doing and where you were four days earlier to convince the police interviewer of your innocence of a house break-in that took place in your street. Specifically, you are being asked to provide an *alibi* (Burke et al., 2007). Being motivated to convince the interviewer of your innocence, you are probably certain that you will be able to provide a convincing alibi. However, that might not be the case. In this chapter, I will describe the processes of alibi generation and provision and present factors that may hinder and improve innocent alibi providers' ability to provide a complete and accurate alibi. I will then discuss interviewing techniques that may improve the processes of alibi generation and provision for innocent suspects. Finally, I will discuss the implications of existing research on innocent suspects' alibis for practice and theory and suggest future directions for researchers who wish to contribute to this under-studied research domain.

Generating and providing an alibi: one can never fail?

The process by which suspects of a crime provide an alibi has been identified as the generation domain of alibis, which comprises the story phase and the validation phase (Burke et al., 2007). In the story phase, suspects provide their alibi by reporting their actions and whereabouts during the critical time frame of the crime. After suspects provide their alibi, they enter the validation phase, in which they attempt to corroborate their alibi by offering physical or/and person evidence. Physical evidence may be in the form of objects that support the suspect's presence at a certain place during the time frame of the crime, such as CCTV footage. Person evidence may be individuals, such as family members or even strangers, who can support the suspect's version of events (Burke et al., 2007). In your interview at the police station, you are probably trying to remember what activities you took part in and where you were four days earlier. You may be thinking about what you usually do on that specific day (Leins & Charman, 2016). Maybe you took part in an out-of-the-ordinary activity? This would likely pop out and make it easier for you to provide your alibi (see Burke et al., 2007). However, it may be that you simply cannot remember what you did four days ago; this is not surprising, as alibi provision

DOI: 10.4324/9781003308546-12

involves reliance on one's memory (Strange et al., 2014). While suspects may use their agenda or other memory aids to provide their alibi, these may not help them if they did not document their activities in such aids. Moreover, suspects likely need to rely on their memory to combine the details retrieved from their memory aids to create a coherent account of their whereabouts (see Burke et al., 2007).

Research has supported that generating an alibi can be challenging for innocent suspects. For example, in a study by Olson and Charman (2012), participants were asked to rely on only their memory to provide four initial alibis for four time periods. Specifically, participants generated distant-past alibis for two time periods on a date six to 14 weeks prior to the study session and near-past alibis for two time periods on a date three days prior to the session. Then, participants were given 48 hours to corroborate their alibis by locating evidence they had mentioned during alibi provision. It was found that participants generated fewer distant-past than near-past alibis. Moreover, after locating the evidence that could be used to support their alibis, it transpired that 36% of the alibis provided were inaccurate. Similarly, Strange et al. (2014) asked participants to provide an alibi for a timeframe three weeks prior to the study session, followed by allowing them a week to locate corroborating evidence. Then, participants provided their alibi for the same time frame. It was found that both alibis were consistent on only 53% of the details, suggesting that the initial alibis provided by participants were substantially inaccurate. Culhane et al. (2008) demonstrated that innocent individuals may struggle with providing an alibi even for a more recent time frame. The researchers found that 10.9% of participants who were asked to report their actions and whereabouts for a time frame only two days prior to the study session reported that they lacked memory for their actions during that specific time.

How can it be that innocent people, who would do anything to tell the truth, would not remember details about a certain day or remember them incorrectly? As briefly mentioned, innocent alibi providers, like all rememberers, rely on their autobiographical memory (often termed 'episodic memory') to recall and report information about past events. This memory 'storage' is prone to errors, inconsistencies, and suggestibility (Schacter, 1999). For example, innocent suspects may not encode details of a certain event or day, especially if they participated in a routine task, such as grocery shopping. If they do encode and store event details, accessibility to such details may decrease over time (see Pertzov et al., 2017), especially if they lack the motivation to report those details until being interviewed by the police (see Schacter, 1999). In fact, motivation to provide an accurate and informative alibi may not necessarily result in the provision of such an alibi (Kassam et al., 2009).

The generation domain of alibis is followed by the believability domain. This domain is comprised of the evaluation phase and ultimate evaluation phase (Burke et al., 2007). During the evaluation phase, legal personnel such as police officers evaluate the credibility of the alibi. Finally, if the suspect is not believed by the police and if other incriminating evidence exists, the ultimate evaluation phase takes place in court. There, the credibility of the alibi is assessed together with the rest of the evidence that exists against the defendant to determine the defendant's guilt (Burke et al., 2007). For more information on the believability domain of alibis, see Culhane and Hosch (2012) and Olson and Wells (2004).

The problem is clear: while innocent alibi providers may be able to provide an alibi, they are likely to struggle with providing an accurate and complete one. Unfortunately, police interviewers may think that an inaccurate alibi means that the suspect is lying, and hence guilty, and innocent suspects may be prosecuted and falsely convicted for a crime they did not commit (Olson & Charman, 2012). In the next section, I present and discuss research on interviewing techniques that may enhance innocent suspects' memory performance during police interviews.

Enhancing memory processes during alibi generation and provision

To support truthful alibi providers during police interviews, some countries have presented new interviewing protocols that address the memory problems that may arise with the use of less optimal interviewing techniques. Such interviewing protocols were required due to miscarriages of justice that occurred partly due to biased and unethical interviews conducted by police interviewers. For example, in 1992, the PEACE interview model was presented in the United Kingdom (U.K.; Central Planning and Training Unit, 1992a, 1992b). The PEACE model is comprised of five stages (that stand for its acronym): Planning and preparation; Engage and explain; Account; Closure; Evaluation. By encouraging the use of open-ended interviewing prompts, this model allows suspects to present their version of events (cf. the confrontational Reid technique, which is widely used during American police interviews; Inbau et al., 2013). The PEACE model aims to eliminate false confessions by encouraging police interviewers trained with this model (as are most police officers in the U.K.; see Clarke & Milne, 2001) to avoid guilt assumptions and maintain open-mindedness (Griffiths & Milne, 2006). This model and its adaptations have been in use in other countries such as New Zealand (Bull & Soukara, 2010) and Norway (which uses the KREATIV model; Fahsing & Rachlew, 2009).

Alongside the use of ethical information-gathering interviewing techniques by some police organisations, researchers have been examining the effects of various interviewing techniques on alibi generation and provision by innocent suspects to further improve suspect interview outcomes. While such research has been scarce, a few notable exceptions can be mentioned.

Leins and Charman (2016) examined if using time cues to prompt an alibi by mentioning the time of the critical event to the alibi provider resulted in mistaken alibis more often than when location cues were used. The researchers noted that time cues are ineffective in promoting accurate alibis mainly because these do not allow the formulation of associations between time and other event details. Participants indicated their usual activities for various weekday time frames, including that of the study session, followed by completing several filler tasks. Approximately one week later, participants provided an alibi to convince an 'investigator' of their innocence of crimes allegedly committed during the first study session. The alibis were provided following one of three recall cues: time-only cue, location-only cue, and combined time-and-location cue. The cues informed participants only of the time in which the alleged crimes happened, only of their location, or of both their timing and location (respectively). Findings demonstrated that alibis were more accurate in the location-only condition than in the time-only and time-and-location conditions. One of Leins and Charman's (2016) explanations for the similarity in alibi accuracy between the time-only and time-and-location conditions was that, in the combined condition, the time cue presented first likely 'overshadowed' the location-cue's ability to produce memories for the critical time frame. Consequently, the time cue in this combined condition affected memory retrieval similarly to how the individual time cue did, resulting in similar alibi accuracy between the time-only and time-and-location conditions. Leins and Charman's (2016) findings are important as they demonstrate that memory-based interview prompts may affect and even improve alibi provision by innocent suspects.

Following the promising findings of Leins and Charman (2016), in my doctoral research, I examined the effects of pre-alibi instructions on innocent suspects' alibis informativeness and accuracy (Portnoy, 2019). After completing a series of neutral tasks, participants attempted to convince an interviewer of their innocence by providing an alibi that was as accurate as possible, as informative as possible, or both as accurate and as informative as possible; control participants received no accuracy or informativeness pre-alibi instructions. Findings demonstrated that participants provided more correct details when instructed to focus on both the informativeness and accuracy of information compared with the control condition, without compromising alibi accuracy. Similarly to Leins and Charman (2016), these findings demonstrate that pre-alibi reporting instructions can facilitate innocent suspects' memory performance. The relative improvement in alibi informativeness in the informativeness and accuracy instructions condition was evident even with the short time interval employed between task completion and alibi provision. In such short time intervals, memory is likely to be relatively adequate already (Ebbinghaus, 1885/2013), yet alibis provided in the combined instructions condition were more complete compared with those provided in the control condition, in which only general alibi provision instructions were provided to participants. Such findings may be relevant to instances whereby individuals are interviewed at the crime scene or nearby by a frontline police officer shortly after a crime has been committed.

More recently, Cardenas et al. (2020) examined the efficacy of mental reinstatement of context (MRC; Memon et al., 2010) in eliciting accurate alibis. MRC encourages rememberers to recall not only the physical environment in which the critical event took place but also their emotional and psychological states during that event (Geiselman et al., 1986). In two experiments, participants reported their typical activities (i.e. schemas) for 15 blocks of one hour for each weekday. Participants were then contacted several times a day for approximately two weeks using text messages to query regarding their current activities. Next, participants were asked to imagine they were suspected of involvement in several robberies and to generate alibis for four time periods to prove their innocence. Critically, participants provided an alibi for one schema-consistent event and one schema-inconsistent event using a time cue and for one schema-consistent event and one schema-inconsistent event using MRC. Across both experiments, Cardenas et al. (2020) did not find that alibi accuracy, measured as consistency between participants' responses to the text messages and their alibis, differed between interviewing technique conditions. The researchers suggested that the time delay administered between the critical events and the memory test could account for the findings. This time delay was longer than the usually shorter time frame that passes between a witnessed event and the interviewing of eyewitnesses—the type of rememberers with which the efficacy of MRC has been examined thus far (Memon et al., 2010). Nonetheless, Cardenas et al.'s (2020) research is an important contribution to the slowly growing body of research on alibi generation and provision by innocent suspects.

The research findings described thus far present mixed results regarding the effects of pre-alibi instructions on innocent suspects' alibis completeness and accuracy. This ambivalence, combined with the scarcity of research on alibi generation and provision, should stimulate researchers to develop and examine more interviewing techniques and prompts that could support the memory of truth-tellers.

Additional factors to consider in alibi research

As we continue to develop and examine interviewing techniques to support innocent alibi providers, I suggest that we also start to examine the potential effects of other factors that may emerge during police interviews on alibi generation and provision. For example, we should also focus on how interviewers treat suspects during interviews. Imagine that, as you are struggling with providing your alibi, but before you get to say anything, the police interviewer already communicates to you that they believe you are guilty of the break-in. Would you then provide more or less accurate information?

Police interviewers may approach suspect interviews while believing that a suspect is guilty even before interviewing them. While this presumption likely starts as a belief, research has supported that it may be communicated to suspects during interviews. For example, Kassin et al.'s (2003) interrogator-participants were led to believe that they would interrogate a guilty or innocent 'suspect'. To prepare for the interrogation, they were asked to choose, from a list, the questions they would ask the 'suspect'. Findings demonstrated that participants who expected to interrogate a guilty 'suspect' chose more guilt-presumptive questions compared with participants who expected to interrogate an innocent 'suspect'. Then, neutral participants who listened to audio recordings of the interrogations judged more 'suspects' interrogated by guilt-presumptive interrogatiors as guilty compared with 'suspects' interrogated by innocence-presumptive interrogatiors. Later, Hill et al. (2008) found that interviewer-participants who were led to believe that they would interview a guilty 'suspect' freely generated a higher proportion of guilt-presumptive questions compared with participants who expected to interview an innocent 'suspect'. In a follow-up study, new participants were accused of alleged cheating of which they were either guilty or innocent and were then interviewed regarding this 'cheating' with questions generated in the first study. Compared with 'suspects' interviewed using neutral questions, 'suspects' interviewed using guilt-presumptive questions reported that, during the interview, they felt more pressure to confess. Then, neutral participants who listened to audio recordings of the interviews rated innocent 'suspects' interviewed using guilt-presumptive questions as more guilty compared with guilty 'suspects' interviewed using such questions.

Kassin et al. (2003) and Hill et al. (2008) demonstrated the potential effects of guilt presumption on the behaviour of interviewers and, ultimately, on interviewees' subjective experience during guilt-presumptive interviews and the perceptions of neutral observers of such interviewees. However, research on the effects of police interviewers' presumption of guilt on suspects' verbal behaviour during alibi provision has been lacking. This research avenue is important considering that an interviewer's presumption of guilt can affect innocent suspects' behaviour in ways which neutral observers, such as jurors at a real trial, may perceive as indicating guilt.

To contribute to this research avenue, Portnoy et al. (2019) explored the effects of an interviewer's presumption of guilt on alibi accuracy and informativeness. After completing several non-criminal tasks, participants were accused of stealing a wallet from the task room. To convince an interviewer of their innocence, participants were asked to provide an alibi. Prior to alibi provision, the interviewer communicated to participants that she believed they were either guilty or innocent of the 'theft' or that she had no specific belief about their guilt. The findings were surprising: a manipulation check confirmed that participants in the guilt-belief and innocence-belief conditions perceived that the interviewer had believed they were guilty and innocent (respectively) of the 'theft' before alibi provision. However, the number of correct details provided by participants and detail accuracy did not differ significantly between the guilt-belief conditions. Portnoy et al. (2019) suggested that it may be that participants in the guilt-belief condition did respond to the interviewer's guilt-led behaviour by attempting to 'prove her wrong'; thus, they provided an informative and correct alibi (see Snyder & Stukas, 1999). However, it is likely that participants in the innocence-belief condition attempted to ensure that their innocence was shown (see Kassin & Norwick, 2004); thus, they provided alibis that were as informative and accurate as those of participants in the guilt-belief condition. Portnoy et al. (2019) were the first to examine the effects of an interviewer's presumption of guilt on innocent suspects' alibi quality and completeness. These findings support the need to continue to examine the effects of the many factors that emerge during suspect interviews on alibis, as I discuss in more detail in the next section.

Implications for practice and theory

The few studies I have mentioned in this chapter all demonstrate one thing: even when innocent suspects are motivated to provide their best alibi, pre-alibi instructions may help them provide a better one. This should motivate researchers to continue to develop and examine interviewing techniques that could enhance innocent suspects' memory processes during alibi provision. One could claim that we could easily extrapolate findings from research on eyewitness interviewing, which is abundant, to suspect interviewing. However, that conclusion may be inaccurate. Eyewitnesses who unintentionally provide incorrect information are likely to suffer no legal consequences. However, as described, if suspects unintentionally provide mistaken details in their alibis, the interviewer may think that they are lying, which may lead to the wrongful prosecution and conviction of innocent people (Burke et al., 2007). This difference between eyewitnesses and suspects in the motivation to provide correct information is sufficient to conduct separate research on suspect interviewing.

Research on suspect interviewing in the context of the alibi quality and informativeness should not be confused with research on suspect interviewing in the context of the elicitation of cues to deception. When studying deception detection, researchers use various experimental manipulations to examine whether statements provided by truth-tellers can be differentiated from those of liars or whether both types of suspects behave differently in response to such manipulations. As such, this line of research is focused on assisting interviewers with differentiating between truthful and deceptive suspects (Vrij, 2008) and barely—or not at all—on assisting innocent suspects in providing correct alibis that may exonerate them. Researchers must keep that distinction in mind when planning research on suspect interviewing and declaring research aims.

With the research findings we currently have on suspect alibis, we may be able to carefully suggest optimal and less optimal interviewing techniques to use during suspect interviews. However, such research is still scarce, and we are less knowledgeable about the effects of other aspects of interviews on alibis. As I have already suggested, in the future, I see research on suspect alibis focusing not only on the effects of interviewing techniques on alibi quality and completeness but also on the effects of factors emerging during the use of such interviewing techniques on alibis. If we want to ensure that we do everything we can to promote accurate and complete reporting by innocent alibi providers, we must cover all aspects of the interview process that may affect their ability to provide correct and comprehensive statements. Such perspective should promote a better understanding of the processes of alibi generation and provision and allow researchers to inform practitioners about optimal interviewing techniques. Portnoy et al.'s (2019) research addressed one such aspect that concerns the interviewing environment, namely an interviewer's presumption of guilt. Similar research could be conducted on, for example, the timing of the interview (day versus night).

Moreover, we seem to be moving towards a broader definition of an alibi. People may be asked to explain their presence at the crime scene or nearby to convince a police interviewer of their innocence of a crime that occurred in that location. As this statement may be used by suspects to exonerate themselves, it is an alibi, just as the common 'I was someplace else' statement is. This broader definition of an alibi is relevant to applied contexts whereby people may be initially questioned regarding their presence at the crime scene or nearby by a frontline police officer (Portnoy, 2019). Thus, when planning research on suspect alibis, we should consider all the contexts in which innocent suspects may be asked to provide their alibi and not limit research and practice to the traditional alibi definition.

Concluding remarks

The rise in the number of studies on alibi generation and provision by innocent suspects may lead to a more basic change that concerns how suspects are viewed in the legal system and by the public. It has been suggested that the mere use of the word 'alibi' can lead people to think that the person providing it is guilty (Sommers & Douglass, 2007). The growth in the number of studies dedicated to innocent suspects' alibis conveys the message that people interviewed by the police about their whereabouts during a critical time are not necessarily guilty and that they have something to say that does not necessarily mean 'I did something bad'. That is, published research on alibis of innocent suspects is slowly but surely speaking on behalf of such suspects, reminding the legal system and the public that the presumption of innocence should be respected.

Unethical and biased suspect interviewing occur despite interviewing protocols guiding otherwise, and we might not become aware of such interviews unless they become public. As members of the public, we can stand by the wrongfully incarcerated. As researchers, we can contribute to the elimination of miscarriages of justice by keeping in mind the butterfly effect that can start with one interaction with a biased police interviewer and may continue with the many other elements that emerge during the interview process.

References

Bull, R., & Soukara, S. (2010). Four studies of what really happens in police interviews. In G. D. Lassiter & C. A. Meissner (Eds.), *Police interrogations and false confessions* (pp. 81–95). American Psychological Association.

Burke, T. M., Turtle, J. W., & Olson, E. A. (2007). Alibis in criminal investigations and trials. In M. P. Toglia, J. D. Read, D. F. Ross, & R. C. L. Lindsay (Eds.), *Handbook of eyewitness psychology: Memory for events* (Vol. 1, pp. 157–174). Lawrence Erlbaum Associates.

Cardenas, S. A., Crozier, W., & Strange, D. (2020). Right place, wrong time: The limitations of mental reinstatement of context on alibi-elicitation. *Psychology, Crime & Law*, *27*(3), 201–230.

Clarke, C., & Milne, R. (2001). *National evaluation of the PEACE investigative interviewing course. Police Research Award Scheme*. Report No. PRAS/149: Institute of Criminal Justice Studies, University of Portsmouth.

CPTU (Central Planning and Training Unit). (1992a). *A guide to interviewing*. Home Office.

CPTU (Central Planning and Training Unit). (1992b). *The interviewer's rule book*. Home Office.

Culhane, S. E., & Hosch, H. M. (2012). Changed alibis: Current law enforcement, future law enforcement and layperson reactions. *Criminal Justice and Behavior*, *39*(7), 958–977.

Culhane, S. E., Hosch, H. M., & Kehn, A. (2008). Alibi generation: Data from U.S. Hispanics and U.S. non-Hispanic whites. *Journal of Ethnicity in Criminal Justice*, *6*(3), 177–199.

Ebbinghaus, H. (2013). Memory: A contribution to experimental psychology. *Annals of Neurosciences*, *20*(4), 155 (Original work published 1885).

Fahsing, A., & Rachlew, A. (2009). Investigative interviewing in the Nordic region. In T. Williamson, B. Milen, & S. P. Savage (Eds.), *International development in investigative interviewing* (pp. 39–65). Willan Publishing.

Geiselman, R. E., Fisher, R. P., Mackinnon, D. P., & Holland, H. L. (1986). Enhancement of eyewitness memory with the cognitive interview. *American Journal of Psychology*, *99*(3), 385–401.

Griffiths, A., & Milne, R. (2006). Will it all end in tiers? Police interviews with suspects. In Britain. In T. Williamson (Ed.), *Investigative interviewing: Rights, research, regulation* (pp. 189–211). Willan Publishing.

Hill, C., Memon, A., & McGeorge, P. (2008). The role of confirmation bias in suspect interviews: A systematic evaluation. *Legal and Criminological Psychology*, *13*(2), 357–371.

Inbau, F. E., Reid, J. E., Buckley, J. P., & Jayne, B. C. (2013). *Criminal interrogation and confessions*. Jones & Bartlett Learning.

Kassam, K. S., Gilbert, D. T., Swencionis, J. K., & Wilson, T. D. (2009). Misconceptions of memory: The Scooter Libby effect. *Psychological Science*, *20*(5), 551–552.

Kassin, S. M., Goldstein, C. C., & Savitsky, K. (2003). Behavioural confirmation in the interrogation room: On the dangers of presuming guilt. *Law and Human Behaviour*, *27*(2), 187–203.

Kassin, S. M., & Norwick, R. J. (2004). Why people waive their Miranda rights: The power of innocence. *Law and Human Behavior*, *28*(2), 211–221.

Leins, D. A., & Charman, S. D. (2016). Schema reliance and innocent alibi generation. *Legal and Criminological Psychology*, *21*(1), 111–126.

Memon, A., Meissner, C. A., & Fraser, J. (2010). The cognitive interview: A meta-analytic review and study space analysis of the past 25 years. *Psychology, Public Policy, and Law*, *16*(4), 340–372.

Olson, E. A., & Charman, S. D. (2012). 'But can you prove it?'—examining the quality of innocent suspects' alibis. *Psychology, Crime & Law*, *18*(5), 453–471.

Olson, E. A., & Wells, G. L. (2004). What makes a good alibi? A proposed taxonomy. *Law and Human Beahvior*, *28*(2), 157–176.

Pertzov, Y., Manohar, S., & Husain, M. (2017). Rapid forgetting results from competition over time between items in visual working memory. *Journal of Experimental Psychology: Learning, Memory, and Cognition*, *43*(4), 528–536.

Portnoy, S. (2019). *Memory-based approaches to the examination of alibis provided by innocent suspects* (Doctoral dissertation). University of Portsmouth & University of Gothenburg.

Portnoy, S., Hope, L., Vrij, A., Granhag, P. A., Ask, K., Eddy, C., & Landström, S. (2019). "I think you did it!": Examining the effect of presuming guilt on the verbal output of innocent suspects during brief interviews. *Journal of Investigative Psychology and Offender Profiling*, *16*(3), 236–250.

Schacter, D. L. (1999). The seven sins of memory: Insights from psychology and cognitive neuroscience. *American Psychologist*, *54*(3), 182–203.

Snyder, M., & Stukas, A. A. (1999). Interpersonal processes: The interplay of cognitive, motivational, and behavioral activities in social interaction. *Annual Review of Psychology*, *50*, 273–303.

Sommers, S. R., & Douglass, A. B. (2007). Context matters: Alibi strength varies according to evaluator perspective. *Legal and Criminological Psychology*, *12*(1), 41–54.

Strange, D., Dysart, J. E., & Loftus, E. F. (2014). Why errors in alibis are not necessarily evidence of guilt. *Zeitschrift für Psychologie*, *222*(2), 82–90.

Vrij, A. (2008). Nonverbal dominance versus verbal accuracy in lie detection: A plea to change police practice. *Criminal Justice and Behavior*, *35*(10), 1323–1336.

10 Interviewing suspects with the Strategic Use of Evidence (SUE) technique

Serra Tekin

Imagine a murder case in which a suspect is interviewed. CCTV footage shows the suspect rushing out of the building where the crime occurred shortly after the crime. The suspect denies having killed the victim, and more evidence needs to be gathered to understand what happened. This is an example of a relatively common case where the police possess evidence suggesting that the suspect may have been involved. However, it is also possible that the evidence is a result of an innocent activity. For instance, the suspect may have wished to surprise a friend who lives in the same building, but the friend was not home, and the suspect was running to catch the bus. One of the tasks the police have here is to collect information from the suspect to determine whether they should pursue the investigation of the suspect. Then the question arises as to how the police should conduct the suspect interview to find out the truth. Research shows that if an interviewer adopts a non-coercive, open-minded, and respectful style of interviewing, as opposed to using physical and/or psychological coercion, a suspect is more likely to provide information that will help the investigation (Alison et al., 2013). However, this style of interviewing is broad, and the police require more specific techniques that can be tailored to individual cases. For instance, how and when should the interviewer inform the suspect of the CCTV footage in the interview? The Strategic Use of Evidence (SUE) technique is one of such specific techniques and offers ways to use the evidence in a strategic manner. By using the evidence strategically, an interviewer can detect deception and gather new information from the suspect.

This chapter aims to provide an overview of research into the SUE technique. The first section summarises the technique and demonstrates how it can be used to detect deception. The second section lays out the principles behind the technique that constitute the SUE framework. These principles are key to understanding the various strategic ways an interviewer can utilise the evidence in an interview. Finally, the third section presents a new line of SUE research that aims to enhance information elicitation.

The SUE technique and detecting deception

Evidence can be disclosed to the suspect at different times during an interview. The interviewer may inform the suspect of the existing evidence before posing

DOI: 10.4324/9781003308546-13

any questions (Early Disclosure of Evidence), drip-feed the evidence through-out the interview (Gradual Disclosure of Evidence), or disclose it towards the end of the interview (Late Disclosure of Evidence). The SUE technique guides an interviewer to determine when it is best to disclose a piece of evidence to achieve interview goals such as deception detection and information elicita-tion. This section focuses on deception detection and how using the evidence strategically can increase the differences between statements of lying and truth-telling suspects.

An interviewer who uses the SUE technique first obtains the suspect's statement via open-ended questions and explores alternative explanations via specific questions before disclosing the evidence (Hartwig et al., 2005). This translates to the following interview structure for the case provided previously. The interviewer first invites the suspect to provide an account of their activities on the day of the murder. They then ask specific questions such as where the suspect has been, what the suspect has been wearing that day etc. Only then the interviewer informs the suspect of the CCTV footage.

Obtaining the suspect's side of the story before disclosing the evidence assists with deception detection as doing so leads to liars and truth-tellers adopting different strategies as a response to the questions. Research shows that a guilty suspect who is motivated to convince the interviewer that they are innocent typically withhold information that will give away their guilt. On the other hand, an innocent suspect who is typically motivated to demonstrate their innocence is likely to be forthcoming with information to show that they are not guilty (Hartwig et al., 2010; Strömwall et al., 2006). In the SUE interview, regardless of veracity, the suspect is unaware of the evidence whilst provid-ing their statement. If the suspect is guilty, they will typically be withholding and leave out the activities that led to the evidence ("I was home all day"). Consequently, the statement will contradict what the evidence suggests, and the interviewer will elicit a statement-evidence inconsistency. If the suspect is innocent, they will be more likely to share the activity that led to the evidence ("I wanted to surprise a friend who lives at XX, but she wasn't home. So, I took the bus back home"). This will result in a statement-evidence consist-ency. In contrast to the SUE interview, when the interviewer discloses the evidence early on (Early Disclosure of Evidence), lying and truth-telling sus-pects' statements should look more similar. An innocent suspect will likely be forthcoming and provide the reason why the evidence exists. However, a guilty suspect, knowing what evidence exists against them, will be more likely to make up an innocent excuse as to why the evidence exists ("I knew the victim and wanted to surprise her that day by showing up unannounced. She didn't answer the door, so I head back home"). This statement will be consistent with the evidence and will sound similar to a statement obtained from a truth-teller.

The SUE studies use a mock crime paradigm and compare the SUE inter-view to other interview protocols. In the mock crime paradigm, participants are assigned to either the guilty group and commit a mock crime (e.g., steal-ing a wallet) or the innocent group and perform a non-criminal act requiring activities similar to those performed for the mock crime (e.g., moving the wallet to reach another object). The criminal or non-criminal activities generate the same pieces of evidence (e.g., fingerprints on the wallet) indicating potential guilt. The participants are then interviewed as suspects under the suspicion of a crime (e.g., stealing money from a wallet) and are instructed to deny having committed the crime in the interview. Thus far, the findings consistently show that guilty suspects are indeed more inconsistent with the evidence than innocent suspects when the evidence is used strategically, but there is no difference in statement-evidence inconsistencies in innocent and guilty suspects' statements in the Early Disclosure interviews. The innocent suspects are found to be forthcoming in both interview conditions, and guilty suspects adopt forthcoming strategies in the Early Disclosure interviews and withholding strategies in the SUE interviews (for a meta-analysis, see Oleszkiewicz & Watson, 2021). In summary, the SUE research demonstrates that the degree of statement-evidence inconsistencies can be used as a cue to deception or truth (Hartwig et al., 2014).

The SUE technique has been tested in various other situations. Some examples include deception detection with children, uncovering suspects' true and false intentions and eliciting cues to deceit and truth in cases with multiple suspects (Granhag & Hartwig, 2015). Researchers have also been exploring strategies that take into consideration the strength and specificity of evidence in evidence disclosures (e.g., Granhag et al., 2013). The results are quite robust in the ability of the SUE interview to differentiate liars and truth-tellers in these situations. However, some avenues within SUE research are less known or unexplored. One such research avenue concerns innocent suspects. Innocent suspects are assumed to have nothing to hide and that they reveal as much information as they can in an interview. Although this may be the case for some, others may have valid reasons not to cooperate and/or lie in an interview. Clemens and Grolig (2019) found that when interviewed strategically, innocent suspects who had not committed the crime in question but engaged in another unlawful activity at the crime scene were inconsistent with the evidence more than innocent suspects who did not commit the crime nor the unlawful activity. This may have implications such as mistaking innocent individuals as deceivers in an interview. For instance, if the suspect in the example case mentioned previously wasn't involved in the murder but bought an illegal item from the victim before she was murdered, it is possible that they will conceal being in the victim's building. This will result in a statement-evidence inconsistency. Therefore, it is important to continue exploring innocent suspects' motivation and behaviour in SUE interviews.

SUE framework

The SUE interviews can be flexible when it comes to how the interviewer uses the evidence. To understand the various ways to disclose the evidence strategically, it is necessary to understand the principles behind the technique. These principles constitute the SUE framework: (1) suspects' perception of the evidence; (2) suspects' counter-interrogation strategies; and (3) suspects' verbal responses (Granhag & Hartwig, 2015). This section briefly explains the principles and then demonstrates how they are at play when the interviewer aims to detect deception.

Suspects' perception of the evidence

Suspects typically attempt to estimate what the interviewer knows about the crime in question. The result of that estimation can be referred to as a suspect's perception of the evidence. The interviewer's knowledge is especially critical for a guilty suspect who denies the criminal act and is motivated to get away with the crime by appearing innocent (e.g., Moston & Engelberg, 2011). If the guilty suspect accurately estimates the interviewer's knowledge of the crime, they will be better able to manage their statement content. That is, they can manipulate their stories to address the evidence held by the interviewer. This is typically done by providing innocent explanations to potentially incriminating information while avoiding the information they perceive the interviewer not to know. However, making an accurate estimation is difficult unless the suspect is informed about what the interviewer knows. In cases where the suspect is unaware of the interviewer's knowledge, their perception of the evidence will derive from an underestimation (thinking the interviewer has less evidence than they actually have) or an overestimation (thinking the interviewer has more evidence than they actually have).

Suspects' counter-interrogation strategies

This principle refers to suspects' information management strategies to achieve a goal, such as convincing the interviewer that they are innocent. As mentioned before, being innocent or guilty informs suspects' strategies in an interview. Studies exploring mock suspects' strategies show that guilty suspects believe that disclosing too many details would damage their credibility, whereas innocent suspects believe that providing as much information as possible would reveal their truthfulness (Colwell et al., 2006).

Suspects' verbal responses

Suspects' verbal responses refer to the verbal outcome of the interview. For the SUE research, the possible interview outcomes are cues to deceit and information unknown to the interviewer. The SUE principles are related to each other. A suspect's perception of the evidence influences their counter-interrogation strategies, and their strategies influence their verbal responses (Granhag & Hartwig, 2015). Therefore, by affecting the suspect's estimation of how much the interviewer knows, it is possible for the interviewer to steer the interview towards the interview goal.

SUE principles and deception detection

Sharing the available evidence with the suspect at the onset of the interview, as in the Early Disclosure of Evidence interview, will lead to a rather accurate perception of the evidence. A guilty suspect, aware of what the interviewer knows, will try to account for the evidence and choose a forthcoming counter-interrogation strategy. Consequently, the suspect's statement will match the evidence, and the suspect's verbal response will result in a statement-evidence consistency. In the SUE interview, however, the suspect is unaware of the evidence whilst answering the interviewer's questions. In this case, the guilty suspect is expected to estimate the interviewer's knowledge as little or none. This inaccurate perception of the evidence will likely result in a withholding counter-interrogation strategy. By not giving away incriminating details, the suspect will be working towards the goal of deceiving the interviewer, but their story will not match the evidence. The verbal response will then be a statement-evidence inconsistency, a cue to deceit. The SUE research on deception detection supports this reasoning for guilty suspects (Hartwig et al., 2014); however, the relationship between the principles has not been directly examined in this line of research.

The SUE technique and information gathering

The ability to detect deception can be helpful in investigations; however, simply determining one's veracity does not fully serve the needs of an investigation when further information is required regarding the crime. For instance, it may be clear that the suspect is lying about their whereabouts despite the CCTV footage showing they were at the crime scene, but this is still insufficient to determine whether the suspect had been involved in the crime. It then becomes important to elicit further information from the suspect. If the suspect is innocent, they will likely volunteer information; however, this does not apply to a guilty suspect who may withhold information to avoid self-incrimination (Hartwig et al., 2014). A recent development within the SUE research attempts to explore whether strategic evidence disclosure can be used to elicit new information from guilty suspects (see Tekin, 2016). New information here refers to information that can help make connections between the crime and the guilty suspect (e.g., mentioning meeting the victim on the day of the crime without admitting to murdering her) or information that can help rule out the innocent as suspects (e.g., pointing out that they were on a bus on the way to the victim's place when the crime was taking place). By using the SUE principles, Tekin and colleagues developed a new tactic within the SUE research, called the SUE-Confrontation tactic, and tested the tactic's ability to enhance information gathering.

SUE principles and the SUE-Confrontation tactic

A guilty suspect is likely to be forthcoming with information they believe the interviewer to hold because they are motivated to avoid contradicting the interviewer's knowledge. If this forthcoming strategy is informed by an overestimation of what the interviewer knows about the crime, some of the information disclosed by the suspect will be new to the interviewer. The key here is to find a way of influencing a suspect's perception into an overestimation without deceiving the suspect about the existing evidence. Tekin and colleagues (2015) were the first to test the SUE-Confrontation tactic designed to make the suspect overestimate the amount of evidence in a case and consequently reveal information. The study by Tekin et al. (2015), as well as the ones that followed (e.g., Tekin et al., 2016), examined the SUE-Confrontation interview by splitting the crime into phases such as the following three: the suspect's activities before the crime, during the crime, and after the crime. One of the phases is deemed the "critical phase". This is the phase for which the interviewer has no information, and it commonly concerns the time of the crime. This phase is critical mainly because the police need to have an accurate account of what happened. The other phases are "less critical phases" for which the interviewer holds potentially incriminating evidence (e.g., eyewitness testimony suggesting that the suspect was following the victim the day before the crime and CCTV footage suggesting that the suspect was around the crime scene after the crime had occurred). These two phases are less critical as the evidence raises suspicion but cannot be used to make a connection between the crime and the suspect.

In the SUE-Confrontation interview, the interviewer questions the suspect about each phase of the crime separately and handles the less critical phases first. For one of these less critical phases, the interviewer uses the evidence strategically (asks open-ended and specific questions about the suspect's activities before disclosing the evidence in this phase). At this point, a guilty suspect is expected to perceive the interviewer to have little or no information and provide a statement inconsistent with the evidence. The interviewer then confronts the suspect with the inconsistency and emphasises the seriousness of being inconsistent. The interviewer repeats this process for the other less critical phase. This interviewing process is expected to teach the suspect that the interviewer knows more even if they do not share this knowledge with the suspect at the onset of the interview. A suspect initially believing that the interviewer has little or no information may now start thinking the interviewer knows more. Moreover, confrontations with inconsistencies are unwanted as they attack a guilty suspect's credibility. As a response, the suspect is expected to try to restore their diminished credibility by preventing further confrontations. It is at this point (when the suspect overestimates the evidence and is motivated to avoid contradictions) that the interviewer questions the suspect about the critical phase by asking an open-ended question about their activities. The suspect may then share some of their activities during this critical time even if they do not admit guilt. The verbal response to this forthcoming strategy will be new information.

Tekin et al. (2015) compared the SUE-Confrontation interview to two control interviews: Early Disclosure interview and No Disclosure interview (the interviewer did not disclose any evidence and asked only about the critical phase). Mock suspects' statements were coded for statement-evidence inconsistencies for the two less critical phases and new information for the critical phase. Suspects in the SUE-Confrontation interview were more inconsistent with the evidence than suspects in the Early Disclosure interview. Suspects also revealed more new information in the SUE-Confrontation interview compared to the two control interviews. This was new information, such as the suspect mentioning being at the crime scene. Considering that the interviewer did not know what the suspect was doing around the time of the crime, finding out that they were with the victim is an important piece of information. Tekin et al. also examined the assumptions made by the SUE principles. First, the participants who were interviewed with the SUE-Confrontation interview perceived the interviewer to know more about what they did during the crime compared to the participants who were interviewed with the control interviews. This means the suspects' perceptions were influenced by the SUE-Confrontation interview. Second, suspects' strategies were examined. One-third of the withholding suspects switched to a forthcoming strategy as the SUE-Confrontation interview progressed. It is important to note, however, that some did not show this trend and stayed withholding throughout the interview. Nevertheless, this study was the first to show that by using evidence strategically, an interviewer can affect a suspect's decision-making during an interview and obtain new information.

It is an interesting question why some suspects remained withholding when interviewed with the SUE-Confrontation interview. These suspects may have interpreted the confrontations as damaging to their credibility to the point of no return and saw no need to restore it. In a follow-up study, Tekin et al. (2016) gave suspects more opportunities to rebuild their credibility by allowing them to address statement-evidence inconsistencies following confrontations. Suspects who took the opportunity to explain the inconsistencies were found to switch to a more forthcoming strategy and revealed more new information, compared to suspects who chose not to explain inconsistencies. So, again, a portion of the suspects stayed withholding despite being able to account for the inconsistencies. It is possible that explaining statement-evidence inconsistencies did not seem like a feasible way to restore credibility for this group. Such explanations may require changing one's initial story, and these suspects may have believed this change to be more damaging. Although it is still unknown why this bimodal pattern occurs, it is possible that suspects switch from a less to a more forthcoming strategy when they stay motivated to pursue the goal of appearing innocent. If the interview is a game, the interviewer needs to ensure that the suspect stays motivated to continue playing the game (Tekin, 2016). This is important to take into consideration when preparing for an interview.

In an attempt to keep more suspects "in the game", May et al. (2017) added a social component to the SUE-Confrontation interview. The interviewer focused on emphasising their non-guilt assumptive attitude towards suspects throughout the interview. This way of interviewing resulted in more new information about the critical phase compared to the Early Disclosure interview but did not outperform the original SUE-Confrontation interview. However, when faced with this more open-minded atmosphere, suspects believed the interviewer to be friendlier and more respectful. A friendly interviewer is likely to lead to a more cooperative suspect (e.g., Alison et al., 2013); therefore, keeping this component as part of the SUE-Confrontation tactic seems like a good idea. Moreover, Luke and Granhag (2022) found that responding to and pointing out each statement-evidence inconsistency during the interview, as opposed to reacting only to some of the inconsistencies, resulted in the suspects sharing more information. This can be attributed to the fact that the suspects got more feedback on their "performance" and adjusted their strategies accordingly. These studies do not only show how the SUE-Confrontation interview is flexible in handling the evidence, but they also contribute to interviewing practice by testing ways to improve information elicitation.

Overall, the results in this new area of research are promising. The SUE-Confrontation tactic is the first to provide a way of eliciting new and accurate information by using the evidence strategically. This is especially important in the absence of any other evidence to connect the suspect to the crime. The research also provides support to the relationship between the SUE principles. That is, guilty suspects' perceptions of the evidence affect their counter-interrogation strategies, and these strategies, in return, affect the verbal outcome of the interview. Such knowledge is important in allowing interviewers to use the principles to develop more tactics. It is also noteworthy that the SUE-Confrontation tactic does not only elicit new information but also leads to cues to deception or truth. Both verbal outcomes are important in an investigation and for the prosecution to build a solid case. Moving forward, it seems essential to study ways of keeping more suspects motivated in the interview so that they continue playing the "game". Exploring the best way to confront suspects with statement-evidence inconsistencies and how to handle these inconsistencies may be beneficial in enhancing information gathering with the SUE technique.

Concluding remarks

This chapter intended to provide an overview of the SUE research. The SUE technique adopts a non-coercive style of interviewing and offers specific ways of utilising the evidence in an interview. The chapter first introduced the SUE technique and demonstrated how it can help detect deception by magnifying the differences between truth-telling and lying suspects' statements. Next, the principles constituting the SUE framework were described. These principles help develop various strategies to achieve interview goals. A new line of research concerns information elicitation in interviews by using the SUE-Confrontation tactic, which is developed based on these principles. The last section focused on the research findings on this tactic. The findings demonstrate the possibility of influencing guilty suspects' perceptions of the evidence by using the evidence strategically, making them adopt more forthcoming strategies and consequently gather new information that can be useful in an investigation. The findings are promising; however, more research is needed to find ways of encouraging more guilty suspects to switch from less to more forthcoming strategies in interviews. Nevertheless, the SUE technique can be used flexibly to meet the needs of interviewers, whether this is deception detection and/or information elicitation.

References

Alison, L. J., Alison, E. E., Noone, G., Elntib, S., & Christiansen, P. (2013). Why tough tactics fail and rapport gets results: Observing rapport-based interpersonal techniques (ORBIT) to generate useful information from terrorists. *Psychology, Public Policy, and Law*, *19*(4), 411–431.

Clemens, F., & Grolig, T. (2019). Innocent of the crime under investigation: Suspects' counter-interrogation strategies and statement-evidence inconsistency in strategic vs. non-strategic interviews. *Psychology, Crime & Law*, *25*(10), 945–962.

Colwell, K., Hiscock-Anlsman, C., Memon, A., Woods, D., & Michlik, P. M. (2006). Strategies of impression management among deceivers and truth-tellers: How liars attempt to convince. *American Journal of Forensic Psychology*, *24*(2), 31–38.

Granhag, P. A., & Hartwig, M. (2015). The strategic use of evidence technique: A conceptual overview. In P. A. Granhag, A. Vrij, & B. Verschuere (Eds.), *Detecting deception: Current challenges and cognitive approaches*. Wiley.

Granhag, P. A., Strömwall, L. A., Willén, R. M., & Hartwig, M. (2013). Eliciting cues to deception by tactical disclosure of evidence: The first test of the evidence framing matrix. *Legal and Criminological Psychology*, *18*(2), 341–355.

Hartwig, M., Granhag, P. A., & Luke, T. (2014). Strategic Use of Evidence during investigative interviews: The state of the science. In D. C. Raskin, C. R. Honts, & J. C. Kircher (Eds.), *Credibility assessment: Scientific research and applications* (pp. 1–36). Elsevier Academic Press.

Hartwig, M., Granhag, P. A., Strömwall, L. A., & Doering, N. (2010). Impression and information management: On the strategic self-regulation of innocent and guilty suspects. *The Open Criminology Journal*, *3*(2), 10–16.

Hartwig, M., Granhag, P. A., Strömwall, L. A., & Vrij, A. (2005). Detecting deception via strategic disclosure of evidence. *Law and Human Behavior*, *29*(4), 469–484.

Luke, T. J., & Granhag, P. A. (2022). The shift-of-strategy (SoS) approach: Using evidence strategically to influence suspects' counter-interrogation strategies. *Psychology, Crime & Law*, 1–26.

May, L., Granhag, P. A., & Tekin, S. (2017). Interviewing suspects in denial: On how different evidence disclosure modes affect the elicitation of new critical information. *Frontiers in Psychology*, *8*, 1154.

Moston, S., & Engelberg, T. (2011). The effects of evidence on the outcome of interviews with criminal suspects. *Police Practice and Research*, *12*(6), 518–526.

Oleszkiewicz, S., & Watson, S. J. (2021). A meta-analytic review of the timing for disclosing evidence when interviewing suspects. *Applied Cognitive Psychology*, *35*(2), 342–359.

Strömwall, L. A., Hartwig, M., & Granhag, P. A. (2006). To act truthfully: Nonverbal behaviour and strategies during a police interrogation. *Psychology, Crime and Law*, *12*(2), 207–219.

Tekin, S. (2016). *Eliciting admissions from suspects in criminal investigations* (Doctoral dissertation). University of Gothenburg & University of Portsmouth.

Tekin, S., Granhag, P. A., Strömwall, L. A., Giolla, E. M., Vrij, A., & Hartwig, M. (2015). Interviewing strategically to elicit admissions from guilty suspects. *Law and Human Behavior*, *39*(3), 244–252.

Tekin, S., Granhag, P. A., Strömwall, L. A., & Vrij, A. (2016). How to make perpetrators in denial disclose more information about their crimes. *Psychology, Crime and Law*, *22*(6), 561–580.

Part III

Deception detection and legal decision making

11 Lie detection in forensic interviews

Haneen Deeb and Aleksandras Izotovas

On the night of September 7, 1988, 17-year-old Marty Tankliff woke up in his house to discover that his mother had been stabbed to death and his father was severely beaten and in a critical condition (he later died in hospital). When Detective James McCready arrived at the crime scene, he thought that Tankliff was very calm for someone whose parents had been attacked, so he believed that Tankliff was guilty. McCready, invested in his beliefs when interviewing Tankliff, kept accusing him of murdering his parents. Eventually, Tankliff confessed to the crime and was convicted. He was later exonerated after serving 17 years in prison (Seigel, 2021).

While McCready used emotions as a cue to deception, there is no single cue for detecting lies, and the long-held myth of Pinocchio's nose is not empirically valid (Luke, 2019). Empirical evidence shows that cues such as nervousness, gaze aversion, and contradictions that are commonly perceived to be indicative of deception are not necessarily diagnostic (DePaulo et al., 2003; Global Deception Research Team, 2006). Innocent suspects who tell the truth may become nervous if they fear the investigator does not believe they are innocent. Also, an innocent suspect may look away from an investigator due to cultural differences rather than deceptive behaviour. For example, black suspects are less likely than white suspects to look at others in a conversation which may be misinterpreted by investigators as deception (Granhag et al., 2015). Where lie detection is important, such as in forensic settings, verbal cues (e.g., amount of detail) embodied in a verbal account are more diagnostic than nonverbal cues (e.g., gaze aversion) embodied in body language. See Box 12.1 for verbal cues that received empirical support in meta-analyses.

An additional verbal cue that has received attention in the deception literature is consistency, which may be labelled differently depending on context (Vredeveldt et al., 2014). When multiple accounts are provided by the same person at different points in time (between-statement consistency) or when accounts from two accomplices (within-suspect consistency) are given, lie tellers are at least as consistent (repeating the same information) as truth tellers. Also, when more than one event is reported in a single interview (within-statement consistency), lie tellers who report a truthful and a deceptive event are more likely to be consistent (providing the same amount of detail about the

DOI: 10.4324/9781003308546-15

Table 11.1 Empirically supported verbal cues. Compiled from research by Amado et al., 2016; DePaulo et al., 2003; Leal et al., 2018; Verschuere et al., 2021; Vrij et al., 2020, 2021.

Verbal cues that are more likely to be found in truth tellers' accounts than in lie tellers' accounts

Logical structure: Accounts that are coherent
Unstructured production: Accounts that include details not reported in chronological order
Quantity of details: Accounts that include a high number of details
Contextual embeddings: Accounts that include a high number of temporal, spatial, and perceptual details
Reproduction of conversations: Accounts in which conversations that occurred during the target event are reported verbatim
Complications: Accounts that include details that make the reported event more complex
Spontaneous corrections: Accounts in which previously reported details are corrected
Details characteristic of the offence: Accounts that mainly include details related to the target event
Verifiable details: Accounts that include details that can be checked and verified
Plausibility: Accounts that appear realistic and believable and include unusual details
Involvement: Accounts that include expressive language
Immediacy: Accounts that are direct and include active language

Verbal cues that are more likely to be found in lie tellers' accounts than in truth tellers' accounts

Common knowledge details: Accounts involving details that are typically known surrounding an event
Self-handicapping strategies: Accounts in which the speaker provides justifications for not providing relevant information
Peripheral details: Accounts that include details that are non-central to the target event
Negative accounts and complaints: Accounts characterised by negative affect

two events) than truth tellers who are completely truthful. Lie tellers also aim to be consistent with the evidence (evidence-statement consistency) when it is uncovered early in an interview. Therefore, despite the widely held belief that truth tellers are consistent and lie tellers are inconsistent, research shows limited support of these beliefs, with lie tellers becoming particularly consistent if they have time to prepare prior to providing their account.

Beliefs about cues to deception

Laypeople and professionals tend to detect lies at chance levels, but professionals such as police officers are often more confident in their judgements (Bond & DePaulo, 2006). Laypeople and professionals share the global belief that nonverbal cues such as gaze aversion and nervousness are more diagnostic than verbal cues. When they report relying on verbal cues, contradictions and inconsistencies are the most frequently reported cues that are associated with deception (Global Deception Research Team, 2006).

Criminals tend to have different beliefs about cues to deception (Granhag et al., 2004). Unlike laypeople and professionals, criminals are less likely to believe that truth tellers are more consistent than lie tellers, and their views are more likely to match research findings. Criminals' experiences with lie telling seem to help them to understand what works to evade being detected and to identify cues that decision-makers rely on when detecting lies.

Incorrect beliefs held among law enforcement personnel may be attributed to professional manuals and investigative interviewing training that advocate nonverbal cues to deception (Vrij, 2008). Investigators employing accusatory interviews, for example, tend to interview suspects with the presumption that they are guilty. That, in turn, makes the innocent suspect feel defensive and nervous, a cue commonly associated with deception, which ultimately results in investigators judging the suspect as guilty. Consequently, police officers are more sceptical than laypeople, and they show a lie bias, a tendency to judge others' accounts as deceptive (Meissner & Kassin, 2002). That contrasts with laypeople's truth bias, a tendency to judge others' accounts as truthful because the presumption that others would be lying to them does not automatically come to mind (Levine, 2014). These incorrect beliefs and biases have practical significance, especially in forensic settings where false positives lead to the conviction of an innocent person and false negatives result in freeing a guilty person, which is detrimental to societal safety.

Countermeasures employed by lie tellers

The differences between truth tellers and lie tellers are small, so it is difficult to use deception cues to judge whether a person is lying or telling the truth (Hartwig & Bond, 2011). One explanation for the lack of substantial differences is that lie tellers recognise people's assumptions about verbal and nonverbal cues to deception, and they try to behave in a manner that matches those assumptions by controlling their verbal and nonverbal behaviour. For example, lie tellers tend to prepare their stories, keep their stories simple, report embedded lies, provide consistent accounts, refrain from reporting verifiable (i.e., checkable) details or complications, and maintain eye contact (Rosenfeld, 2018). These strategies help them to provide a convincing account, avoid forgetting their account should they need to provide another one in the future, and evade providing possibly incriminating details.

Within terrorist settings, terrorist organisations produce manuals (e.g., The Al-Qaeda's Manchester Manual and the Irish Republican Army's Green Manual) that help their members prepare for interviews by illustrating questions they may be asked at airports or during interviews and by instructing members on how to respond. A field study on terrorists' strategies during interviews revealed that paramilitary groups and right-wing extremists in the United Kingdom remain passive or provide information that is already known to the police, whereas Al-Qaeda terrorists refuse to comment or redact their accounts after they are interviewed (Alison et al., 2014).

Nevertheless, lie tellers cannot always counter interviews. For example, lie tellers cannot reduce body rigidity even after learning that rigidity is correlated with deception. With regards to verbal cues, embedded lies are not necessarily of the same high quality as truthful accounts (Verigin et al., 2020). When lie tellers familiarise themselves with the alibi setting, their statements may become as consistent with the evidence as truth tellers' statements, but they tend to provide more details than truth tellers, which gives their lie away (Deeb et al., 2018). Also, instructing lie tellers that their accounts will be scanned for complications and verifiable details does not result in lie tellers reporting these cues because they want to keep their stories simple and avoid incriminating themselves.

Given poor lie detection rates and lie tellers' countermeasures, it is important to enhance lie detection by developing innovative interview techniques and looking for different cues of deception that cannot be countered by lie tellers.

Interview techniques to detect deception

Some known interrogation manuals, such as Inbau et al.'s (2013) or the U.S. Army Field Manual (United States, 2006), present interview techniques to infer deception without empirical support. An important reason for the low effectiveness of lie detection of these techniques is that they are not created to elicit verbal differences between truth tellers and lie tellers.

The innovative interviewing approach called Cognitive Credibility Assessment (CCA; Vrij et al., 2017) is used to elicit differences between truth tellers and lie tellers by focusing on verbal cues to deception. The CCA is based on the assumption that in interview settings, lying is typically more mentally demanding than truth telling (Buller & Burgoon, 1996) and that the difference can be further enhanced through specific interventions. Elements that contribute to a lie teller's enhanced cognitive load are preparing a convincing story, suppressing the truth, remembering what was said earlier, controlling their verbal and nonverbal behaviour, monitoring an investigator's reactions, reminding themselves to act and role play, and providing justification for their lies.

The CCA is comprised of three interview techniques: imposing cognitive load, asking unexpected questions, and encouraging suspects to say more (Vrij, 2018). Imposing cognitive load refers to situations where investigators can exploit the different mental states of truth tellers and lie tellers by making interview settings more cognitively challenging. For example, suspects can be asked to engage in a concurrent, second task when reporting the event (e.g., telling what happened while gripping an object; Visu-Petra et al., 2013). The mental resources of lie tellers are more depleted than those of truth tellers, so they tend to be less able to cope with additional requests than truth tellers (Debey et al., 2012). Another technique, asking unexpected questions, is based on the assumption that lie tellers prepare themselves to answer questions they expect to be asked (Hartwig et al., 2007). Therefore, they experience more difficulties when responding to unexpected questions than to expected questions or tasks, whereas truth tellers answer with similar ease to both question types as they rely on their real experiences (Lancaster et al., 2013). Finally, the 'encouraging suspects to say more' technique is related to creating a setting in which suspects are encouraged to provide more details. Truth tellers then tend to report more details than lie tellers because lie tellers are not inclined to say much out of fear that the additional details they report will give leads to investigators and hence uncover their lies (Granhag & Hartwig, 2008).

Studies on these interview techniques have shown medium to large effects. Also, empirical reviews demonstrated that human observers can accurately detect lies and truths with up to 75% accuracy when they look at the verbal cues that these techniques elicit (e.g., Mac Giolla & Luke, 2021). This accuracy rate is higher than the chance levels of 50% and is better than the accuracy rates (48–56%) achieved in traditional interview techniques.

The use of mnemonics in forensic interviews

Memory-enhancing techniques, also called mnemonics, were developed to enhance memory and facilitate accurate and complete accounts from witnesses (Fisher et al., 1989). They are currently being used for lie detection purposes as well. Mnemonics are part of the CCA approach to encouraging suspects to say more.

Recent findings have shown that mnemonics differentiate between truthful and deceptive statements. When participants were interviewed shortly after a stimulus event using either context reinstatement (mentally recreating the to-be-recalled event), sketch (drawing of a location of the event in question), or event-line (reproducing temporal context and sequence of actions in an event) mnemonics, truth tellers reported more visual, spatial, temporal, and action details than lie tellers (Izotovas et al., 2018). Furthermore, the differences between truth tellers and lie tellers in the number of these details were more pronounced when the 'report everything' mnemonic (prompting suspects to disclose all information they can remember) was employed compared to a set of standard questions (Izotovas et al., 2020). Overall, the enhanced discrimination between truth tellers and lie tellers demonstrates that mnemonics facilitate the retrieval of information for truth tellers, but lie tellers may lack the imagination or are reluctant to reveal as much information as truth tellers because of the risk that it can be checked by the police (Vrij et al., 2017).

The experimental findings of the benefits of different interview techniques may not apply across settings because, in these studies, the interviews are typically conducted shortly after the event in question. Memory research has shown that memory traces weaken, and the amount of recalled information can systematically decrease after a time delay (Pansky et al., 2005). Therefore, it is reasonable to expect detrimental effects of delay on verbal lie detection.

Lie detection in delayed interviewing

Research has shown the negative effects of delay on differentiating between truth tellers and lie tellers. In one study, pairs of participants were asked either to have lunch together (truth tellers) or to commit a mock theft and then create an alibi of having had lunch together (lie tellers; Vrij et al., 2009). Participants were interviewed either immediately or after a one-week delay. Results showed that truthful pairs reported more details than deceptive pairs in the immediate interview. That difference, however, was no longer significant in the delayed interview. Similarly, in a recent study in which participants carried out a mock intelligence operation, it was found that truth tellers reported more details than lie tellers when they were interviewed immediately, but there was no difference in the number of details after a three-week delay (Harvey et al., 2017). Nahari (2018) found that truth tellers demonstrated larger variability than lie tellers in the number of details they reported over different delay periods. Specifically, truth tellers provided more information when they were interviewed immediately compared to when they were interviewed two weeks after the event. However, lie tellers reported a similar number of details, regardless of the retention interval between the incident and the interview.

In addition, some studies have shown that delay can negatively affect the efficacy of credibility assessment tools. For example, physiological electrodermal measures and symptom validity tests (Nahari & Ben-Shakhar, 2011) were more efficient lie detection tools for eliciting differences in peripheral (unrelated to the crime) details among truth tellers and lie tellers when tested immediately compared to after a one-week delay. In another study by McDougall and Bull (2015), the verbal quality of statements provided by truth tellers and lie tellers was assessed using two credibility tools: criteria-based content analysis (CBCA; Steller & Köhnken, 1989) and reality monitoring (RM; Johnson & Raye, 1981). Truthful statements achieved higher RM and CBCA scores than deceptive statements but only when interviews were conducted shortly after the mock crime event. The RM and CBCA scores did not differ across veracity conditions when suspects were questioned after 7–10 days.

Overall, findings of previous research show that a time delay between an event and an interview may hamper discrimination between truthful and deceptive accounts based on the number of provided details. In the studies discussed previously, the differences between truth tellers and lie tellers tended to produce medium to large effects in the immediate interviews. However, the effect sizes decreased in the delayed interviews. A possible explanation for this is that delay affects the memory of truth tellers, i.e., they remember less information over time, but that fabricated accounts do not depend to the same extent on the passage of time after the event because lie tellers can fabricate information. A study by Nahari (2018) demonstrated that lie tellers' accounts were affected less by time delay than truth tellers' accounts. However, when lie tellers incorporate truthful elements in their stories, they could also experience a decline in truthful details after the delay. Nonetheless, lie tellers resolve the problem by adding false and unverifiable details to their stories to make an honest impression (Nahari, 2018). Lie tellers' tendency to add details could be explained through 'the stability bias'. They typically experience difficulties in understanding the real nature of memory, including the effects of a time delay (Harvey et al., 2017). It is more important for lie tellers to provide enough detail in their story to be believed by the investigator (Hartwig et al., 2007). Therefore, after a time delay, they may be unwilling to reduce the amount of detail below a threshold perceived as necessary to appear genuine.

One possible solution against the negative effects of delay is early and high-quality questioning of suspects. Retrieval practice, or testing effect, refers to an act of recalling a previously experienced event or learned information (Roediger & Butler, 2011). Retrieval practice strengthens memory traces to recall information later. Witness research has shown that memory testing soon after an event may have beneficial effects of 'inoculating' witness memory against forgetting (Pansky & Nemets, 2012). In addition, high-quality interviewing (i.e., eliciting accurate and complete accounts from suspects) proved to be beneficial for witness memory performance after a delay (Hope et al., 2014). If immediate and appropriate interviewing may help to maintain rich memories of a genuinely experienced event over time, it is reasonable to predict differences between truth tellers and lie tellers in terms of the number of details in repeated delayed interviews. Indeed, mnemonics such as context reinstatement, sketch, even-line, and report everything instruction were found to enhance lie detection after a two-week interview if they were introduced in an immediate interview (Izotovas et al., 2018, 2020).

Theoretical and practical implications

Interview techniques promoting complete and accurate accounts from suspects are beneficial for criminal investigations (Hope et al., 2014). These techniques have also shown benefits in discriminating between truth tellers and lie tellers (Vrij et al., 2017). Furthermore, interviewing methods facilitating detailed responses can be helpful for the investigation in that they allow investigators to compare information in the suspect's account with the available evidence concerning the case. This provides wider opportunities for investigators to plan the upcoming interview and to employ specific questions and tactics (e.g., *when* and *how* to disclose the evidence) to challenge potential lie tellers with contradictions or inconsistencies between their responses and actual evidence.

Researchers are developing new interview techniques to enhance lie detection, which is significant for practical applications such as in law enforcement settings. The most important requirement to employ these techniques, for instance, mnemonics, is to produce speech from the suspects. The recent research focus on verbal techniques and on looking for different cues to deception seems to be going in the right direction, but there is still more to be done to understand deceptive behaviour and how to enhance lie detection.

Training investigators in these interview techniques is important for enhancing lie detection. By informing investigators about cues that received strong empirical evidence and tackling any myths they hold about cues to deception (such as those relevant to nonverbal cues), investigators may be able to resolve cases more quickly and save time and financial resources, which are two crucial resources in forensic settings. Also, directing investigators to cues that are particularly resistant to countermeasures such as verifiable details may aid them in weighing these cues against other diagnostic cues (e.g., consistency) and available evidence to make more informed decisions.

Concluding remarks

Lie telling is not uncommon in forensic settings and identifying lie tellers is important for making informed decisions. Verbal cues to deception have shown more promise than nonverbal cues in enhancing lie detection, so investigators need to look at these cues and ignore widely held myths about deceptive behaviours. Recently developed interview techniques that have been shown to magnify differences between truth tellers and lie tellers and to elicit diagnostic verbal cues that are resistant to countermeasures may enhance lie detection. Also, techniques that employ mnemonics to prompt suspects to report more information are effective for lie detection purposes, but they are best used in the very first interview.

References

Alison, L., Alison, E., Noone, G., Elntib, S., Waring, S., & Christiansen, P. (2014). Whatever you say, say nothing: Individual differences in counter interrogation tactics amongst a field sample of right wing, AQ inspired and paramilitary terrorists. *Personality and Individual Differences, 68*, 170–175.

Amado, B. G., Arce, R., Farina, F., & Vilarino, M. (2016). Criteria-based content analysis (CBCA) reality criteria in adults: A meta-analytic review. *International Journal of Clinical and Health Psychology, 16*(2), 201–210.

Bond Jr, C. F., & DePaulo, B. M. (2006). Accuracy of deception judgments. *Personality and Social Psychology Review, 10*(3), 214–234.

Buller, D. B., & Burgoon, J. K. (1996). Interpersonal deception theory. *Communication Theory, 6*(3), 203–242.

Debey, E., Verschuere, B., & Crombez, G. (2012). Lying and executive control: An experimental investigation using ego depletion and goal neglect. *Acta Psychologica, 140*(2), 133–141.

Deeb, H., Granhag, P. A., Vrij, A., Strömwall, L. A., Hope, L., & Mann, S. (2018). Visuospatial counter-interrogation strategies by liars familiar with the alibi setting. *Applied Cognitive Psychology, 32*(1), 105–116.

DePaulo, B. M., Lindsay, J. L., Malone, B. E., Muhlenbruck, L., Charlton, K., & Cooper, H. (2003). Cues to deception. *Psychological Bulletin, 129*(1), 74–118.

Fisher, R., Geiselman, R. E., & Amador, M. (1989). Field test of the cognitive interview: Enhancing the recollection of actual victims and witnesses of crime. *Journal of Applied Psychology, 74*(5), 722–727.

Global Deception Research Team. (2006). A world of lies. *Journal of Cross-Cultural Psychology, 37*(1), 60–74.

Granhag, P. A., Andersson, L. O., Strömwall, L. A., & Hartwig, M. (2004). Imprisoned knowledge: Criminals' beliefs about deception. *Legal and Criminological Psychology, 9*(1), 103–119.

Granhag, P. A., & Hartwig, M. (2008). A new theoretical perspective on deception detection: On the psychology of instrumental mind-reading. *Psychology, Crime & Law, 14*(3), 189–200.

Granhag, P. A., Vrij, A., & Verschuere, B. (2015). *Detecting deception: Current challenges and cognitive approaches*. John Wiley & Sons.

Hartwig, M., & Bond Jr, C. F. (2011). Why do lie-catchers fail? A lens model meta-analysis of human lie judgments. *Psychological Bulletin*, *137*(4), 643–659.

Hartwig, M., Granhag, P. A., & Strömwall, L. A. (2007). Guilty and innocent suspects' strategies during police interrogations. *Psychology, Crime & Law*, *13*(2), 213–227.

Harvey, A., Vrij, A., Leal, S., Hope, L., & Mann, S. (2017). A stability bias effect amongst deceivers. *Law and Human Behavior*, *41*(6), 519–529.

Hope, L., Gabbert, F., Fisher, R. P., & Jamieson, K. (2014). Protecting and enhancing eyewitness Memory: The impact of an initial recall attempt on performance in an investigative interview. *Applied Cognitive Psychology*, *28*(3), 304–313.

Inbau, F. E., Reid, J. E., Buckley, J. P., & Jayne, B. C. (2013). *Criminal interrogation and confessions*. Jones & Bartlett Learning.

Izotovas, A., Vrij, A., Hope, L., Mann, S., Granhag, P. A., & Strömwall, L. A. (2018). Facilitating memory-based lie detection in immediate and delayed interviewing: The role of mnemonics. *Applied Cognitive Psychology*, *32*(5), 561–574.

Izotovas, A., Vrij, A., Hope, L., Strömwall, L. A., Granhag, P. A., & Mann, S. (2020). Deception detection in repeated interviews: The effects of immediate type of questioning on the delayed accounts. *Journal of Investigative Psychology and Offender Profiling*, *17*(3), 224–237.

Johnson, M. K., & Raye, C. L. (1981). Reality monitoring. *Psychological Review*, *88*(1), 67–85.

Lancaster, G. L., Vrij, A., Hope, L., & Waller, B. (2013). Sorting the liars from the truth tellers: The benefits of asking unanticipated questions on lie detection. *Applied Cognitive Psychology*, *27*(1), 107–114.

Leal, S., Vrij, A., Deeb, H., & Jupe, L. (2018). Using the model statement to elicit verbal differences between truth tellers and liars: The benefit of examining core and peripheral details. *Journal of Applied Research in Memory and Cognition*, *7*(4), 610–617.

Levine, T. R. (2014). Truth-default theory (TDT): A theory of human deception and deception detection. *Journal of Language and Social Psychology*, *33*(4), 378–392.

Luke, T. J. (2019). Lessons from Pinocchio: Cues to deception may be highly exaggerated. *Perspectives on Psychological Science*, *14*(4), 646–671.

Mac Giolla, E., & Luke, T. J. (2021). Does the cognitive approach to lie detection improve the accuracy of human observers? *Applied Cognitive Psychology*, *35*(2), 385–392.

McDougall, A. G., & Bull, R. (2015). Detecting truth in suspect interviews: The effect of use of evidence (early and gradual) and time delay on criteria-based content analysis, reality monitoring and inconsistency within suspect statements. *Psychology, Crime & Law*, *21*(6), 514–530.

Meissner, C. A., & Kassin, S. M. (2002). "He's guilty!": Investigator bias in judgments of truth and deception. *Law and Human Behavior*, *26*(5), 469–480.

Nahari, G. (2018). Reality monitoring in the forensic context: Digging deeper into the speech of liars. *Journal of Applied Research in Memory and Cognition*, *7*(3), 432–440.

Nahari, G., & Ben-Shakhar, G. (2011). Psychophysiological and behavioral measures for detecting concealed information: The role of memory for crime details. *Psychophysiology*, *48*(6), 733–744.

Pansky, A., Koriat, A., & Goldsmith, M. (2005). Eyewitness recall and testimony. In N. Brewer & K. D. Williams (Eds.), *Psychology and law: An empirical perspective* (pp. 93–150).

Pansky, A., & Nemets, E. (2012). Enhancing quantity and accuracy of eyewitness memory via initial memory testing. *Journal of Applied Research in Memory and Cognition*, *1*(1), 2–10.

Roediger, H. L. III, & Butler, A. C. (2011). The critical role of retrieval practice in long-term retention. *Trends in Cognitive Sciences, 15*(1), 20–27.

Rosenfeld, J. P. (Ed.). (2018). *Detecting concealed information and deception: Recent developments.* Academic Press.

Seigel, J. (2021, March 25). The truth about lying. *Knowable Magazine.*

Steller, M., & Köhnken, G. (1989). Criteria-based statement analysis. In D. C. Raskin (Ed.), *Psychological methods in criminal investigation and evidence* (pp. 217–245). Springer.

United States. (2006). *FM 2–22.3 (FM34–52) human intelligence collector operations.* Headquarters, Department of the Army.

Verigin, B. L., Meijer, E. H., & Vrij, A. (2020). Embedding lies into truthful stories does not affect their quality. *Applied Cognitive Psychology, 34*(2), 516–525.

Verschuere, B., Bogaard, G., & Meijer, E. (2021). Discriminating deceptive from truthful statements using the verifiability approach: A meta-analysis. *Applied Cognitive Psychology, 35*(2), 374–384.

Visu-Petra, G., Varga, M., Miclea, M., & Visu-Petra, L. (2013). When interference helps: Increasing executive load to facilitate deception detection in the concealed information test. *Frontiers in Psychology, 4,* 146.

Vredeveldt, A., van Koppen, P. J., & Granhag, P. A. (2014). The inconsistent suspect: A systematic review of different types of consistency in truth tellers and liars. In R. Bull (Ed.), *Investigative interviewing* (pp. 183–207). Springer.

Vrij, A. (Ed.). (2008). *Detecting lies and deceit: Pitfalls and opportunities.* John Wiley & Sons.

Vrij, A. (2018). Verbal lie detection tools from an applied perspective. In P. Rosenfeld (Ed.), *Detecting concealed information and deception* (pp. 297–327). Academic Press.

Vrij, A., Deeb, H., Leal, S., Granhag, P. A., & Fisher, R. P. (2020). Plausibility: A verbal cue to veracity worth examining? *European Journal of Psychology Applied to Legal Context, 13*(2), 47–53.

Vrij, A., Fisher, R., & Blank, H. (2017). A cognitive approach to lie detection: A meta-analysis. *Legal and Criminological Psychology, 22*(1), 1–21.

Vrij, A., Leal, S., Granhag, P. A., Mann, S., Fisher, R. P., Hillman, J., & Sperry, K. (2009). Outsmarting the liars: The benefit of asking unanticipated questions. *Law and Human Behavior, 33*(2), 159–166.

Vrij, A., Palena, N., Leal, S., & Caso, L. (2021). The relationship between complications, common knowledge details and self-handicapping strategies and veracity: A meta-analysis. *The European Journal of Psychology Applied to Legal Context, 13*(2), 55–77.

12 Trust, doubt, and symptom validity

Irena Bošković

The topic of symptom fabrication does not need an elaborate introduction. If you just think about the last time you were invited to a Zoom drinks session or to yet another family group video call, you will also remember that you were probably tempted to suddenly "develop" a horrible headache. Even while watching a football match, you will most likely witness a player throwing himself on the ground screaming (it is usually a *he*), although he is perfectly able to continue playing after the referee whistled fault in his favour.

A recent study confirmed that the majority of the general public had some experience with symptom fabrication, implying that it is part of our general behavioural repertoire (Dandachi-FitzGerald et al., 2020). Even a vast majority (97%) of psychology students would, to some degree, engage in malingering if an appealing incentive is present (Boskovic, 2020). The severity of such deception, however, can vary depending on its consequences. In clinical and legal settings, the intentional symptom fabrication or gross exaggeration of symptoms for external incentives, defined as *malingering* (American Psychiatric Association, 2013), can lead to serious issues, not only for the malingerers but also for the genuine patients and society in general.

The estimated prevalence of malingered symptom reports varies between 0 and 40%, depending on the context in which it occurs (e.g., civil or criminal) and on the type of reported complaints (Mittenberg et al., 2002; Young, 2015). The consequences following malingering are usually, but not necessarily, proportional to the incentives that motivate a person to fabricate their symptoms. In the *civil setting*, one of the main reasons behind symptom fabrication is to obtain monetary compensation. For an example, see Case box 12.1. If only 25% of all benefit-receiving individuals are malingering, both from the general public and among war veterans, there would be a loss of approximately 20 billion dollars in the U.S. alone (Chafetzl & Underhill, 2013). That estimation is even higher when considering the Veteran Affairs system in the U.S. An eligible veteran can obtain an annual compensation in the amount of 36 thousand dollars (tax-free) for their entire lifetime. Hence, it is easy to assume, as it has been documented in many cases (see Guilmartin et al., 2000), that many would engage in malingering to receive such financial benefit. As the compensation funds are limited, fraudsters directly jeopardize the possibility of helping people with genuine health issues.

DOI: 10.4324/9781003308546-16

Case box 12.1   "Push through the pain"

Mark, a former war veteran, also known as the Action Man Mark, claimed to be unable to walk more than 50 meters due to the excruciating lower back pain after his return from a military tour in Afghanistan. Mark was captured dragging his legs out of the courtroom after he was declared disabled, thus, eligible for the compensation. Yet, he seemed not to have any health issues while using the obtained funds to swim with sharks, climb Mt Kilimanjaro, and participate in a triathlon. The source of his activities? His Facebook account. Mark's defence stated that he was able to "push through the pain" because of his prior military training. Yet, Mark was found guilty of fraud (see Joseph, 2017).

Malingering happens in the *criminal setting* as well, although on a smaller scale (Merten & Merckelbach, 2013). For a perpetrator, reporting severe mental health issues could significantly influence the outcome of their trial. Thereby, thanks to the fabricated symptom reports, a perpetrator could be considered as less or not at all criminally responsible for the committed act (McDermott et al., 2013). Thus, the consequences of malingering in the criminal setting include healthy perpetrators remaining free or occupying spots at forensic hospitals in which they will undergo unnecessary treatments. Although clinicians often claim that it is against professional conduct not to provide treatment to people who claim to need it, it is necessary to first ensure that a treatment receiver could benefit from it (see McNally & Frueh, 2012). For instance, treating malingerers with antipsychotic medication can be detrimental to their health (see van der Heide et al., 2020). Further, malingerers might join various treatment programs so as to secure proof of their claims. However, their participation could undermine the evaluations of such treatments as it is not in the malingerer's best interest to report recovery (Van Egmond & Kummeling, 2002).

A similar, distorting effect of malingering can also be found on research outcomes. Rienstra et al. (2013) tested the association between the hippocampal volume and memory performance among patients of a memory clinic. Despite strong theoretical and empirical arguments for such association, their initial data indicated no relationship between this brain region and an individual's memory. Yet, when the participants with extreme scores on symptom fabrication checks were excluded, a positive correlation between the hippocampal volume and memory performance appeared significant. Therefore, undiscovered malingerers in the patient samples can seriously distort both the treatment evaluations and research outcomes.

For the reasons discussed previously, it is of key importance to encourage psychologists and practitioners in related domains to (1) recognize the scale of the problem malingering presents, (2) explore methods for its detection, and (3) employ such methods in their assessments. Hence, in the following text, I will present some of the most frequently used methods for the detection of fabricated symptoms, as well as some novel approaches that require further investigation.

Trust vs. doubt

The majority of practitioners underestimate the prevalence of symptom fabrication and, thus, do not employ checks for symptom fabrication (Allcott et al., 2014). Such lack of scepticism is particularly problematic when assessing claims of Posttraumatic Stress Disorder (PTSD), which due to its subjective symptoms, is one of the most frequently fabricated disorders in both civil and criminal contexts (see Young, 2016). Yet, the resistance to addressing the magnitude and severity of malingering is especially strong in cases involving veterans. Thus, despite the awareness that malingering directly takes away the help from genuine patients, service providers are usually reluctant to upset their clients, especially when those clients claim to be war veterans. For instance, Poyner (2010) described that even when she, as the psychologist in Veterans Affairs, tried to draw attention to this issue and proposed including assessment measures that could serve as a check for exaggeration or fabrication of symptoms, she was soon removed from the cases and eventually asked to leave. So, even when practitioners might be willing to further investigate the possibility of malingering, it appears that those in charge are not. And without such support, it is understandable that practitioners will lack the initiative to test for symptom fabrication.

Unfortunately, the ground for the trusting attitude of service providers and their dismissal of malingering as an issue is based on omnipresent myths about malingering. For instance, it is often believed that malingerers cannot keep up with their fabrication for a prolonged period of time (Jelicic et al., 2017). Following that reasoning, the employment of symptom validity checks is futile as the exposure of a malingerer is just a matter of time. However, that is not true, as some of the documented cases, such as the case of Rudolf Hess, indicate that people who fabricate their symptoms can do so for years (see Case box 12.2).

Case box 12.2   "My memory will again respond to the outside world"

Rudolf Hess, a leading member of the Nazi party in Nazi Germany, was brought to court during the Nuremberg trials. For the majority of the trial, he claimed to suffer from amnesia. This claim made him officially incompetent to stand trial. Hence, he was not allowed to defend himself. After receiving that information, he, after more than three years of claiming complete amnesia for all of the war crimes he committed, declared that "[. . .] from this moment on, my memory will again respond to the outside world". Hence, he admitted to simulating amnesia. He received a life sentence in prison. In 1987, Rudolf hanged himself while in custody when he was 93 years of age (for a video of Rudolf's confession, see Jackson, 2008).

An assumption that malingering, if present, can easily be detected using a clinical interview is yet another myth that discourages clinicians from including symptom validity tests in their assessments (Jelicic et al., 2017). Possibly the best example was provided in the study conducted by Hickling and colleagues (2002), who hired actors to attempt to be admitted to a psychiatric hospital by claiming symptoms of PTSD. Despite the standard clinical assessment in place, none of the actors were initially detected as feigners. Further, even when Hickling informed the staff about the presence of actors among the patients, the additional screening led to the detection of only three actors (Hickling et al., 2002), indicating a presence of a blind spot in the assessment. Another finding that casts doubt on the legitimacy of the assumption that clinical interview alone can serve as a detection method for malingering is that only 4% of practitioners reported feeling confident in their ability to detect symptom fabrication (Cohen & Appelbaum, 2016).

Finally, many practitioners might be biased against symptom validity tests by thinking about possible consequences they would have to confront if it is established that they made a mistake (i.e., false positive). Besides the embarrassment, practitioners could, in certain jurisdictions, also face lawsuits for defamation of character or for malpractice (Knoll & Resnick, 1999). However, it should be clear that decisions about malingering are never based on just one test score or weak evidence. Because of the potentially severe legal and personal consequences for both the evaluee and the evaluator, decisions about malingering always require enough proof to indicate certainty. Even in case of erroneous outcomes of the assessment, making a false negative decision (not detecting malingering when it is present) is certainly preferable to a false positive decision (claiming that a patient is malingering when they are not). Hence, the reasons clinicians typically use as justification for not employing the Symptom Validity Tests do not hold ground, as they are based on misconceptions.

Symptom validity testing

It is important to clarify that Symptom Validity Tests (SVTs) are not aimed at detecting malingering but rather the presence of *response bias*. The misunderstanding about the goal of employing SVTs might also be one of the reasons why practitioners are reluctant to implement them. Hence, including SVTs in the assessment should not by itself mean that a practitioner has doubts about the honesty of their patients but rather that the practitioner wants to establish the validity of patients' reporting styles. It is important to establish the presence of either negative response bias (i.e., presenting your health as worse than it is) or positive response bias (i.e., presenting your health as better than it is; Rogers, 2018), not only because it signals how valid the assessments' results are but also because it provides an understanding of patients' reporting tendencies. The reporting tendencies (e.g., overreporting or underreporting) are not always related to an intentional behaviour such as malingering but could rather reflect the presence of certain personality traits such as dissociation

(Merckelbach et al., 2017), fantasy proneness (Boskovic, Ramakers et al., 2020; Merckelbach, 2004), and alexithymia (Merckelbach et al., 2018). Specifically, people who score higher on some of these traits show a tendency to amplify their health complaints. Furthermore, negative response bias can be driven by an internal, rather than an external, incentive, such as taking on a "patient role" or attention-seeking behaviour, which presents an actual disorder (i.e., factitious disorder; see Drob et al., 2009). Hence, the employment of SVTs enhances the quality of an assessment rather than simply serving a potential "accusatory" purpose.

Recently, Merten et al. (2016) proposed a categorization of SVTs into two main categories defined by the rationale behind the tests: (a) Performance Validity Tests (PVTs) and (b) Self-Report Validity Tests (SRVTs; Merten et al., 2016). As the name suggests, the PVTs measure both the effort and performance that a person exhibits during the assessment. The rationale behind the majority of PVTs is that, when given a task and two possible answers (from which always one is correct and one incorrect), a person, just by guessing, performs on a chance level (i.e., 50% of correct answers). Thus, underperforming on PVTs is indicative that a person knew the correct answer but intentionally chose the incorrect options. The SRVTs have a slightly different way of detecting response bias. The rationale behind them is that people who intentionally wish to present their health as worse than it is will endorse many items pertaining to different complaints. Hence, it is likely that those people will also endorse items that describe unlikely symptoms ("My headaches are so strong that my feet hurt"). Such bizarre claims are a typical part of SRVTs. Research shows that bizarre items are cross-culturally stable, meaning that it is unlikely that bizarre items would be mistaken for genuine complaints (Boskovic, van der Heide et al., 2017; Merckelbach et al., 2017). Yet, endorsing just a couple of these items is not diagnostically important, as it can reflect, for instance, inattentive responding and other issues rather than malingering (e.g., poor language proficiency; see Merckelbach et al., 2019). That is why it is especially important to validate SRVTs in a variety of populations so that the established cut-off points increase the certainty of making correct diagnostic decisions.

Many of the recently developed SRVTs include checks for random responding, such as the Self-Report Symptom Inventory (SRSI; Merten et al., 2016) and the Inventory of Problems-29 (IOP-29; Viglione et al., 2017). Introducing such checks increases the confidence with which the SRVT scores reflect intentional response bias rather than noise. Another benefit of these newly developed measures is that they move away from the bizarre quality of items, which can often be easily recognized by an evaluee, thus making them suspicious about the aim of the assessment. For instance, the SRSI includes a mix of items describing genuine complaints that are mixed with implausible symptoms rarely to be found among real patients. Despite the qualities one SVT might include, the results on a single measure are never enough to indicate response bias. Rather, a forensic psychologist should always apply multiple tests to secure the optimal cross-benefit in terms of the tests' sensitivity (true positive outcomes) and specificity (true negative outcomes), applying the so-called "multiple failure" rule (see Larrabee et al., 2019). Also, it is important to note that the performance of the SVTs will vary depending on the presented pathology. Certain issues are easier to detect than others, depending on their subjectivity and prevalence. For instance, whereas detecting fabricated anxiety-related claims is quite successful (> 77%), even psychometrically well-equipped measures underperform when it comes to detecting fictitious claims of chronic pain (<50%; Boskovic, Merckelbach et al., 2020).

Finally, without a proper indication of an external benefit driving the biased response style, regardless of the SVT scores, an argument about malingering cannot be made. This is exceptionally important to note because, contrary to its description in the Diagnostic and Statistical Manual of Mental Disorders (DSM-5; American Psychiatric Association, 2013), malingering is *not* a dichotomous phenomenon. Rather, the assessment outcome should always reflect the likelihood of the obtained SVT scores in two competing scenarios: that a person is malingering vs. that they are experiencing genuine symptoms.

Alternative approaches to the detection of fabricated symptoms

Besides the SVTs, the utility of other methods was also tested in the detection of symptom fabrication. For instance, one of those alternative methods was a *reaction time task* which measures attentional bias, such as the Modified Stroop Task (MST). During this task, a series of neutral and psychopathology-related words are presented in different colours, and an evaluee is asked to name the colour of the words as fast as possible. It is assumed that a person who claims to have certain psychological issues will need a longer time to identify the colour of the words related to their complaints due to the attention bias (i.e., the MST effect). Hence, the absence of the MST effect among people who claim certain issues would suggest fabrication (Buckley et al., 2002). Yet, our research disproved that assumption, as it was repeatedly shown that malingerers can easily generate the MST effect, even without any prior information about the task. Therefore, using the MST to determine symptom fabrication is discouraged (Boskovic et al., 2018; Boskovic, Hope et al., 2019).

Another tested method, originating from the lie detection field, is the Verifiability Approach (VA; Nahari et al., 2014a, b). This approach is in accordance with the Undeutsch hypothesis (Steller, 1989). Undeutsch postulated that the content of fabricated statements is typically different from genuine stories. The creators of the VA specifically focused on the possibility of verifying provided content. In particular, they proposed that truth-tellers, both spontaneously and when prompted (see Nahari et al., 2014b), report more details that, in principle, can be verified. Verifiable details are defined as the pieces of information that could potentially be (a) documented, (b) vouched for by another identifiable person with whom the activity was performed, (c) witnessed by another identifiable person, or (d) recorded (Nahari et al., 2014b; for more details see Nahari et al., 2019). Liars, however, cannot disclose such information without the danger of being revealed as deceivers. Hence, liars resolve this dilemma by providing details that are closed to verification (i.e., unverifiable information; Nahari et al., 2014a). The main hypothesis behind the VA, namely that truth-tellers provide more verifiable details whereas liars increase the amount of unverifiable information, has been supported by the majority of VA studies in the lie detection domain (for an overview, see Nahari et al., 2019). Yet, the so-called VA effect varies drastically between studies, as shown in a recent meta-analysis (Verschuere et al., 2021).

Applying the VA in the symptom validity field required a slight adjustment of the criteria of verifiable details. Namely, we also included the information concerning taking medication as verifiable because it could potentially be checked via blood analyses. The overall results of our work did not fit well with the previously reported lie-detection findings. That is, multiple studies indicated that verifiable details mostly do not aid the detection of fabricated symptoms but rather the abundance of non-verifiable information signals feigning (Boskovic, Bogaard et al., 2017; Boskovic, Gallardo et al., 2019; Boskovic, Diebets et al., 2019). It is important to note that, when talking about internal experiences such as symptoms, providing verifiable (health-related) information might be exceptionally difficult for genuine patients as health issues cannot always be externally observed. Nevertheless, malingerers were shown to provide an overwhelming amount of vague, subjective, and thus, non-verifiable information when explaining their fictitious complaints. For actual statements and coding, see Case box 12.3. That is an important finding, especially when considering many descriptions of malingerers as people who will be reluctant to elaborate on their issues and who would be uncooperative (see DSM-5; APA, 2013).

Case box 12.3 *"What do I do with that pain?"*

Statement 1: I got up normally, despite the pain, because I am used to it. After having breakfast, the pain did not disappear, so I took one ibuprofen, 400mg; half an hour later, I took two more ibuprofens, 400mg (the procedure was prescribed by my doctor). I slept the whole day. Had dinner and went to bed again because the headache was still there.

Statement 2: I felt a strong, stinging pain in my head. I hoped it was only temporary and that I only need to drink enough fluids for it to go away. After taking a shower, the pain was still present, coming in waves, some stronger than others. Trying to ignore the headache as well as I could. It was not that salient while being "active". I had a very hard time concentrating because the headache was quite distracting. The stinging feeling did not go away, and I did not have access to any medication, so I kept drinking water. I did not see myself being able to attend the exam, so I made the decision to go to see a doctor and from there home to rest. The headache was too strong, mainly located in my forehead, making it sometimes difficult to keep reading for a bit. <u>I went to the doctor</u>, he wrote me a <u>prescription,</u> and <u>I got</u> some <u>medication at the pharmacy</u>. At home, I took the dose and hoped for it to relieve my pain. I lay down in bed to rest. By that time, the headache was still coming in waves like in the morning, pulsating pain. I slept for around 3 hours and felt better after that. I got up and made myself some dinner and realized the headache was gone, thanks to the medication.

Note: Case information provided by author. Statement 1 is from a truth-teller, whereas the second statement was provided by an instructed malingerer. Verifiable information is underlined.

However, the prior-mentioned research mostly included pain-related symptom reports, as they are highly problematic to detect. Also, it is important to note that symptom reports are, content-wise, far from the reports VA was originally designed for. Hence, further investigation of the utility of VA is necessary.

A multi-method approach

A multi-method approach implies the employment of different methods that could screen for symptom fabrication. In one of our previous studies, we tested the combination of the SVT (SRSI) and the VA (Boskovic, Diebets et al., 2019). We specifically investigated PTSD claims because they must include two main parts: trauma narrative (i.e., traumatic event; for example, see Case box 12.4) and trauma-related symptoms. Trauma narratives pertaining to external events are closer in their quality to statements inspected in the lie-detection field; therefore, they are more suitable for the VA. Simultaneously, it was also important to test the utility of the SRSI in detecting fabricated PTSD symptoms, especially because that measure includes subscales that cover PTSD-related symptoms (Merten et al., 2016). Healthy young adults were given a newspaper article about a traffic accident in which many people died. Then, one group of participants was exposed to the (trauma-inducing) scene of that accident via virtual reality, whereas the members of the other group were not provided further information. The second group was instructed to lie about being members of the first group and to report experiencing severe consequences from the virtual reality exposure. All participants wrote the trauma narratives about what happened and reported their symptoms. The results of the study confirmed malingerers' tendency to be elaborative and vague in their (trauma) reports, whereas genuine patients provide more verifiable information. However, the difference between groups in terms of verifiable information was only found when inspected in terms of proportions, thus, taking into account the length of reports (i.e., verifiable details/total details).

Case box 12.4   Grenfell Tower, London, 2017

In 2017, the Grenfell Tower in London suddenly burned down. As this building was full of residents, officially, 72 people died in the fire. After the incident, more than a thousand people claimed to suffer from severe trauma. More than 67% were diagnosed with PTSD, which is the largest prevalence ever documented in Europe. Up to April 2019, the U.K. has spent 16.5 million pounds on provided care for these individuals. At the same time, there are numerous cases in which it was found that many of these individuals lied in their reports; thus, they were never living near the Grenfell Tower nor had any family members who lived or died there. The estimated loss is more than 2 million pounds (see Clark, 2018).

Therefore, truth-tellers would report more checkable information but only when taking the length of the statement into account. Despite significant findings, it is important to note that these differences are far from convincing enough to support implementing VA in practice where practitioners lack a referencing point to which individuals' reports can be compared. Regarding SVT scores, it was confirmed that malingerers tend to over-endorse symptoms, regardless of their (im)plausibility.

Looking into the detection rates, it was evident that a multi-method approach to the detection of fabricated symptoms resulted in the optimal cross-benefit in terms of sensitivity and specificity, correctly detecting 76% of malingerers. Hence, applying these two methods together could lead to more valid decision-making regarding symptom fabrication in PTSD claims (Boskovic, Diebets et al., 2019). Although further effort needs to be put into the investigation of these measures together, it is important to stress that different methods could be combined depending on their utility alone and on the tested pathology. Therefore, we encourage practitioners (and practitioners to be) to use multiple different methods when screening for symptom fabrication. If exaggeration (i.e., *hyperbolism*) is demonstrated on multiple different measures, the chance that a person is intentionally fabricating symptoms is significantly increased. Though, this conclusion can be drawn only once all possible confounding factors (e.g., poor language skills) are excluded.

Concluding remarks

This chapter was written for psychologists in training, psychologists who are not familiar with symptom validity research, and those who hold certain biases about this field. The main goal behind writing this text was to nudge current and future professionals towards the mindset known as *thinking dirty* (see Beach et al., 2017), meaning that the approach towards the client should always contain some dose of healthy scepticism. The take-home message of this text contains three major points: (1) Malingering occurs on a non-trivial level and, as such, should be screened for, not just in forensic contexts but in the clinical contexts as well; (2) There are many available (scientifically supported) methods for detecting symptom fabrication, among which SVTs are the most appropriate, and their implementation can significantly increase the quality of any health-related assessment; (3) Decisions about the veracity of symptom reports are not lightly made, nor are they based on one source alone. Hence, implementing a multi-method approach and a multiple failure rule are necessary ways of conducting proper symptom validity assessment.

References

Allcott, D., Anderson, S., Friedland, D., Leng, N., Gross, M., Skelton-Robinson, M., & Weller, M. (2014). How do experts reporting for the legal process validate symptoms? The results of a survey. *Medicine, Science and the Law, 54*(2), 68–73.

American Psychiatric Association. (2013). *Diagnostic and statistical manual of mental disorders, DSM 5-TR*. American Psychiatric Association.

Beach, S. R., Taylor, J. B., & Kontos, N. (2017). Teaching psychiatric trainees to "think dirty": Uncovering hidden motivations and deception. *Psychosomatics, 58*(5), 474–482.

Boskovic, I. (2020). Do motives matter? A comparison between positive and negative incentives in students' willingness to malinger. *Educational Psychology, 40*(8), 1022–1034.

Boskovic, I., Biermans, A. J., Merten, T., Jelicic, M., Hope, L., & Merckelbach, H. (2018). The modified Stroop task is susceptible to feigning: Stroop performance and symptom over-endorsement in feigned test anxiety. *Frontiers in Psychology, 9*, 1195–1210.

Boskovic, I., Bogaard, G., Merckelbach, H., Vrij, A., & Hope, L. (2017). The verifiability approach to detection of malingered physical symptoms. *Psychology, Crime and Law, 23*(8), 717–729.

Boskovic, I., Diebets, P., Bogaard, G., Hope, L., Jelicic, M., & Orthey, R. (2019). Verify the scene, report the symptoms: Testing the verifiability approach and SRSI in the detection of fabricated PTSD claims. *Legal and Criminological Psychology, 24*(2), 241–257.

Boskovic, I., Gallardo, C. T., Vrij, A., Hope, L., & Merckelbach, H. (2019). Verifiability on the run: An experimental study on the verifiability approach to malingered symptoms. *Psychiatry, Psychology and Law, 26*(1), 65–76.

Boskovic, I., Hope, L., Ost, J., Orthey, R., & Merckelbach, H. (2019). Detecting feigned high impact experiences: A symptom over-report questionnaire outperforms the emotional Stroop task. *Journal of Behavior Therapy and Experimental Psychiatry, 65*, 101483.

Boskovic, I., Merckelbach, H., Merten, T., Hope, L., & Jelicic, M. (2020). The self-report symptom inventory as an instrument for detecting symptom over-reporting. *European Journal of Psychological Assessment, 36*(5), 730–739.

Boskovic, I., Ramakers, A., & Emre Akca, A. Y. (2020). Dull versus creative liars—Who deceives better? Fantasy proneness and verifiability of genuine and fabricated accounts. *Journal of Investigative Psychology and Offender Profiling, 18*(1), 56–67.

Boskovic, I., van der Heide, D., Hope, L., Merckelbach, H., & Jelicic, M. (2017). Plausibility judgments of atypical symptoms across cultures: An explorative study among Western and Non-Western experts. *Psychological Injury and Law, 10*(3), 274–281.

Buckley, T. C., Blanchard, E. B., & Hickling, E. J. (2002). Automatic and strategic processing of threat stimuli: A comparison between PTSD, panic disorder, and nonanxiety controls. *Cognitive Therapy and Research, 26*(1), 97–115.

Chafetzl, M., & Underhill, J. (2013). Estimated costs of malingered disability. *Archives of Clinical Neuropsychology, 28*(7), 633–639.

Clark, N. (2018, March 11). £1million Grenfell fraud investigation underway after 15 people claimed they lived in ONE flat. *The Sun.*

Cohen, Z. E., & Appelbaum, P. S. (2016). Experience and opinions of forensic psychiatrists regarding PTSD in criminal cases. *Journal of the American Academy of Psychiatry and the Law, 44*(1), 41–52.

Jackson, R. H. (2008). Nuremberg day 9 hess at nuremberg, admitting he faked loss of memory. [Video]. *YouTube.*

Joseph, A. (2017, August 3). Ex-Paratrooper dubbed 'Action Man' who said he could barely walk to get disability benefits then climbed Kilimanjaro is jailed as judge brands him 'completely and utterly fanciful'. *Dailymail.*

Dandachi-FitzGerald, B., Merckelbach, H., Bošković, I., & Jelicic, M. (2020). Do you know people who feign? Proxy respondents about feigned symptoms. *Psychological Injury and Law, 13*(3), 225–234.

Drob, S. L., Meehan, K. B., & Waxman, S. E. (2009). Clinical and conceptual problems in the attribution of malingering in forensic evaluations. *Journal of the American Academy of Psychiatry and the Law, 37*(1), 98–106.

Guilmartin, J. F., Burkett, B. G., & Whitley, G. (2000). Stolen Valor: How the Vietnam generation was robbed of its heroes and its history. *The Journal of American Culture, 23*(2), 96.

Hickling, E. J., Blanchard, E. B., Mundy, E., & Galovski, T. E. (2002). Detection of malingered MVA related posttraumatic stress disorder: An investigation of the ability to detect professional actors by experienced clinicians, psychological tests and psychophysiological assessment. *Journal of Forensic Psychology Practice, 2*(1), 33–53.

Jelicic, M., Merckelbach, H., & Boskovic, I. (2017). Seven myths about feigning. In H. Otgaar & M. L. Howe (Eds.), *Finding the truth in the courtroom: Dealing with deception, lies, and memories* (pp. 128–131). Oxford University Press.

Knoll IV, J. L., & Resnick, P. J. (1999). USV Greer: Longer sentences for malingerers. *The Journal of the American Academy of Psychiatry and the Law, 27*(4), 621–625.

Larrabee, G. J., Rohling, M. L., & Meyers, J. E. (2019). Use of multiple performance and symptom validity measures: Determining the optimal per test cutoff for determination of invalidity, analysis of skew, and inter-test correlations in valid and invalid performance groups. *Clinical Neuropsychologist, 33*(3), 1354–1372.

McDermott, B. E., Dualan, I. V., & Scott, C. L. (2013). Malingering in the correctional system: Does incentive affect prevalence? *International Journal of Law and Psychiatry, 36*(3), 287–292.

McNally, R. J., & Frueh, B. C. (2012). Why we should worry about malingering in the VA system: Comment on Jackson et al. (2011). *Journal of Traumatic Stress, 25*(4), 454–456.

Merckelbach, H. (2004). Telling a good story: Fantasy proneness and the quality of fabricated memories. *Personality and Individual Differences, 37*(7), 1371–1382.

Merckelbach, H., Boskovic, I., Pesy, D., Dalsklev, M., & Lynn, S. J. (2017). Symptom over-reporting and dissociative experiences: A qualitative review. *Consciousness and Cognition, 49*, 132–144.

Merckelbach, H., Dandachi-FitzGerald, B., van Helvoort, D., Jelicic, M., & Otgaar, H. (2019). When patients overreport symptoms: More than just malingering. *Current Directions in Psychological Science, 28*(3), 321–326.

Merckelbach, H., Prins, C., Boskovic, I., Niesten, I., & À Campo, J. (2018). Alexithymia as a potential source of symptom over-reporting: An exploratory study in forensic patients and non-forensic participants. *Scandinavian Journal of Psychology, 59*(2), 192–197.

Merten, T., & Merckelbach, H. (2013). Symptom validity testing in somatoform and dissociative disorders: A critical review. *Psychological Injury and Law, 6*(2), 122–137.

Merten, T., Merckelbach, H., Giger, P., & Stevens, A. (2016). The self-report symptom inventory (SRSI): A new instrument for the assessment of distorted symptom endorsement. *Psychological Injury and Law, 9*(2), 102–111.

Mittenberg, W., Patton, C., Canyock, E. M., & Condit, D. C. (2002). Base rates of malingering and symptom exaggeration. *Journal of Clinical and Experimental Neuropsychology, 24*(8), 1094–1102.

Nahari, G., Ashkenazi, T., Fisher, R. P., Granhag, P. A., Hershkowitz, I., Masip, J., . . . Vrij, A. (2019) 'Language of lies': Urgent issues and prospects in verbal lie detection research. *Legal and Criminological Psychology, 24*(1), 1–23.

Nahari, G., Vrij, A., & Fisher, R. P. (2014a). Exploiting liars' verbal strategies by examining the verifiability of details. *Legal and Criminological Psychology, 19*(2), 227–239.

Nahari, G., Vrij, A., & Fisher, R. P. (2014b). The verifiability approach: Countermeasures facilitate its ability to discriminate between truths and lies. *Applied Cognitive Psychology, 28*(1), 122–128.

Poyner, G. (2010). Psychological evaluations of veterans claiming PTSD disability with the department of veterans affairs: A clinician's viewpoint. *Psychological Injury and Law, 3*(2), 130–132.

Rienstra, A., Groot, P. F. C., Spaan, P. E. J., Majoie, C. B. L. M., Nederveen, A. J., Walstra, G. J. M., . . . Schmand, B. (2013). Symptom validity testing in memory clinics: Hippocampal-memory associations and relevance for diagnosing mild cognitive impairment. *Journal of Clinical and Experimental Neuropsychology, 35*(1), 59–70.

Rogers, R. (2018). An introduction to response styles. In R. Rogers & S. D. Bender (Eds.), *Clinical assessment of malingering and deception* (pp. 3–18). The Guildford Press.

Steller, M. (1989). Recent developments in statement analysis. In C. Yuille (Ed.), *Credibility assessment* (pp. 135–154). Springer.

van der Heide, D., Boskovic, I., van Harten, P., & Merckelbach, H. (2020). Overlooking feigning behavior may result in potential harmful treatment interventions: Two case reports of undetected malingering. *Journal of Forensic Sciences, 65*(4), 1371–1375.

Van Egmond, J., & Kummeling, I. (2002). A blind spot for secondary gain affecting therapy outcomes. *European Psychiatry, 17*(1), 46–54.

Verschuere, B., Schutte, M., van Opzeeland, S., & Kool, I. (2021). The verifiability approach to deception detection: A preregistered direct replication of the information protocol condition of Nahari, Vrij, and Fisher (2014b). *Applied Cognitive Psychology, 35*(1), 308–316.

Viglione, D. J., Giromini, L., & Landis, P. (2017). The development of the inventory of problems—29: A brief self-administered measure for discriminating bona fide from feigned psychiatric and cognitive complaints. *Journal of Personality Assessment, 99*(5), 534–544.

Young, G. (2015). Malingering in forensic disability-related assessments: Prevalence 15 ± 15 %. *Psychological Injury and Law, 8*(3), 188–199.

Young, G. (2016). PTSD in court I: Introducing PTSD for court. *International Journal of Law and Psychiatry, 49*, 238–258.

13 Risk assessment and the influence of bias

Jennifer Kamorowski

Many decisions in legal and correctional settings implicitly or explicitly involve an estimation of risk. Estimations of the risk of violent, criminal, or sexual recidivism or failure to appear can influence decisions such as pretrial detention/release (bail), sentencing, parole, level of supervision, and long-term detention of criminal offenders. Estimating the risk of recidivism or failure to appear is commonly accomplished through the use of risk assessment instruments (RAIs). The proliferation and ubiquity of RAIs are illustrated by the fact that they are in use in at least 44 countries and, worldwide, there are over 200 commercially available RAIs and an additional 200 or more that have been locally developed in use in forensic and correctional settings (Singh et al., 2014).

The popularity of RAIs is based, in part, on beliefs that their use will: (1) increase efficiency, transparency, consistency, and fairness in decision-making; (2) reduce the influence of bias; (3) promote accuracy in risk estimations through the use of statistical models; and (4) enable decision-makers to devise individual interventions to make effective use of limited resources, reduce individual risk, and thereby promote public safety. Moreover, decades of research in a variety of domains indicate that risk estimations based on structured and formalized lists of risk factors improve the accuracy of risk predictions over human judgements based solely on intuition and experience, which are susceptible to various cognitive biases. For example, a meta-analysis of 136 empirical studies by Grove and Meehl (1996) compared clinical predictions to predictions based on statistical methods and revealed that only eight of those studies suggested greater accuracy of the clinical predictions.

In fact, it has been suggested that bias contributes to errors in unstructured judgments of recidivism risk and that RAIs mitigate biased evaluations of risk by limiting evaluator discretion (Hannah-Moffat et al., 2009). Yet, there is relatively little research examining the effect of an RAI-based risk estimate on decision-makers in criminal justice settings. In this chapter, I present recent research that examines whether and how decisions of judges, corrections officials, and jurors are affected by RAI-based risk estimates, including early indications that how RAI-based risk estimates are interpreted and applied is not immune to the influence of bias.

DOI: 10.4324/9781003308546-17

Types of risk assessment instruments

There are two primary types of structured risk assessment instruments. *Actuarial* RAIs employ statistical models of risk factors that are most predictive of recidivism. Developers of actuarial RAIs assign numerical values and weighting to the risk factors, which are then summed to arrive at a risk score. The risk score is often associated with a risk estimate, or likelihood percentage, that is determined by observed recidivism rates of individuals with the same score. As a class, actuarial RAIs include the use of algorithms and machine learning for risk prediction. The second type of RAI utilizes *structured professional judgement*. Like actuarial RAIs, structured professional judgement instruments include a set of empirically validated risk factors. However, in contrast to an actuarial RAI, in which the relative weight of a specific risk factor is based on a statistical model, the relevance and importance of each risk factor are determined by the risk evaluator and their own expertise and discretion.

Risk assessment is also commonly classified by "generations". The first generation of risk assessment is characterized by a professional's (e.g., judge, psychologist, probation/parole officer) unstructured, subjective evaluation of risk. The second generation of risk assessment refers to RAIs that include static or historical risk factors (e.g., age, criminal history, gender). Third-generation RAIs include both static factors and dynamic risk factors, or risk factors that can change and are sometimes referred to as criminogenic needs (e.g., education, employment, substance abuse). Fourth-generation RAIs include measures of responsivity, or characteristics of the individual being evaluated that may inform potentially useful interventions for risk reduction. Third- and fourth-generation RAIs are based on the Risk, Needs, Responsivity (RNR) principle proposed by Andrews and Bonta (1998), which suggests that criminal behaviour is predictable and that the risk of reoffending can be reduced by identifying individual needs and utilizing interventions that match the ability and learning style of the offender.

Social and political context, as well as the stage of criminal case processing at which a decision-maker is considering risk, is likely to affect whether the focus is on the prediction, management, or reduction of risk. In addition, despite the delineated classifications of approaches to risk assessment and research indicating the superiority of structured RAIs for estimating the likelihood of recidivism, it appears that decision-makers in the criminal justice system incorporate their own judgment in evaluating risk and making risk-related decisions, regardless of whether a risk estimate derived from an RAI is available to them. The RAI-based risk estimate may inform their judgment, but it is likely not the only consideration, nor does it supplant their judgment in risk-related decisions. The following discussion of risk-based decisions in criminal justice systems will help provide more concrete examples of how RAIs are employed.

Risk assessment in criminal justice applications

One of the first decisions in the process of a criminal case is whether the accused should be held in pretrial detention or released on personal recognizance or money bail. When considering this decision, a judge is likely to consider the risk of criminal offending, as well as the risk that the defendant will not appear for future court proceedings. Many state and federal jurisdictions, as well as the federal court system in the United States (U.S.), use a pretrial RAI for the purpose of estimating risk. For example, the Pretrial Risk Assessment is used by federal probation and parole officers in the U.S. as a method to assess a defendant's risk of failing to appear for court, a new arrest, or committing a technical violation for which their pretrial release would be revoked.

In one of the more controversial applications of RAIs in legal decision-making, judges may use risk scores or risk categories in deciding upon the nature and length of a criminal defendant's sentence, particularly in the U.S. (Monahan et al., 2018). However, the use of RAI information at sentencing is generally advisory, meaning that a judge is not required to use this information in her sentencing decision. In addition, there may be little guidance (or restrictions) regarding how judges should use RAI information at sentencing. Therefore, whether and how a risk estimate is incorporated into a judge's decision-making is widely discretionary. While researchers have begun to study how an RAI influences judges' decisions, this body of research is recent and relatively sparse.

RAIs are also often used by probation/parole officers and other correctional professionals to identify offender risks and needs and to develop strategies to manage risk. For example, probation officers in the Netherlands use an RAI to inform case management plans, presentence reports, and offender supervision (Bosker & Witteman, 2016). The case management plan contains information about offender needs, treatment targets, and interventions that should support offender change. In addition, the probation officer may provide information to the court about sanctions or conditions that could be imposed on the offender and the intensity of the level of supervision and controls thought to be likely to reduce the likelihood of criminal recidivism. The same basic principles employed by probation officers in the Netherlands are typical of probation officers in other countries, such as England and Wales, the United States, Sweden, Belgium, Barbados, and numerous others.

In summary, risk estimates derived from an RAI are used to inform various decisions throughout the life cycle of a criminal case. Whether an RAI risk estimate is effective in mitigating bias on the part of the decision-maker is understudied, particularly in light of claims that mitigating bias is one of the arguments in favour of widespread implementation of RAIs in criminal justice decision-making. Rather than adopting a binary view of whether an RAI is or is not effective in mitigating the influence of bias, researchers and decision-makers should consider the use of RAI-based risk estimates in the context of how risk is estimated and how it affects decision-making.

Risk assessment and risk management in context

A risk estimate derived from an RAI does not appear from thin air—there are a series of stages and decisions that may be opaque or unconsidered by legal

decision-makers and the public. In fact, an RAI risk estimate and related decisions about risk management should be understood as a process that involves
several steps, any of which may be susceptible to the influence of bias: (1) RAI
development; (2) RAI completion; (3) RAI interpretation; and (4) RAI risk
estimate application. The first step involves the development of the RAI and
the type of information input into the models. Second, the completion of an
RAI often involves the evaluator's discretion in the scoring of specific items.
Third involves the interpretation of the risk estimate by the evaluator and the
decision-maker. Finally, the decision-maker applies the risk estimate, in combination with other information they deem relevant, to choose from a range of
available options for managing or reducing risk.

Bias and risk assessment instrument completion

While there is an extensive body of research related to the development and
predictive validity of RAIs, whether bias influences other steps in the process of risk assessment and decision-making has received little attention from
researchers. Some notable exceptions include research related to bias and completion of an RAI, indicating that variance in scores on RAIs in an adversarial
system depends on whether the evaluator works for the prosecution or the
defence (e.g., Murrie et al., 2008, 2009, 2013). Another example is research
conducted by Kamorowski and colleagues (2020), in which they found that
forensic mental health evaluators' risk judgments about violent recidivism in
a specific case were significantly related to their individual general attitudes
towards offenders. Specifically, evaluators who had more positive attitudes
judged the risk of violent recidivism to be lower than did evaluators who held
more negative attitudes towards offenders. In short, there are relatively few
published studies about the effects bias may have on the completion of an RAI,
indicating the need for researchers to directly examine this question. Moving
to the next steps of the process, the following section highlights some of the
main findings from research about the interpretation and application of RAI
risk estimates in criminal justice settings.

Bias and interpretation and application of risk estimates

The interpretation and application of risk estimates is carried out by criminal
justice professionals, as well as in the legal context in which judges or juries
make risk-related decisions. For example, correctional professionals such as
probation and parole officers and prison administrators may be involved in
both the completion of RAIs and the application of an RAI-based risk estimate
in decision-making. Evidence from research suggests that bias can influence
these stages of the process. For example, Miller and Maloney (2013) found that
a large sample of U.S.-based probation and parole officers often employed discretionary adjustments or overrides to RAI-based risk scores. A small percentage of the officers admitted to intentionally manipulating the information to

complete the RAI so as to achieve the "desired" outcome, which often meant more restrictive supervision for the offender.

Furthermore, other studies indicate that correctional officers more commonly use overrides to increase (rather than decrease) the risk level, particularly when applied to non-white offenders and people convicted of sexual offences. The use of overrides is a practice that is known to reduce the predictive validity of an RAI, with limited exceptions, and research suggests bias against particular groups or types of offenders when overrides are used to increase risk scores. The findings from research related to how RAIs are interpreted and translated to decisions among probation and parole officers suggest the operation of cognitive bias despite the readily available, more objective risk estimate derived from the RAI.

Given the prevalence and ongoing expansion of the use of RAIs with respect to decision-making in the legal system, researchers have begun to examine how the availability of an RAI-based risk estimate affects judges' decisions. In a recent survey that included 42 U.S. judges, nearly all of the judges agreed that a pretrial RAI informs their decisions at least sometimes (DeMichele et al., 2019). The implication is that judges also use their discretion to depart from the recommendation based on an RAI risk estimate. However, the fact that judges sometimes follow recommendations derived from an RAI provides no insight into the reasons why judges depart from those recommendations.

Yet, there is relatively little research related to how RAIs influence judges' decisions, with the exception of some recently published work. In one of the first studies about the impact of risk assessment in judges' decision-making, Stevenson (2018) concluded that information from an RAI did not increase racial disparities in bail decisions relative to the status quo. However, further analysis of the same data by Albright (2019) demonstrated that judges were more likely to override the risk estimate in favour of harsher bail conditions for Black defendants as compared to white defendants. Moreover, judges were more likely to override scores for moderate-risk Black defendants than for similar white defendants, suggesting that race played a role in judges' decisions. Taken together, these findings indicate that while an RAI may not increase the racial disparity in judges' bail decisions, the availability of an RAI risk estimate was not effective in mitigating the influence of apparent racial bias in bail decisions.

Relatedly, Stevenson and Doleac (2019) conducted a study in which they examined the effects of risk assessment on judges' sentencing decisions in Virginia. They found that white defendants were more likely to be classified as low-risk than Black defendants, despite the fact that state sentencing guidelines indicated the same sentence was recommended for both. This finding suggests that if a judge made an adjustment to the sentence recommended based on state guidelines in light of a higher RAI risk estimate, Black defendants would be disadvantaged by such a departure. In fact, the results of the study indicated that in courts where risk assessment was used most, it was more likely that Black defendants would receive a longer prison sentence relative to white defendants.

In another example of research examining the potential for bias to affect judges' sentencing decisions, Skeem and colleagues (2020) conducted an experimental study to examine whether risk assessment information interacts with a defendant's socioeconomic status on judges' decisions to sentence the defendant to probation or incarceration. Their results indicated that risk information decreased the likelihood of incarceration for a relatively affluent defendant but increased the probability of incarceration for a relatively poor defendant. Taken together, the extant research in both real-world and experimental settings related to how RAI risk estimates combine with other defendant characteristics highlights the need to further examine the claim that an RAI risk estimate reduces the effects of bias. The findings from the cited studies demonstrate that an RAI risk estimate combined with judges' discretion, at best, fail to eliminate bias and, at worst, can lead to disproportionately negative impacts for minority and poor defendants. In other words, in combination with potentially biasing information about the defendant, it appears that an RAI risk estimate may be interpreted and translated into judges' decision-making in a manner that fails to correct bias.

Finally, judges are not the only decision-makers in the legal system who have an RAI-based risk estimate available for consideration. In countries that utilize the jury system, it is important to study how an RAI risk affects jurors' translation of risk and potentially biasing information about risk and decisions that result therefrom. In a series of three experimental studies, Kamorowski and colleagues (2021, 2022a, 2022b) examined the extent to which an actuarial risk score mitigated the influence of bias among mock jurors on their estimates of sexual recidivism risk. Kamorowski and colleagues utilized a case vignette to invoke a bias about the "likability" of an individual being considered for civil commitment (hereafter, the respondent) under a "sexually violent predator" statute. They presented the participants with information from a sexual recidivism risk assessment instrument, the Static-99R (Helmus et al., 2012). In one study, the researchers found that information from the Static-99R was effective in mitigating the likability bias, irrespective of the individual jurors' level of need for cognition (Kamorowski et al., 2021).

In a subsequent study, Kamorowski and colleagues examined whether jurors exhibited asymmetrical scepticism towards the Static-99R information when such information contradicted their pre-existing perceptions of the respondent (2022a). Again, the Static-99R information appeared to mitigate the influence of the likability bias, and there was no evidence that asymmetrical scepticism towards the Static-99R information negatively affected jurors' integration of the risk estimate in their own estimates of the respondent's risk of sexual recidivism.

However, in one study, Kamorowski and colleagues found that jurors' pre-existing attitudes towards sexual offenders significantly predicted their estimates of sexual recidivism risk after reviewing the Static-99R information, such that jurors with more negative attitudes rendered significantly higher risk estimates than those with less negative attitudes (2022b). In other words, jurors' pre-existing bias exerted a negative influence on their willingness or ability to integrate information derived from a risk assessment instrument. Moreover, a negative bias towards sexual offenders significantly predicted the likelihood that jurors voted for the civil commitment of the respondent.

Apart from the research conducted by Kamorowski and colleagues, there appears to be no published research about how jurors integrate RAI-based risk estimates in rendering their decisions, nor whether RAI-based risk estimates are effective in mitigating bias with respect to how risk information is applied by jurors in legal decision-making. In addition, there are few studies in which researchers have attempted to examine whether RAI-based risk estimates are effective in mitigating the operation of bias among criminal justice professionals, such as probation and parole or correctional officers or among judges with respect to the translation or application of these estimates.

Concluding remarks

RAIs are rapidly gaining widespread acceptance at all stages of criminal case processing in a number of countries. Given the rapid pace at which RAIs are being implemented in legal systems, research to rigorously examine the effectiveness of RAI risk estimates in mitigating bias is of critical importance. Without such knowledge, the simple fact that an RAI-based risk estimate was available to decision-makers can give the mistaken impression that a decision was reached in an objective manner.

Given that one of the most often-cited arguments in favour of expanding the use of RAIs in legal decision-making is that they promote more objective evaluations of the risk of recidivism, it is critical to empirically test this assumption by comparing decisions made with and without risk assessment information, as well as research aimed at uncovering how risk assessment information tends to be integrated along with other information about the individual who is subject to a deprivation of liberty based on their predicted recidivism risk. Taken together, the studies discussed in this chapter indicate that we know relatively little about the influence of RAIs on decision-making. Furthermore, what little research has been conducted on this topic suggests that bias may influence the completion of RAIs as well as the interpretation and application of risk assessment information.

It is not only imperative to establish that RAIs should be the preferred method of risk assessment but also to evaluate the impact RAIs have on decision-making in legal settings, as well as the impact these decisions have on the individuals who are the targets of such decisions. RAIs have been implemented in many countries and for a variety of purposes, in some cases with alarming speed and with a rather sparse research base to support all of the uses for which RAIs are employed. Given the significant effects risk assessment can have on individuals and on public safety, researchers should make concerted efforts to study the impact of RAI-based risk estimates on criminal justice professionals and legal decision-makers with a particular focus on the effectiveness of RAI-based risk estimates on mitigating the influence of bias in decision-making.

References

Albright, A. (2019). If you give a judge a risk score: Evidence from Kentucky bail decisions. Harvard John M. *Olin Fellow's Discussion Paper, 85*, 16.

Andrews, D. A., & Bonta, J. (1998). *The psychology of criminal conduct* (2nd ed.). Anderson Publishing.

Bosker, J., & Witteman, C. (2016). Finding the right focus: Improving the link between risk/needs assessment and case management in probation. *Psychology, Public Policy, and Law, 22*(2), 221–233.

DeMichele, M., Baumgartner, P., Barrick, K., Comfort, M., Scaggs, S., & Misra, S. (2019). What do criminal justice professionals think about risk assessment at pretrial? *Federal Probation, 83*(1), 32–41.

Grove, W. M., & Meehl, P. E. (1996). Comparative efficiency of informal (subjective, impressionistic) and formal (mechanical, algorithmic) prediction procedures: The clinical—statistical controversy. *Psychology, Public Policy, and Law, 2*(2), 293–323.

Hannah-Moffat, K., Maurutto, P., & Turnbull, S. (2009). Negotiated risk: Actuarial illusions and discretion in probation. *Canadian Journal of Law & Society/Revue Canadienne Droit et Societe (University of Toronto Press), 24*(3), 391–409.

Helmus, L., Thornton, D., Hanson, R. K., & Babchishin, K. M. (2012). Improving the predictive accuracy of static-99 and static-2002 with older sex offenders: Revised age weights. *Sexual Abuse: A Journal of Research and Treatment, 24*(1), 64–101.

Kamorowski, J., Ask, K., Schreuder, M., Jelícic, M., & de Ruiter, C. (2021). "He seems odd": The effects of risk-irrelevant information and actuarial risk estimates on mock jurors' perceptions of sexual recidivism risk. *Psychology, Crime & Law*, 1–30.

Kamorowski, J., Ask, K., Schreuder, M., Jelícic, M., & de Ruiter, C. (2022a). *Asymmetrical Skepticism toward actuarial risk information and mock jurors' estimates of sexual recidivism risk.* Manuscript.

Kamorowski, J., Ask, K., Schreuder, M., Jelícic, M., & de Ruiter, C. (2022b). *Who's the most dangerous of them all? Risk-irrelevant information and mock jurors' attitudes bias sexual recidivism risk estimates.* Manuscript.

Kamorowski, J., de Ruiter, C., Schreuder, M., Jelícic, M., & Ask, K. (2020). *The effect of negative media exposure and evaluators' attitudes toward offenders on violence risk assessment with the HCR-20v3.* PsyArXiv.

Miller, J., & Maloney, C. (2013). Practitioner compliance with risk/needs assessment tools: A theoretical and empirical assessment. *Criminal Justice and Behavior, 40*(7), 716–736.

Monahan, J., Metz, A. L., & Garrett, B. L. (2018). Judicial appraisals of risk assessment in sentencing. *Behavioral Sciences & the Law, 36*(5), 565–575.

Murrie, D. C., Boccaccini, M. T., Guarnera, L. A., & Rufino, K. A. (2013). Are forensic experts biased by the side that retained them? *Psychological Science, 24*(10), 1889–1897.

Murrie, D. C., Boccaccini, M. T., Johnson, J. T., & Janke, C. (2008). Does interrater (dis) agreement on psychopathy checklist scores in sexually violent predator trials suggest partisan allegiance in forensic evaluations? *Law and Human Behavior, 32*(4), 352–362.

Murrie, D. C., Boccaccini, M. T., Turner, D. B., Meeks, M., Woods, C., & Tussey, C. (2009). Rater (dis)agreement on risk assessment measures in sexually violent predator proceedings: Evidence of adversarial allegiance in forensic evaluation? *Psychology, Public Policy, and Law, 15*(1), 19–53.

Singh, J. P., Desmarais, S. L., Hurducas, C., Arbach-Lucioni, K., Condemarin, C., Dean, K., Doyle, M., Folino, J. O., Godoy-Cervera, V., Grann, M., Ho, R. M. Y., Large, M. M., Nielsen, L. H., Pham, T. H., Rebocho, M. F., Reeves, K. A., Rettenberger, M., de Ruiter, C., Seewald, K., & Otto, R. K. (2014). International perspectives on the practical application of violence risk assessment: A global survey of 44 countries. *International Journal of Forensic Mental Health, 13*(3), 193–206.

Skeem, J. L., Scurich, N., & Monahan, J. (2020). Impact of risk assessment on judges' fairness in sentencing relatively poor defendants. *Law and Human Behavior, 44*(1), 51–59.

Stevenson, M. T. (2018). Assessing risk assessment in action. *Minnesota Law Review, 103*(1), 303–384.

Stevenson, M. T., & Doleac, J. L. (2019). Algorithmic risk assessment in the hands of humans. *IZA Discussion Papers No. 12853, IZA – Institute of Labor Economics.*

14 Tunnel vision and falsification in legal decision-making

Enide Maegherman

Although the decision on the guilt of a defendant is one of the most important aspects of legal proceedings, little is known about how it is made. Legal decision-making has been studied from several perspectives. In the current chapter, theories on legal decision-making will be discussed, including the danger of tunnel vision and potential remedies. Naturally, legal scholars and practitioners have an interest in the topic of legal decision-making. Nevertheless, due to the often limited legal regulations on how evidence should be weighed in order to make a decision on guilt (Anderson et al., 2005), psychological theories are also essential in understanding how evidence is integrated into a final dichotomous decision. Within the theories on legal decision-making, a distinction can be made between story-based theories and argument-based theories, with the former being mainly used by psychologists (Bex, 2010).

For instance, according to the story model devised by Pennington and Hastie (1986), evidence is evaluated through the form of a story. The organisation of the story is based on relations which imply cause and intentions of actions, according to the jurors' general knowledge concerning action sequences. Although several stories may be constructed, one will be preferable to others. Further development of the story model can be seen in the theory of anchored narratives (Wagenaar et al., 1993). According to that theory, the different elements of the indictment need to be anchored in commonly accepted knowledge. The story of the indictment forms the main story to be anchored. The evidence anchors elements of the story into rules that are commonly accepted. As various types of evidence differ in what is commonly accepted, the number of sub-stories required to anchor the evidence also differs. Unsafe anchors, such as confessions under pressure or interpretation of activity based on DNA evidence, can result in unsafe convictions.

The importance of studying legal decision-making has been demonstrated by miscarriages of justice, where a piece of problematic evidence often receives a lot of attention. Nevertheless, there is often also evidence for the suspect's innocence that was ignored. The cognitive process that can cause such evidence to be ignored is known as tunnel vision. Tunnel vision starts with a belief in something. In miscarriages of justice, that belief would be that the suspect is the perpetrator of the crime he or she is charged with. When presented with

DOI: 10.4324/9781003308546-18

information that contradicts the belief, an uneasy feeling, known as cognitive dissonance, arises (Festinger, 1957). To avoid that negative feeling, the initial belief should be maintained, and consonance should be achieved. Holding on to the initial belief, despite contradictory information, is known as belief perseverance, which is closely related to confirmation bias. Confirmation bias is the tendency to look for and interpret information in such a way that the theory one holds can be supported while paying less attention to information that could contradict that theory (Nickerson, 1998). Findley and Scott (2006) argued that the criminal justice system is particularly vulnerable to the influence of tunnel vision.

Tunnel vision within judicial decision-making has been a cause for concern, as can be seen in many miscarriages of justice. For instance, in the Netherlands, tunnel vision received a lot of attention after the miscarriage of justice in the Schiedam Park Murder. In that case, where an innocent man was convicted for the murder of a 10-year-old girl, evidence that supported his innocence was disregarded. The commission that investigated the miscarriage of justice concluded that tunnel vision had played a role in the wrongful conviction (Posthumus, 2005; van Koppen, 2003). Following the publication of the commission's findings, several changes were implemented in the police and prosecution organisations to reduce the risk of tunnel vision. In the Dutch judicial system, which is mainly inquisitorial in nature, the court must determine whether the defendant committed the crime he is accused of. There must be sufficient legal evidence against the defendant, and the court has to be convinced the defendant is guilty. If either of these requirements is not fulfilled, the court must acquit (Dubelaar, 2014). The court has to motivate its decision to convict using the evidence the decision could rest upon (Reijntjes & Reijnjes-Wendenburg, 2018) and explain why the decision deviated from explicitly supported points raised by either the defence or the prosecution (Art. 359 DCCP). As the judge in the adversarial system does not decide or investigate in the same way as the judge in the inquisitorial system (van Koppen & Penrod, 2003), the more dominant role of the judge in the inquisitorial system was largely the subject of the research.

Falsification and alternative scenarios

One aspect that has been argued to be key in avoiding tunnel vision is to engage in falsification. Falsification involves looking for evidence that can disprove a theory (Popper, 1959/2005). Several failed attempts at falsification make it more likely that a theory is true (Crombag et al., 1992/2006). If, on the other hand, one only looks for evidence that can confirm their theory, that theory will be accepted until someone finds contradictory evidence that was not looked for. Falsification can also be related to the consideration of alternative scenarios. For instance, trying to support an alternative scenario could be considered an attempt at falsifying the original scenario. Similarly, trying to disprove an alternative scenario would result in trying to confirm the original scenario. Therefore, it is essential that evidence that can both confirm and falsify the scenario should be sought for each scenario.

Ideally, evidence will discriminate between the several scenarios (van Koppen & Mackor, 2020). If evidence can confirm one scenario while disconfirming another, it, therefore, has strong evidential value. An example of such evidence would be CCTV footage showing the suspect at another location than the crime scene at the time of the crime. In that case, the scenario for the suspect's guilt would be falsified, while the scenario in which the suspect is innocent has been supported.

Many years after the publication of the report on the Schiedam Park Murder, it was investigated to what extent judges in the Netherlands are now aware of the problem of tunnel vision and to what extent they engage in falsification and the consideration of alternative scenarios (Maegherman, 2021). In general, judges had a good understanding of the concept of falsification and acknowledged its importance, often relating it to the avoidance of tunnel vision. In line with the findings by Rachlinski (2012), Dutch judges also performed relatively well on hypothesis testing tasks. However, based on their experiences, there seemed to be a focus on excluding alternative scenarios rather than on the consideration of evidence for and against all possible scenarios. Furthermore, judges also acknowledged that they do not feel able to falsify in every case. That was due to various reasons, including the lack of exonerating information in the case file. Moreover, there was a difference in the extent to which judges felt they should consider alternative scenarios when these were not mentioned by the defence or when these scenarios were not investigated by the police. Such actions can be considered the role of the 'active judge'.

Active judges and lawyers

The concept of an active judge can be considered a key element of the inquisitorial system (Strier, 1992). Although it is commonly accepted by Dutch judges that the court should be active in its role (Cleiren & Dubelaar, 2014), previous research has shown that there is no clear consensus on what the role of an active judge entails or how it should be fulfilled (Ferdinandusse, 2018; De Weerd, 2013). These findings were also supported by the respondents of our survey. The role of the active judge can be related to the use of falsification and to the consideration of alternative scenarios. For instance, there is a big difference between excluding alternative scenarios that were proposed by the defence and investigating whether there is any evidence for an alternative scenario that was not necessarily explicitly brought forward by any of the parties. Whereas the former, whereby the court is essentially trying to disprove an alternative scenario, cannot be considered a serious attempt at falsification, the latter can. As confirmed by the respondents, whether or not the court feels obliged to investigate, or to even exclude, scenarios that seem plausible but were not raised by either the defence or the prosecution depends on their interpretation of their role. Similarly, the consideration of exonerating evidence also varied between judges. Judges also showed variation in the extent to which they consider it their role, or necessary, to request or conduct further investigation (Maegherman, 2021).

Related to the role of the active judge is also the role of the lawyer, as even judges who have a restrictive view of what an active judge should do will have to consider alternative scenarios when those scenarios are raised and substantiated by the defence lawyer. Based on several experimental studies with law students, it was hypothesised that law students, as future lawyers, may be more able to consider alternative scenarios and apply falsification than the average population or judges (Maegherman, 2021). That hypothesis was based on several studies in which, despite using a similar methodology to other studies on confirmation bias (e.g., Ask et al., 2008), law students did not show a preference for the scenario suggested to them. Future research should therefore focus on testing that hypothesis with practising lawyers, as their use of alternative scenarios may increase the attempts at falsification in practice.

Researching legal decision-making

In several studies, support has been found for confirmation bias affecting the evaluation of evidence, as well as for the use of alternative scenarios in countering the influence of confirmation bias. In one of the few studies conducted in practice with judges, Schünemann and Bandilla (1983 as cited in cited in Schünemann & Bandilla, 1989) found the decision by judges to be affected by how incriminating the evidence they received prior to trial was. O'Brien (2009) found that expressing a hypothesis about a prime suspect caused participants to focus on information supporting that suspect's guilt. That effect was diminished by having to consider why the hypothesis of guilt may be wrong. Rassin (2018) also observed confirmation bias in participants, which was reduced by an active consideration of how well each piece of evidence fit with different scenarios but not by the mere presentation of an alternative scenario. Although some studies have been conducted using judges as participants, there are limitations in the extent to which most researchers have access to judges or case files, which often makes studying legal decision-making in practice challenging.

The only insight into decisions often comes from the written verdict, which is not a representation of the decision-making process but rather what the decision could be based on—justification rather than the description of the discovery process (Reijntjes & Reijnjes-Wendenburg, 2018). Falsification is usually not evident from a written case verdict when the suspect was convicted, as the only requirement is to account for the decision that was made, not for all scenarios that were possibly considered. Thus, if falsification does happen, it will not necessarily become clear from the written verdict. Nevertheless, the verdict provides insight into the decision, as the evidence construction used to reach a decision may, for instance, not discriminate between scenarios. In the following exploration of a recent case from Dutch criminal law, a critical examination of the court's decision, on the basis of the written decision and motivation (Rechtbank Limburg, 2020), will be explained.

The Nicky case

In 2018, a suspect was arrested for the murder and sexual abuse of a young boy, Nicky Verstappen. In the early morning of August 10th, 1998, Nicky's tent mates at a summer camp noticed he was missing. The camp leaders assumed Nicky had run away because he was homesick. The previous day, he also had a fight with his campmates and said that he wanted to go home. In the evening of August 11th, Nicky's body was found approximately 1200m from the campsite. In 2018, a suspect was identified based on a DNA match and arrested. He continues to deny being responsible for Nicky's death.

It has to be noted that in this case, the defendant was convicted by the court of first instance. At the time of writing, appeal proceedings and potential cassation proceedings have not yet been completed. Nevertheless, the decision in the case can be used as an example of legal decision-making and evidence consideration in practice. Of course, the discussion of the case here will be limited. However, based on the written verdict in the case, it can be argued that the court's reasoning insufficiently included consideration of alternative explanations. For further information and analysis on the case, see van Koppen et al. (2022).

The indictment stipulated that the suspect, in the period of August 10th–11th, 1998, intentionally killed Nicky. The killing was preceded by, or occurred simultaneously with, sexual abuse of the victim. The aim of the killing was to facilitate the abuse or to escape punishment after the fact. In doing so, the suspect also deprived the victim of his liberty, according to the prosecution. The court answered three questions in their verdict. Firstly, whether Nicky had been raped or sexually abused by the defendant. Secondly, whether the defendant had unlawfully deprived the victim of his liberty. Lastly, the court answered whether the defendant was responsible for Nicky's death.

Sexual abuse

To answer the first question, the court used the results of the physical examination and the related opinions of experts, as well as trace evidence that was found on the victim's body. According to the pathologists, there were small scratches on the anus that could be an indication of penetration and were thus considered an indication of a sexual act. Medical experts who later examined photos of the body could not exclude that there were signs of penetration. At trial, one of the experts was heard. According to a court reporter present at the trial, the expert stated that sexual abuse was unlikely (Belleman, 2020). Another court reporter cited the conclusion of the expert as saying that the physical deformations he saw on the boy indicated absolutely nothing about whether or not he had been sexually abused (Dingemanse, 2020). Even the spokesperson for the victim's family confirmed that that was the expert's conclusion but argued that the conclusion was based on autopsy photos of very poor quality. The defence lawyer also referred to the expert's testimony when arguing why his client should be acquitted of the first charge. However, in its written decision, the court simply states that the defence misunderstood the testimony, thereby dismissing the potential support for the scenario in which no sexual abuse happened.

Although it could indeed be argued that the statement at trial was discrepant from the opinions of other experts, the court chose not to explore reasons for that discrepancy, instead dismissing the interpretation by the defence, despite the support of that interpretation by several independent media reporters. Overall, the court concludes that there could have been sexual abuse in the form of penetration of the anus and based this conclusion fully on the original report of the pathologist. It appears the court was here selective in the information it used and chose to interpret it in such a way that it supported the guilt of the suspect, despite contradictions. That could be considered an example of confirmation bias.

The court then went on to consider the facts and circumstances relevant to the conclusions of the experts. When Nicky was found, he was only wearing pyjama trousers and underwear, both of which were inside out and back to front. The court, therefore, concluded that Nicky's clothes were taken off and then put on again, the wrong way around. An alternative explanation could be that he got dressed in the dark in a tent shared with others. It is, therefore, not clear how the clothes can discriminate between several scenarios, limiting their value (van Koppen & Mackor, 2020). The court furthermore considered the position Nicky was found in, which according to the movement expert, was a consequence of the fact that he had been laid down there. According to the court, the fact that the clothes were inside out, and the fact that the body was laid down in a covered location, made an innocent explanation for the injuries to the anus less likely. How one follows from the other was not explained further by the court, although this would have been beneficial considering the potential alternative explanations.

The third factor used by the court to determine whether Nicky had been sexually abused was the trace evidence that was found on Nicky's clothes. DNA evidence matching the suspect's DNA was found on the underwear and the pyjama trousers. According to the Dutch forensic institute, the trace evidence found on the underwear, which was found on the waistband and the front of the underwear, could be expected if an assailant made contact with a victim. According to the expert, the amount of trace evidence found is more likely in case of longer or intensive contact than in case of singular superficial contact. The court also found that the locations of the traces indicated actions with a sexual motive. Thus, bearing in mind the traces found in the crotch area on the inside of the underwear, there is no other explanation than that the suspect put his hand in the underwear in the pubic area. That conclusion fits with the earlier conclusion that Nicky's clothes had been removed and now leads to the conclusion that the suspect took Nicky's clothes off and/or on. Taken together with the indications of penetration discussed earlier, the court concluded that the suspect touched and penetrated Nicky. Therefore, the interpretation of the DNA evidence seems to have been affected by the disputed conclusion of sexual abuse, which can also be considered an example of confirmation bias.

An alternative scenario for the DNA was given by the suspect. He claimed he found the body lying on the stomach, turned him around a little, listened for a heartbeat on Nicky's chest, and straightened out Nicky's clothes. The suspect did not answer any further questions relating to his actions with the body or clothing. The court concluded that the straightening of the clothes, as described by the suspect, could not have resulted in the trace evidence that was found. In relation to that scenario, the defence also pointed out that transference of the physical material could have occurred during the investigation of the clothing, as the regulations and safeguards for dealing with trace evidence were not yet up to the standards of today. The court did not follow the defence's reasoning and argued that investigations done on the underwear in 2006 and 2008 were done in accordance with the current knowledge. The acknowledgement that less stringent measures were used in 1998 and that biological material of several of the employees of the institute had been found among the collected samples, as well as mentions of contamination in other reports, does—according to the court—not result in the trace on the underwear being unreliable. Scientific publications in which various scenarios of contamination and secondary transference are discussed do not, according to the court, provide sufficient support for a concrete scenario of contamination or transference in this case. An example of such scientific publications might include the review conducted by Burrill et al. (2019), who state that, with increasing sensitivity of testing, even tertiary and subsequent transference can result in DNA profiles that can be detected. Furthermore, researchers have also found that the duration of contact does not appear to affect the amount of DNA deposited (Sessa et al., 2019). Although those scientific publications could undermine the conclusions of the court, the court's interpretation of the evidence does not seem to have been affected, again suggesting their interpretation of the information was affected by their belief that Nicky has been sexually abused. How the court determined that the trace evidence was reliable, despite the accepted occurrences of contamination in this and other cases (for a strange example, see the phantom of Heilbronn), could have been explained further to rule out a biased interpretation.

In addition to the scenario in which an innocent activity led to the transfer of DNA onto the body, several other (partial) DNA profiles were found on the underwear. Although these were compared to a number of people over the years, no matches were found that were related to the case, as stated by the court in its decision. These were either found on locations later determined not to be related to the crime, or there was insufficient material found on places that could not be related to sexual abuse. Therefore, the court seems to be using the abuse they considered to be proven to determine which traces of

DNA found on the body were relevant to the death of Nicky. That gives the impression that the interpretation of the relevance of the other DNA evidence would have been different if sexual abuse had not been found proven, again suggesting an interpretation of the information in line with confirmation bias.

Deprivation of liberty

The second question the court had to answer was whether Nicky was unlawfully deprived of his liberty by the suspect. The court states there was no indication that Nicky voluntarily agreed to be sexually abused by the suspect. As the victim and the suspect did not know each other, there must have been some form of coercion or physical violence from the side of the suspect for Nicky to allow the abuse. According to the court, the lack of evidence for physical violence does not mean that no physical violence took place. Essentially, the court states that even though there is no evidence that the suspect used violence or coercion against Nicky, they assume there was violence or coercion, again based on the fact that they found abuse by the suspect to be proven.

The court finds that the actions of the suspect must mean that Nicky was deprived of his liberty, at least for the duration of the abuse. To come to this conclusion, the court provides no other evidence other than what they had previously determined to be proven. The court does not explain how or where the suspect met Nicky. It does not provide a scenario for how Nicky left the tent, or was taken from the tent, without his tent mates noticing. It also does not explain how the physical violence didn't only not leave marks or wounds but also did not leave additional DNA on Nicky's body. The scenario of the court, therefore, seems incomplete and unsafely anchored. Furthermore, there is very little verification of the scenario beyond the fact that Nicky was abused. To try to falsify the limited scenario, attempts should be made to try and disconfirm the scenario. For instance, the lack of DNA found on the body could contradict the scenario of physical violence. The fact that the court considered this element of the charge to be proven appears to have been based mainly on their conviction that the suspect was guilty of the element of abuse. The lack of both verification and falsification in this example contradicts the theoretical understanding of logical reasoning in determining whether a theory is true.

Responsible for Nicky's death

The third question the court answered was whether the suspect was also responsible for Nicky's death. No cause of death could be determined. Medical experts determined it was unlikely that Nicky died due to natural causes. Based on a combination of that conclusion, the sexual abuse, and the location where and the position in which the body was found, the court established that the only possible conclusion was that Nicky did not die due to natural causes but in relation to a crime.

Experts determined which possible causes of death were left after the exclusion of several possibilities. The conclusion was that Nicky was most likely smothered or asphyxiated. The court felt that some of the causes of death suggested by the defence did not require consideration because there were no serious indications for these. Others, such as dehydration or an undiscovered medical condition, were checked and excluded by the medical experts. The court did not comment on what specific actions Nicky had been subjected to, as it could not be determined how the breathing was restricted, for how long, or what the physical reaction of the victim was.

To determine what must have happened to Nicky in 1998, the court used the suspect's *modus operandi* as indicated by two earlier instances of sexual abuse of young boys by the suspect. According to those boys, the suspect put his hand on their mouth, pushed them to the ground, and abused them. The court states that the death could be an unwanted consequence of physically trying to control Nicky. During the sexual abuse, the suspect could have put his hand on the victim's mouth, or laid on top of him, thereby causing pressure on Nicky's chest. The court acquitted the suspect of qualified manslaughter but nevertheless found the suspect responsible for Nicky's death.

The court considered that the suspect's actions in the previous cases of sexual abuse fit with the cause of death considered to be most plausible in Nicky's case, and these actions do not necessarily leave a trace on the victim. The court thus appears to use the previous convictions of the suspect to come to their conclusion on the cause of death in the current case, thereby making it inherently so that the cause of death is consistent with the previous instances in which the suspect abused boys, albeit without the abuse resulting in the boys' deaths. The fact that the suspect in previous cases did not penetrate the boys was also not considered by the court in its written decision. The differences with the earlier cases of abuse do not seem to have received the same attention as the similarities, which could again indicate a biased interpretation.

Upon analysis of the verdict, the construction of evidence used to convict the suspect in Nicky's case seems problematic. Both the unlawful deprivation of liberty and the responsibility for Nicky's death were essentially dependent on the abuse being proven. Such an evidence construction (*schakelbewijs*) becomes problematic when it is used to pass the minimum threshold of evidence legally needed to convict. The construction has previously been compared to a train, whereby the stronger case (with the most evidence) pulls the weaker cases (De Wilde, 2008). In this case, even the evidence for the strongest case, namely the sexual abuse, was relatively weak, as it was based on the injuries to the anus, which do not necessarily have to indicate sexual abuse, as was testified by the expert at trial. The conclusion of sexual abuse was supported by where, and the position in which, Nicky's body was found. The DNA was also used as supporting evidence for the sexual abuse, even though no DNA was found on the body other than skin cells on the chest, and the suspect gave an alternative explanation for the DNA on the clothing. In terms of the theory of anchored narratives, it could be argued that the scenario in which the suspect abused Nicky was unsafely anchored. Subsequently, basing the conviction for the deprivation of liberty, which resulted in the death of Nicky, on that unsafe anchoring also threatens the rest of the evidence construction.

Few alternative scenarios were dismissed by the court. It must be noted that few alternative scenarios were also raised by the defence lawyer, who mainly tried to undermine the evidence the prosecution had presented against his client. Nevertheless, there were a lot of unanswered questions in the case file, such as, for instance, how Nicky met the suspect and ended up where he was found. For instance, the other DNA profiles could have been given further attention. A team leader of the investigation has previously also said that it was possible that there was no perpetrator (Van Dyck & Langenberg, 2001). There was also a fight between Nicky and his tent mates the night before, during which Nicky had been beaten and kicked. Perhaps Nicky suffered injuries there that later led to his death. There was also another camp leader who had previously been accused of sexual abuse (Redactie, 2010). Although his DNA was previously compared to the DNA found on the underwear, it is unclear which sample it was compared to. It is also questionable whether the court would have concluded that the DNA that matched with the convicted man was related to the death of Nicky if the defendant had not previously abused boys of the same age as Nicky. The interpretations of the evidence seem highly interdependent.

Concluding remarks

Although a lot of research has been conducted on the potential influence of tunnel vision, more research should be focused on practice. Several experimental studies on practical elements, such as the order in which the evidence is presented and the accountability requirements, were conducted with law students who did not show confirmation bias (Maegherman, 2021). Although changing the accountability requirement could have a positive influence, it should be determined whether it could protect against bias in real-life situations, where the court might also be under time pressure. Further research on training, for example, on the analysis of competing hypotheses method (Heuer, 1999), has also been unable to provide a clear answer on how tunnel vision could be prevented in the context of legal decision-making. To further develop ways in which bias can be prevented, it is essential to cooperate with practitioners, especially considering the risk of bias that can be found in several cases was not present in law students, and so research in practice seems to be required in order to suggest potential improvements.

References

Anderson, T., Schum, D., & Twining, W. (2005). *Analysis of evidence*. Cambridge University Press.

Ask, K., Rebelius, A., & Granhag, P. A. (2008). The 'elasticity' of criminal evidence: A moderator of investigator bias. *Applied Cognitive Psychology*, *22*(9), 1245–1259.

Belleman, S. [@SaskiaBelleman]. (2020, October 5). *Forensisch arts Rob Bilo in de rechtbank van Maastricht, getekend door @PetraUrban. Volgens Bilo is seksueel misbruik van #Nicky onwaarschijnlijk* [Image attached] [Tweet]. Twitter.

Bex, F. J. (2010). *Evidence for a good story: A hybrid theory of arguments, stories and criminal evidence* (Doctoral dissertation). University of Groningen.

Burrill, J., Daniel, B., & Frascione, N. (2019). A review of trace "Touch DNA" deposits: Variability factors and an exploration of cellular composition. *Forensic Science International: Genetics, 39*(1), 8–18.

Cleiren, C. P. M., & Dubelaar, M. J. (2014). De betekenis van het scenario-denken voor het bewijs op grondslag van de tenlastelegging en de rechterlijke onderzoeksplicht [The meaning of scenario-thinking for the evidence based on the indictment and the judicial duty to investigate]. *Strafblad, 12*(6), 445–446.

Crombag, H. F. M., van Koppen, P. J., & Wagenaar, W. A. (2006). *Dubieuze zaken: De psychologie van strafrechtelijk bewijs [Dubious cases: The psychology of evidence in criminal law].* Olympus (Original work published 1992).

De Weerd, L. (2013). Geen scheidsrechter maar rechter [Not referee but judge]. *Trema, 36*(5), 156–160.

De Wilde, B. (2008). Bewijsminimumregels als waarborgen voor de waarheidsvinding in strafzaken? [Minimum evidence rules as safeguards for finding truth in criminal law cases?] In J. H. Crijns, P. P. J. van der Meij, & J. M. ten Voorde (Eds.), *De waarde van waarheid. Opstellen over waarheid en waarheidsvinding in het strafrecht* (pp. 269–294). Boom Juridische uitgevers.

Dingemanse, B. (2020, October 5). Advocaat over zaak Nicky Verstappen: 'Deze zaak is klaar' [Lawyer on the case Nicky Verstappen: 'This case is done'. *1Limburg.*

Dubelaar, M. J. (2014). *Betrouwbaar getuigenbewijs: waardering en totstandkoming van strafrechtelijke getuigenverklaringen in perspectief* [Reliable witness evidence: evaluation and formation of criminal law witness statements in perspective] (Doctoral dissertation). Leiden University.

Ferdinandusse, W. N. (2018). De actieve rechter [The active judge]. *Strafblad, 16*(2), 22–40.

Festinger, L. (1957). *A theory of cognitive dissonance.* Stanford University Press.

Findley, K. A., & Scott, M. S. (2006). Multiple dimensions of tunnel vision in criminal cases. *Wisconsin Law Review, 2,* 291–398.

Heuer, R. J. (1999). *Psychology of intelligence analysis.* Center for the Study of Intelligence.

Maegherman, E. F. L. (2021). *Facilitating falsification in legal decision-making: Problems in practice and potential solutions* (Doctoral dissertation). Maastricht University & University of Gothenburg.

Nickerson, R. S. (1998). Confirmation bias: A ubiquitous phenomenon in many guises. *Review of General Psychology, 2*(2), 175–220.

O'Brien, B. (2009). Prime suspect: An examination of factors that aggravate and counteract confirmation bias in criminal investigations. *Psychology, Public Policy, and Law, 15*(4), 315–334.

Pennington, N., & Hastie, R. (1986). Evidence evaluation in complex decision making. *Journal of Personality and Social Psychology, 51*(2), 242–258.

Popper, K. (2005). *The logic of scientific discovery.* Routledge (Original work published 1959).

Posthumus, F. (2005). Evaluatieonderzoek in de Schiedammer parkmoord. *Openbaar ministerie.*

Rachlinski, J. J. (2012). Judicial psychology. *Rechtstreeks, 2,* 15–34.

Rassin, E. (2018). Reducing tunnel vision with a pen-and-paper tool for the weighting of criminal evidence. *Journal of Investigative Psychology and Offender Profiling, 15*(2), 227–233.

Rechtbank Limburg. (2020). Uitspraak in de zaak Nicky Verstappen. ECLI:NL:RBLIM: 2020:9077. *Rechtbank Limburg.*

Redactie. (2010, September 24). Graf van kampoudste geopend: Match of geen match [Grave of camp leader opened: Match or no match]. *De Limburger.*

Reijntjes, J. M., & Reijnjes-Wendenburg, C. (2018). De Bewijsconstructie [The evidence construction]. In *Handboek Strafzaken 34: Bewijs* [EPUB version].

Schünemann, B., & Bandilla, W. (1989). Perseverance in courtroom decisions. In H. Wegener, F. Lösel, & J. Haisch (Eds.), *Criminal behavior and the justice system: Psychological perspectives* (pp. 181–192). Springer.

Sessa, F., Salerno, M., Bertozzi, G., Messina, G., Ricci, P., Ledda, C., Rapisarda, V., Cantatore, S., Turillazzi, E., & Pomara, C. (2019). Touch DNA: Impact of handling time on touch deposit and evaluation of different recovery techniques: An experimental study. *Scientific Reports, 9*(1), 1–9.

Strier, F. (1992). What can the American adversary system learn from an inquisitional system of justice. *Judicature, 76*(3), 109–111.

Van Dyck, C., & Langenberg, H. (2001, September 1). De bizarre jacht op de moordenaar van Nicky Verstappen. [The bizar hunt on the murderer of Nicky Verstappen]. *De Limburger.*

van Koppen, P. J. (2003). *De Schiedammer parkmoord: Een rechtspsychologische reconstructie* [The Schiedam park murder: A legal psychological reconstruction]. Ars Aequi Libri.

van Koppen, P. J., Horselenberg, R., & Ebbekink, L. M. (2022). *De fietser op de hei: Scenario's en bewijs in de zaak tegen Jos B* [The cyclist on the heath: Scenarios and evidence in the case against Jos B.]. Boom Criminologie.

van Koppen, P. J., & Mackor, A. R. (2020). A scenario approach to the simonshaven case. *Topics in Cognitive Science, 12*(4), 1132–1151.

van Koppen, P. J., & Penrod, S. D. (2003). Adversarial or inquisitorial: Comparing systems. In P. J. van Koppen, & S. D. Penrod (Eds.), *Adversarial versus inquisitorial justice: Psychological perspectives on criminal justice systems* (pp. 2–20). Plenum.

Wagenaar, W. A., van Koppen, P. J., & Crombag, H. F. M. (1993). *Anchored narratives: The psychology of criminal evidence.* Harvester Wheatsheaf.

15 Fact-finding in asylum cases

Tanja van Veldhuizen

To qualify as a refugee, asylum seekers must have a well-founded fear of persecution in their country of origin due to reasons of race, religion, nationality, sexual orientation, or membership in a particular social group. Assessing the origin and identity of, and alleged acts of persecution against, the applicant is a key element of asylum procedures. Due to a general scarcity of documentary evidence, the decision to grant or deny international protection largely depends on a credibility assessment of the applicant's oral statements. The study of interviewing and decision-making practices in asylum cases is relatively new to legal psychology. Some best practices in criminal fact-finding procedures, however, translate to the assessment of asylum claims. Even though the evidentiary and legal context of asylum procedures differs from criminal proceedings, the investigative tools and decision-making processes also show similarities. I summarize the available empirical evidence and use insights from legal psychological research to discuss the effectiveness of current interviewing practices and credibility assessments in asylum cases.

European asylum procedures typically are divided into two stages: first, the *material facts* in an asylum claim are identified and investigated; and second, in a legal analysis, the substantiality of those elements is assessed. Fact-finding takes place in the first stage. Material facts are those elements of the asylum story that relate to protection grounds explicated in the Geneva Convention, such as nationality, sexual identity, religious identity, and past experiences of persecution. The case officer must investigate each material fact and decide which elements of the asylum story are believed (Qualification Directive, 2011).

Not all material facts are relevant to all cases. For example, proving your nationality, also referred to as origin, sometimes is sufficient to show a well-founded fear of persecution. Eritrean asylum seekers are at risk of persecution by Eritrean authorities simply because fleeing the country is illegal. Yet in most cases, several material facts combine to form the asylum narrative and must be assessed both individually and in conjunction. Read, for example, Gloria's story (see Case box 15.1), who claims to have fled political persecution in the Democratic Republic of Congo (DRC). One material fact in her case is political persecution. Concretely, the validity of the alleged arrest is the subject of investigation because of her involvement in an illegal political group.

DOI: 10.4324/9781003308546-19

Another material fact is her origin from the DRC. In every asylum case, the applicant's alleged origin functions as a frame of reference. Without confirming that Gloria is from the DRC, the authorities cannot assess whether she was indeed persecuted by the Congolese authorities, whether her story fits with knowledge about the political situation and prison system in the DRC, or whether she faces a risk of persecution in her home country for other reasons such as her religion or ethnic identity (i.e., other material facts in her story).

Case box 15.1 *Gloria's Story*

Gloria is a 31-year-old woman applying for asylum in the Netherlands. She claims to have fled the Democratic Republic of Congo (DRC) after being arrested for her involvement in a political youth group. Gloria belongs to the ethnic group Mutela and is a Roman Catholic. She was brought up by her aunt and later lived with her brother. She went to school for eight years.

In her initial interview, Gloria states: In her twenties, Gloria became interested in the political party UDPS (Union pour la Democratie at le Progrès Social), and she joined an activist group of the party. Her name wasn't on the list of members, but she was allowed to participate in the meetings. Together with other members, she gathered information about the occupied territories and spread that information. They used to talk to people about the problems that came with the war, for example, the lack of medical care and medicine. Her problems started when the whole group was arrested. She does not know what became of the others, but she was interrogated and sent to prison without a trial. That was approximately one year after she became involved.

Life in prison was hard. Most days, she had to work in a garden. She would be beaten if she was not fast enough, or sometimes without any reason at all. When asked if she was abused in any other way, she refuses to talk and starts crying. After spending a few years in prison, she managed to escape with help from the prison commander. She is not sure why he helped her but thinks a family member with connections bribed him. After her release, she had to hide inside the commander's house. The commander arranged for her to flee the country.

Her journey from DRC started in 2018. The commander organized the journey and managed to get her ID documents. She travelled with a false passport to Brazzaville, where she was handed over to a smuggler.

Together with the smuggler, she flew to Marocco, where she transited to the Netherlands. She applied for Asylum at Schiphol in 2020. She has no identity documents or other evidence to support her story. She claims that the smuggler took the passport. Gloria claims that she cannot go back to DRC; she would be captured, sent to prison and possibly be executed because she escaped prison and has been working for an illegal party.

In her second interview, Gloria tells a slightly different story: After being released from prison, her brother took her in. She was not allowed to leave his house. He tried to arrange a marriage with an old man, but Gloria refused. After she had beaten the man, he did not want to marry her anymore. After that, her brother sold her to two other men. They came for her and took her away in a minivan. The windows were black, so she had no idea where they had taken her. She was kept in a house with other girls and boys. Often, men would come by, but she does not want to talk about them.

After a while, she thinks a couple of months, she was forced to travel with two other girls, a man, and a woman, to the Netherlands. She had to pretend that the man and woman were her parents. Upon arrival in the Netherlands, she was again kept in a house where men would visit her regularly. She does not know how often or how many men visited her. She had hoped that her life would improve but finally realised that it would not. She managed to escape the house and filed an asylum application

Note. Case information provided by author. This story is inspired by real asylum cases, but details have been changed to ensure anonymity.

Once relevant elements in the asylum story are identified, the next step is to gather and assess supporting evidence. In asylum cases, the burden of proof lies with the applicant; the applicant must provide the determining authority with all evidence at his or her disposal at the earliest time possible. Evidence includes documents and oral statements.

Like Gloria, most asylum seekers do not have identity documents, either because they never had an ID, because the smuggler took the document, or because they lost or destroyed it during their flight. Evidence for other material facts is even rarer. For example, Gloria's story could potentially be supported by an arrest warrant or by a document stating her membership in the illegal political party. In their assessment, case officers generally must rely solely on the applicant's oral statements and country of origin information (COI) to verify those statements. COI reports contain information about, for instance, the political and socioeconomic situation, the rule of law, and the status of specific social groups in a specific country. The reports are made by the European Asylum Support Office (EASO), as well as by individual E.U. member states. The validity of Gloria's statements could be tested against information about the political party she joined and about the treatment of political dissenters by Congolese authorities.

In summary, asylum procedures are characterized by a complex evidentiary context. Because oral statements often are the only available evidence, the decision to grant or deny status largely depends on the extent to which those statements are believed. Therefore, a credibility assessment is at the core of all asylum cases (United Nations High Commissioner for Refugees [UNHCR], 2013).

Similarities and differences between asylum and criminal cases

Fact-finding in asylum and criminal cases is demarcated by different legal frameworks. Where in asylum cases, the burden of proof lies with the applicant, in criminal law, the state must prove the suspect's guilt. However, because, there typically is little evidence in asylum cases, the standard of proof is lower than in criminal cases. Asylum seekers must establish their fear of persecution with a reasonable degree of likelihood rather than beyond a reasonable doubt, which is the standard in criminal cases.

In practice, the process of fact-finding also shows similarities. First, investigative interviews are crucial to fact-finding in almost all cases. In criminal investigations, victim, witness, and suspect statements help to form a comprehensive story about the crime. The content and scope of the interview in criminal investigations differ from asylum interviews, but the memory processes and strategies employed by interviewees are probably similar. In both criminal and asylum procedures, the investigative authority gathers as much detailed and accurate information as possible, reconstructs a timeline, and tries to get a better understanding of specific events. Witnesses in criminal cases rely on autobiographical memory to reconstruct the events leading up to and surrounding the offence. Asylum seekers, in comparison, can be considered witnesses of their own life. They rely on autobiographical memory to tell a coherent and complete story about who they are, where they come from, and what has happened to them in their country of origin (Herlihy et al., 2012). Gloria, for example, was asked to talk about her childhood and life in the DRC, the events that instigated her flight, as well as her journey to Europe.

Based on the information gathered in the interview, authorities attempt to distinguish between truthful and fabricated accounts. In criminal cases, suspects (and even witnesses and victims) sometimes lie, for example, to avoid incriminating themselves or to protect others. Asylum seekers may embellish true events or present false information to increase their chances of acquiring status. Although motives for lying vary, the underlying cognitive processes of suppressing the truth, presenting a false narrative, and monitoring the responses of the interviewer are analogous. In order to succeed, liars typically plan and rehearse their story and keep it simple. In comparison, truthful interviewees tell their story like it is. They reconstruct their story from autobiographical memory and are therefore prone to memory errors. Wrongly, they believe their sincerity will shine through and that authorities can easily tell that they speak the truth (e.g., Granhag & Hartwig, 2008).

In sum, comparable cognitive processes are at play in criminal and asylum interviews, shaping the quality and credibility of statements. Consequently, similar interviewing techniques should be effective in gathering valid and reliable information or eliciting diagnostic cues to deception. Good interviewing practices from the criminal context may be applicable to asylum cases, at least to the extent that they facilitate memory recall and help truthful interviewees to tell a convincing story while also hindering liars in their effort to appear credible (van Veldhuizen, 2017).

Eliciting asylum claims

The goal of asylum interviews is to elicit as much accurate information as possible. To attain that goal, interviewers should ask primarily free recall and open questions in an information-gathering style (Vrij et al., 2014). Free recall and open questions invite the interviewee to tell what they remember about an event, place, people, or object in their own words. Apart from a broad demarcation of the context or topic, the answer is not delimited in any way. Open questions ideally start with one of the invitations: 'tell', 'explain', or 'describe' (i.e., TED questions). Direct and closed questions should be used sparsely. Such questions only require a short factual answer or a simple 'yes' or 'no' and typically yield less information. Yes-or-no questions may even induce guessing and thereby also reduce the validity of the answer. Forced choice questions, which present several options to choose from, and suggestive questions, which steer towards a specific answer or imply information not previously mentioned by the interviewee, should be avoided altogether (Oxburgh et al., 2010).

Interview style is also linked to statement quality (Meissner et al., 2012). Style refers to how questions are posed. Information-gathering questions emphasize truth-gathering and communicate a genuine interest in the interviewee's story. Accusatory questions are confrontational and communicate disbelief. An information-gathering style promotes the working relationship between the interviewer and the interviewee. Resultingly, interviewees provide more comprehensive answers and diagnostic information, even if they are reluctant. Accusatory questions, in turn, create distance between the interviewer and interviewee. Interviewees may become less forthcoming, for instance, because they feel that they will not be believed regardless of what they do or say. As asylum seekers easily mistrust authorities, the negative effect of accusatory questions on their attitude and cooperation presumably is even larger than in criminal investigations.

An additional benefit of open and information-gathering questions is that they are challenging for liars. Liars prefer to keep their answers straight and simple. A strategy that is more difficult to maintain in response to open and inviting questions than to direct, closed, and confrontational questions. When invited to tell more, liars risk contradicting themselves or other available evidence because they must improvise and depart from their rehearsed story (Vrij et al., 2006).

Asking open questions is demanding for interviewers. Even more so when they perform several tasks simultaneously, which is often the case in asylum interviews. Interviewers must formulate and ask questions, listen empathetically, monitor to some extent whether communication through the interpreter goes well, note down the answer, keep track of the narrative, and identify needs for further information. That may be the reason why in practice, closed questions seem to predominate. Studies of casefiles in the Netherlands and Finland showed that the majority of questions in asylum interviews are closed questions, requiring only a short factual (Netherlands 36%; Finland 47.1%) or yes-no (Netherlands 42%; Finland 34.2%) answer. Only 12.2% (Finland) to 18% (Netherlands) of the questions are open or free-recall questions. On the positive side, forced-choice, suggestive, and misleading questions are rare (<4% in both countries), and in both studies, approximately 97% were information-gathering questions. The Finnish study additionally showed that open questions were concentrated at the beginning of the interview (Skrifvars et al., 2020; van Veldhuizen et al., 2018).

Interestingly, a vignette study among Swedish asylum officials showed a better balance of open (75%) vs. closed (18%) questions compared to the Finnish and Dutch studies (van Veldhuizen, Horselenberg, Landström et al., 2017). The results could indicate that Swedish officials are more skilled than Finnish and Dutch interviewers. However, in the vignette study, participants only formulated five questions, had no other simultaneous tasks requiring cognitive resources, and did not interact with an interviewee. Another interpretation is that asylum officials have knowledge of good interviewing practices but experience difficulties translating that knowledge into practice.

Credibility assessments

Both laymen and presumed experts, such as law enforcement personnel, typically perform poorly and only slightly better than chance at distinguishing true from fabricated accounts (Bond & DePaulo, 2006). In line with that finding, a considerable proportion of asylum officials name issues of credibility, that is, 'to decide whether someone tells the truth or not' as the number one problem in asylum decision-making (Granhag et al., 2005).

To make asylum assessments more structured and objective, common credibility indicators are used across Europe. Statements should be detailed and comprehensive, internally consistent within an interview and over multiple interviews, externally consistent with statements made by other witnesses and with COI and knowledge from other sources, and plausible (UNHCR, 2013). Considering the indicators, several elements in Gloria's story are conspicuous. Most striking is perhaps the contradiction in her story about her flight from the DRC between the first and second interviews. Although that part of her story logically must have been false in at least one interview, her story is not necessarily untrue in other aspects. Regardless of how the flight went, the claim of being arrested for her political beliefs may still be true and suffice to grant international protection.

The use of credibility indicators has been widely criticized. A first criticism is that there may be reasons related to autobiographical memory or personal circumstances as to why statements lack detail or are inconsistent or inaccurate. For example, Gloria may feel ashamed of what happened to her after her release from prison and, therefore, reluctant to talk about it. Second, because of the uncertainty surrounding asylum decisions, officials may search for and add up adverse credibility findings to simplify their work. That practice increases the risk of getting bogged down in testing details in the periphery of the story while losing sight of the core elements of the claim. Finally, empirical evidence suggests that the credibility indicators are not assessed independently but in relation to each other, which casts doubt on their objectivity (Maegherman et al., 2018).

To date, there is no alternative assessment tool of exceeding precision. Discarding the credibility indicators altogether would therefore not be prudent. Instead, I argue that asylum officials should be alert to and rule out alternative explanations for adverse credibility findings as much as possible.

Alternative explanations for adverse credibility findings

Ruling out alternative explanations starts with asking the right questions. As outlined previously, free recall and open questions are most effective in gathering detailed, comprehensive, and accurate statements. Translated to credibility assessments, basing a negative asylum decision on a lack of detail or elaboration is unfair if the interviewer primarily asked directive and closed questions.

Question content also is important for effective credibility assessments. Questions must be in line with what the applicant can be expected to know. For example, in Gloria's case, the interviewer may wish to get a more detailed account from Gloria about where she was taken by the two men after her brother sold her. However, as Gloria mentioned, the windows of the minivan were blinded, so she did not know where they had taken her. Nor was she allowed to leave the house, so she had no knowledge of the surroundings. As such, that part of her asylum narrative may be minimal and vague, but she offers a plausible explanation for her lack of knowledge. Her explanation should be explicitly considered when invoking the lack of knowledge as an adverse credibility finding.

That may sound like kicking open doors, but in practice, asylum officials seem to hold unrealistic expectations about what people should know about their home environment. Empirical studies show that when assessing an origin claim, applicants are expected to have ample knowledge about the alleged country of origin (van Veldhuizen et al., 2018; van Veldhuizen, Horselenberg, Landström et al., 2017). Many questions—on average 93 in each case—were asked to assess autobiographical and semantic knowledge of their immediate living environment (e.g., the geography and landmarks), the flight to Europe (e.g., duration, travel route, and transportation), documents (i.e., what they look like and how they are issued), personal background (e.g., ethnicity and major life events), the country of origin (e.g., customs, news and politic, and typical objects). The underlying assumption is probably valid; most individuals have some knowledge about their hometown and country. However, that knowledge is limited and dependent on personal history, relevance, and cognitive abilities. As such, in response to numerous very specific questions, probably every applicant will demonstrate gaps in their knowledge. Indeed, experimental results indicate that, even though truth-tellers know more about their alleged town of origin than liars, accurately distinguishing between individual truth-tellers and liars based on origin knowledge questions is impossible (van Veldhuizen, Horselenberg, Stel et al., 2017).

A study of Finnish case files further indicates that credibility assessments are frequently fuelled by incorrect psychological assumptions about truthfulness and human behaviour (Skrifvars et al., 2021). The first set of assumptions relates to what a truthful account should look like. The account should include specific information about past experiences, including times, durations, and names, but also verbatim wordings of conversations and texts. That is unrealistic in light of human memory capacities. Also, applicants are expected to be willing and able to describe subjective thoughts and feelings regarding sensitive personal experiences. The lack of such information is sometimes considered a sign of deception, even if the disclosure is related to various individual and contextual factors, among which trauma, cultural differences, and interview quality. Finally, in some instances, an adverse credibility finding related to one element undermines the credibility of other elements of the claim when the elements are, in fact, unrelated.

The second set of assumptions relates to the plausibility of the behaviour of individuals and organizations. Asylum officials make assumptions about how state and non-state actors normally function but also about how rational individuals behave in fight or flight situations. Such assumptions are problematic because human behaviour is highly variable, and one cannot predict how individuals react to specific situations or circumstances. Moreover, decision-makers typically judge other people's behaviours based on their own subjective views and cultural norms. Hence, all assumptions discussed here could bias the assessment.

Practical implications

Eliminating error in credibility assessments altogether is a utopia. Yet, enhancing interviewing practices and reducing bias in the assessment may reduce the error margin. The first aim should be to improve the balance of open to closed questions, especially in later parts of the interview. With a free recall model of interviewing, that could be accomplished. Following that model, the interview should start with a broad free recall. In the resulting narrative, topics can be identified for follow-up questions. In Gloria's narrative, the political party and life in prison might be identified as relevant. Each topic should be introduced with another free recall question, for example, 'You told me about your involvement in the UDPS; please tell me more about that party'. Subsequently, open and clarifying questions can be asked, for example, 'Who was the leader of the UDPS'? Only after closing the topic with a summary should the next topic be introduced.

The free recall model is associated with several positive outcomes. First, when executed correctly, the model ensures the use of open questions throughout the interview and increases the use of summaries. Second, by identifying topics based on the free narrative, you start from the applicant's memory rather than using a standardized list of questions. There may still be reasons why the applicant cannot elaborate, but presuming that there is a memory trace for topics introduced by the applicant, the explanation for a succinct statement can be ruled out. Third, instead of starting from available information about the country of origin, the statements can be tested against COI in hindsight. Fourth, an interview following the free recall model has a clear structure and is efficient. Instead of hopping back and forth between topics, topics are systematically questioned, possibly lessening the number of questions needed to elicit the same amount of information. Finally, allowing the applicant to tell as much as possible in their own words is beneficial for estimating the general ability of the applicant to tell a logical and comprehensive story.

A second aim should be to reduce the risk of biased assessments. One way to counteract bias is falsification; that is, actively trying to prove your own wrong. Translated to asylum cases, officials should explicate their reasoning behind each adverse credibility finding and explain which alternative explanations have been considered. Several questions should be addressed in the decision letter: (a) how the lack of specificity, inconsistency, inaccuracy, or implausibility undermines the core of the asylum claim; (b) what are other scenarios that could explain the problem in the story, besides the scenario that the account is (partially) fabricated; and (c) why the adverse credibility finding fits better with the fabrication scenario than with the other scenarios. Thus far, the motivation of asylum decisions and explication of alternative scenarios is limited.

Concluding remarks

Fact-finding in asylum cases is complex. Documents to support the applicant's oral statements are rarely available. Officials must rely on a credibility assessment of the oral statements and general information about the situation in the country of origin to decide on a case. Wrong decisions can have major consequences. Unjustly granting status to undeserving applicants may threaten the stability of the system. However, unjustly returning a refugee may be tantamount to signing their death sentence. Considering the stakes, it is surprising that, to date, little research has focused on interviewing and decision-making in asylum cases. The empirical evidence discussed in this chapter shows that there is room to improve current practice. Legal psychological insights are valuable to the field, but more empirical studies are needed to ground further recommendations in sound evidence.

References

Bond, C. F., & DePaulo, B. M. (2006). Accuracy of deception judgments. *Personality and Social Psychology Review, 10*(3), 214–234.

Granhag, P. A., & Hartwig, M. (2008). A new theoretical perspective on deception detection: On the psychology of instrumental mind-reading. *Psychology, Crime & Law, 14*(3), 189–200.

Granhag, P. A., Strömwall, L. A., & Hartwig, M. (2005). Granting asylum or not? Migration board personnel's beliefs about deception. *Journal of Ethnic and Migration Studies, 31*(1), 29–50.

Herlihy, J., Jobson, L., & Turner, S. (2012). Just tell us what happened to you: Autobiographical memory and seeking asylum. *Applied Cognitive Psychology, 26*(5), 661–676.

Oxburgh, G. E., Myklebust, T., & Grant, T. (2010). The question of question types in police interviews: A review of the literature from a psychological and linguistic perspective. *International Journal of Speech Language and the Law, 17*(1), 45–66.

Maegherman, E., van Veldhuizen, T. S., & Horselenberg, R. (2018). Dropping the anchor: The use of plausibility in credibility assessments. *Oxford Monitor of Forced Migration, 7*(2), 37–56.

Meissner, C. A., Redlich, A., Bhatt, S., & Brandon, S. (2012). Interview and interrogation methods and their effects on investigative outcomes. *Campbell Systematic Reviews, 8*(1), 1–53.

Qualification Directive 2011/95/EU [Recast QD 2004], L336/09 C.F.R. (2011).

Skrifvars, J., Korkman, J., Sui, V., van Veldhuizen, T. S., & Antfolk, J. (2020). An analysis of question style and type in official Finnish asylum interview transcripts. *Journal of Investigative Psychology and Offender Profiling, 17*(3), 333–348.

Skrifvars, J., Sui, V., Antfolk, J., van Veldhuizen, T. S., & Korkman, J. (2021). *Psychological assumptions underlying credibility assessments in Finnish asylum determinations.* PsyArXiv.

United Nations High Commissioner for Refugees. (2013). *Beyond proof: Credibility assessment in EU asylum systems.* United Nations High Commissioner for Refugees.

van Veldhuizen, T. S. (2017). *Where I come from and how I got here: Assessing credibility in asylum cases* (Doctoral dissertation). Maastricht University & University of Gothenburg.

van Veldhuizen, T. S., Horselenberg, R., Landström, S., Granhag, P. A., & van Koppen, P. J. (2017). Interviewing asylum seekers: A vignette study on the questions asked to assess credibility of claims about origin and persecution. *Journal of Investigative Psychology and Offender Profiling, 14*(1), 3–22.

van Veldhuizen, T. S., Horselenberg, R., Stel, M., Landström, S., Granhag, P. A., & van Koppen, P. J. (2017). The provenance of émigrés: The validity of measuring knowledge of places. *Psychology, Crime and Law, 23*(6), 553–574.

van Veldhuizen, T. S., Maas, R. P. A. E., Horselenberg, R., & van Koppen, P. J. (2018). Establishing origin: Analysing the questions asked in asylum interviews. *Psychiatry, Psychology and Law, 25*(2), 283–302.

Vrij, A., Hope, L., & Fisher, R. P. (2014). Eliciting reliable information in investigative interviews. *Policy Insights from the Behavioral and Brain Sciences, 1*(1), 129–136.

Vrij, A., Mann, S., & Fisher, R. P. (2006). Information-gathering vs accusatory interview style: Individual differences in respondents' experiences. *Personality and Individual Differences, 41*(4), 589–599.

Index

Note: Page numbers in **bold** indicates tables on the corresponding page.

accusatorial interviewing 72, 75
accusatory: interviews 119; purpose 131; questions 64, 164
active judge 150–151
acute stress 33–37; and encoding 33–35; and retrieval 36–37
adversarial system 142, 149
alibi 95–102
alternative scenarios 65, 149–151
amnesia 129 (Case box 12.2)
anchoring bias 61
applied: areas 24; contexts 102; findings 59; practice 29; research 1–2, 37; researchers 58; settings 34, 36, 38, 40
asylum: cases 160, 162–164; procedures 160, 163; seekers 52, 160, 162–164
attachment 81–83
attention bias 132
autobiographical memory 50–51, 96, 163–164

behaviour: attention-seeking behaviour 131; criminal behaviour 140; and culture 47–49; deceptive behaviour 117, 123; intentional behaviour 130; interviewer's behaviour 58–61, 73; nonverbal behaviour 61, 64, 119–120; and priming 78–80, 85; suspects' behaviour 89, 100, 107; verbal behaviour 100, 119–120; witness behaviour 71
bias 58–59, 139, 167–168; and risk assessment 142–145
biased: behaviour 63; interpretation 156; lineups 30; thinking 58

calibration 27–29
cognition 49, 59, 61; analytic cognition 49; holistic cognition 49; meta- 23; need for cognition 144

cognitive bias 63, 143
Cognitive Credibility Assessment (CCA) 120–121
cognitive load 61–66, 120
compliance 54–55
confidence 23; confidence-accuracy relationship 25–28; judgements 23–25; level of 12–13
confirmation bias 59–60, 63, 65, 149, 151
consistency: between-statement consistency 117; bias 10; evidence-statement consistency 118; statement-evidence consistency 106, 109; statement-evidence inconsistencies 107, 110–112; within-suspect consistency 117
content analysis 59
cost-benefit 70–73
counter-interrogation strategies 107–109
countermeasures 119–120
co-witness 15
credibility 39, 110–111; of the alibi 97–98; assessment 51–52, 165–167; assessment tools 122
Criteria-Based Content Analysis (CBCA) 122
cross-cultural: deception detection 52; interaction 49; interviews 53–54; investigative interview 47; psychology 47; settings 47, 50–53
cues to deception 52, 101, 107, 112, 117; beliefs about 118–119; nonverbal cues 117–119; verbal cues 117–121
cultural differences 47–52, 71, 117, 167; and investigative interviews 50, 53–54
culture 47; collectivistic culture 48–50; individualistic culture 48–50; and style of communication 49–50

deception 105; detect deception 120–121
deception detection 106–109; *see also*
    lie-detection
decision-making 63–64, 141; and asylum
    165; and judge's 141, 143–144; process
    59–61, 70, 160; and risk assessment
    142; and suspect's 93, 111; *see also* legal
    decision-making
delayed interviewing 121–122
disclosure: of evidence 106–108; facilitating
    disclosure 78, 81, 84; information
    disclosure 59–60, 70, 72–74, 82–83;
    interview 107–111
disputed memories 14
DNA 152–157
doubt 129–130

encoding 10, 23, 25–26, 33–35
episodic memory(ies) 11, 25, 96
estimator variables 12
evidence 3, 25, 39–40, 47, 49; empirical
    evidence 11, 117, 123, 160, 166;
    physical evidence 22, 95; scientific
    evidence 10; video evidence 16
evidence-based: interviewing 68, 73;
    recommendation 75; techniques 58
evidence-disclosure tactics 89, 92–93
expectancy effects 60–61
extraneous load 62
eyewitness 23–24, 35; confidence-accuracy
    26–29; identifications 29; interview 12,
    47; memory 33–34, 36–37, 51; and
    metamemory 25–26; Metamemory Scale
    (EMS) 30; testimony 2, 9, 12, 22

fact-finding 160, 163
false: beliefs 16–18; confessions 54–55, 97;
    memories 13–14; negative 119, 130;
    positive 130
falsification 149–151
flashbulb memories 11
forensic: contexts 40; hospitals 128;
    interviews 21; psychologist 131;
    psychology 1–3; settings 23, 117,
    119, 123
forgetting 10–11
free recall 51, 164–166, 168

germane load 62
guilt-presumptive 59–60, 99–100

helpfullness 83
heuristic cues 26

heuristics 62–63
House of Legal Psychology 3

individualism-collectivism 47
inferences 26, 88–91
information elicitation 53, 61, 64–66,
    71–74, 105–106, 112
information-gathering 60, 72–73, 164–165
innocence-presumptive 100
innocent suspects 22, 90, 95–102
inquisitorial system 149–150
instinctive tactics 58
interrogation 58, 60, 99; manuals 120;
    tactic 88
interviewing techniques 72, 74–75, 164;
    and alibi generation 97
interview techniques to detect deception
    120–121
intrinsic load 61–62
inverse relationship 60
investigation-relevant information (IRI)
    58–59, 61, 63
investigative interview 58–60, 62–64,
    78; and inferences in 88; and priming
    81–83; *see also* cultural differences

lawyers 150–151
legal decision-making 145, 148, 151–152
liars 106–107, 132–133, 164–165, 167
lie bias 119
lie-detection 120–123, 132–134; in
    delayed interviewing 121–123
lie tellers 117–123
likability bias 144
linguistic techniques 59

malingering 127–132
memory 2, 9–12; aids 96; confidence
    judgments 26; contamination 29;
    discontentment 30; distortions 11–13;
    encoding 26; errors 9–10, 164;
    functioning 22; memory formation 61;
    monitoring 23; performance 23, 25–26,
    33–40, 97, 98, 123, 128; processes
    97–99, 163; recall 164; reports 15,
    51–52; retrieval 9, 26; retrieval processes
    24; self-efficacy 24; suggestibility 13;
    system 22–23; trace 25–26; and the
    veracity of 14–16
memory-enhancing techniques 73, 121
mental reinstatement of context (MRC)
    98–99
metacognition 23

metacognitive: functioning 23; judgements 24; monitoring 25; system 23
metamemory 22–24; and eyewitness performance 29–30; and eyewitness testimony 25–26
migration 47
misinformation 9, 11–13; and acceptance 54; effect 12; and parental 13
mnemonics 121, 123
mock 58; crime 1, 15, 36, 51, 122; crime paradigm 106; eyewitnesses 11; intelligence operation 122; interview 62–63; investigation paradigm 73; jurors 144; suspects 108; terror attack 83; terror plot 81; terror threat 82; theft 121; witness 30, 51, 53, 73; witness paradigm 54
moderator variables 27, 29

non-believed memories 16–17

open questions 164–166

PEACE 97
perceived interviewer knowledge (PIK) 89, 92–93
perception-behaviour link 80
police interview 37–38; and alibi 97
Posttraumatic Stress Disorder (PTSD) 129–130, 134–135
power distance (PD) 53
pragmatic: implicature 88–89; inferences 89–90
prime 79–85; prime suspect 60–61, 64, 151; priming 78–85
proactive inhibition 10
psycholinguists 88
publication bias 38–39

racial bias 143
rapport 53, 73–74
rapport-building techniques 54, 73–74
rationalisation 58
reality monitoring (RM) 122
recidivism 139–142, 144–145
reconstructive memory 9–10
recovered memories 14
rehearsal 11
relevance theory 89–90
reliability of priming 80, 84–85

response bias 130–131
retrieval 9, 23–24, 26, 35; induced facilitation 11; induced forgetting 11; practice 123; stress 36–37
retroactive interference 10
risk: assessment 139–145; estimate 139–145
risk assessment instruments (RAIs) 140–145; validity of 142–143

schema 9–10, 62–65; consistent and inconsistent 10, 99
self-: construal 48–49, 54–55; credibility cues 26; efficacy 24–26, 29–30; fulfilling prophecy 61; handicapping strategies **118**; incrimination 71
Self-Report Symptom Inventory (SRSI) 131, 134
Self-Report Validity Tests (SRVT) 131
sensitivity 131, 135, 154
sexual abuse 10, 152–156; child sexual abuse 14
source misattribution 12
specificity 90–91, 107, 131, 135, 168
stability bias 122
statement-evidence inconsistency 106–107, 109–112
Strategic Use of Evidence (SUE) 105–112
stress 33–37
stress-memory relationship 38–39
stressor 90–91; acute stressors 33; laboratory stressors 34–36
suggestibility 12–13, 54, 96
suspects' perception 108–109, 111–112
symptom validity 12, 129; symptom validity test (SVT) 122, 130–132
system variables 12

trauma 134–135
trust 53, 129–130
truth bias 119
truth-tellers 51, 101, 106–107, 117–122, 132–135, 167
tunnel vision 60, 148–150

Verifiability Approach (VA) 132–135
violence 69 (Case box 6.1), 155

witness cooperation 68–75
working memory 61–63